A Personal Devil

FORGE BOOKS BY ROBERTA GELLIS

A Mortal Bane
A Personal Devil

A Personal Devil

ROBERTA GELLIS

A TOM DOHERTY ASSOCIATES BOOK
NEW YORK

This is a work of fiction. All the characters and events portrayed in this novel are either fictitious or are used fictitiously.

A PERSONAL DEVIL

This book is printed on acid-free paper.

A Forge Book
Published by Tom Doherty Associates, LLC
175 Fifth Avenue
New York, NY 10010

www.tor.com

Forge® is a registered trademark of Tom Doherty Associates, LLC.

Library of Congress Cataloging-in-Publication Data

Gellis, Roberta.
    A personal devil / Roberta Gellis.—1st ed.
        p.   cm.
    "A Tom Doherty Associates book."
    ISBN 0-312-86998-3 (acid free : paper)
        1. Great Britain—History—Stephen, 1135–1154—Fiction.   2. Women
detectives—England—Fiction.   3. Knights and knighthood—Fiction.
4. Prostitutes—Fiction.   5. Blind women—Fiction.   I. Title.

PS3557.E42 P47   2001
813'.54—dc21

                                                                00-048418

First Edition: March 2001

Printed in the United States of America

0 9 8 7 6 5 4 3 2 1

To my beloved son, Mark,
and his dear wife, Sandra,
and my darling Elizabeth

A Personal Devil

Prologue

MAINARD'S SHOP
EAST CHEPE

The woman was screaming again. Sabina cocked her head to listen better, but even her keen hearing could not make out words through the thick walls and floor. After a moment she shuddered, stood, and reached for her staff. Moving it gently from left to right, she ascertained that the little girl who served and led her had not accidentally pushed any furniture into her path. The child forgot sometimes that even small displacements of a stool or a little table could trip up a blind woman. However, the path to the door was clear, and Sabina moved to it swiftly and surely.

Her lips, full and normally curved into a gentle smile, thinned as she made out the shrieks of rage more clearly. Then her teeth set into a grimace of determination, and she lifted the latch and pulled the door open. This time she would be ready. If the woman came up to her chamber again to abuse and strike her as she had done during the past week, she would defend herself.

Sabina's breath came quicker. She would do more than defend herself, she thought, changing her grip on the staff she held. She would put her staff into the woman's neck. With any luck, she would crush the Adam's apple and kill the foul bitch. If she missed her aim, at least she could push her attacker right off the small landing of the stair so she would fall into the workshop below. Even at the worst, that should injure her enough to keep her away for weeks. At best, she would break her neck and die.

No one would blame her—a blind woman feeling with her staff and accidentally striking a person she did not expect to be on her landing. And even if someone remembered that she might hold a grudge against the woman, who had made trouble for her, accused her of whoring so that she was almost arrested and punished, Sabina could hope that the good character given her by the journeyman and apprentices as well as by the master of the shop would save her from being accused of murder.

There was a crash, the journeyman cried out as did the voice of a girl child. Sabina gritted her teeth and held the staff steady to strike. The woman deserved to die! Sabina did not even care if she were accused of murder, not even if she were hanged for it. She would at least have freed her lover from the terrible succubus that was sucking out his life, reviling him, blaming him, threatening him—giving him no peace.

The shrieking stopped. Sabina heard footsteps, heard the woman shout one last threat. She gripped her staff more firmly.

One

"Whore!" Sir Bellamy of Itchen bellowed, his fair skin crimson with rage.

Magdalene la Bâtarde, whoremistress of the Old Priory Guesthouse looked up at him, completely unmoved, then uttered a small exasperated sigh.

"Yes," she agreed. "I am a whore. I have been telling you so since the day we met."

"You swore to me you had retired from that work."

Magdalene sighed again. "I did not swear. I said I took no pleasure in making the beast with two backs, and that is true, but I was and am a whore. You know quite well my reasons for taking the man's five pence. We are a woman short since Sabina took Master Mainard's offer and became his leman. I cannot turn away the men accustomed to her service. I run a business and I must pay an exhorbitant rent. I need the money."

For a moment Bell could not speak. He stared down into her exquisitely beautiful face. He could not ever remember seeing a woman so beautiful. The skin was flawless, a translucent, creamy white; the large almond-shaped eyes, framed in golden-brown lashes long enough to touch the fine brown brows above them, were the faintly grayed blue of a misty morning. The nose was straight and fine, the lips full, perfectly shaped, a dark rose. He ground his teeth. Every word she said was true. And he could not bear it.

"Why did you let Sabina go, you fool," Bell snarled.

Magdalene's lips thinned. "First, because Sabina was not a slave. She had long since repaid what I gave her previous whoremistress to let her come to me. Second, and far more important, an unhappy and unwilling whore does not provide the kind of attention to the pleasure of a client for which the Old Priory Guesthouse charges the highest fees in Southwark—"

"So you are not an unhappy and unwilling whore," Bell snapped.

The small sign of temper that Magdalene had displayed a few moments earlier disappeared. She shook her head and laughed. "No, indeed I am not. I feel a sense of virtue and righteousness over the two clients I entertained last week. The one—who really only likes strong and brutal men—can boast in public that the whoremistress herself satisfied him; and the other, who not long ago lost a well-beloved wife and has no chick at home, talked himself out of his loneliness and sorrow and perhaps, at last, is considering taking an indigent sister into his household. These men need my 'services,' such as they are, and I need their five pennies. That is the end of it. The matter is no longer open for discussion. Now, if you wish to dine with us, you will be welcome, but if you only wish to quarrel with me, I have better things to do."

"So you intend to receive clients again?" Bell's voice had dropped to normal, but it was flat and expressionless.

"Until I can find a replacement for Sabina, yes, I do."

Magdalene's voice was equally flat; it was also hard. Bell turned on his heel and went out, slamming the front door behind him. Magdalene sighed. She was very fond of Bell. She would have liked to invite *him* into her bed for far more active entertainment than she had provided for either the young man who desired men or the old widower who needed company, but she did not dare. Bell, she feared, actually cared for her, and in her past experience that bred disaster.

Her husband had been so jealous that he threatened to mutilate her. Her first lover had been slain by the man who wished to keep her in his stead. Her second . . . Magdalene shivered and pushed the memories away. An opening door drew her attention, and she smiled at the adorable face peering timidly around the edge.

"You can come out now, Ella. Bell's gone and he did no harm.

There was no need for you to hide, love. Bell would not be angry at you, and you know his shouting mostly means nothing."

Truly golden curls framed Ella's face and hung below her narrow waist, shining against her dark bedrobe. She emerged cautiously into the corridor that ran from the large front room of the house to the back door. On either side of the corridor three doors broke the wall. Ella looked both ways; her eyes were blue as a clear sky—and just as empty; her nose was short and slightly tip-tilted, her full lips truly the red of ripe wild strawberries. She was still uneasy because things that did not worry Magdalene at all frightened her, and she peered for reassurance at a slightly older woman standing in the doorway across from hers.

Letice, as dark as Ella was fair, with hair hanging to her knees, black and straight as a sheet of silk, nodded at her sister whore and showed her two empty hands. Ella smiled and accepted that as assurance that there was nothing to fear, since Letice, being mute, could not speak any comfort. However, Ella knew that if Letice felt the shouting man to be a threat, she would have been holding a long, wickedly sharp, curved knife concealed along the side of her bedrobe.

Relieved of fear, Ella came into the common room with small bouncing steps. Her perfect lips pouted. There was a tiny frown between her fair brows. "But he might blame me," she said to Magdalene. "In a way, it is my fault. I could take more clients, I am sure I could. . . ."

"Not and give them all the time they want, love."

"Well, I would not tell anyone to go. You are always scolding me for urging my friends to stay longer than they wish. This way, I would not do so."

Magdalene restrained a sigh. Ella was sweet, good, and insatiable for coupling, but she had the mind of a five-year-old. She was not offering to take more clients, as another whore might, because she was greedy for more money. She was paid the same, no matter who or how many slept with her. She was offering out of her excessive eagerness to please everyone and her equally excessive urge for sex.

"Well, that is true, but what if one of your 'friends,' did not wish to leave you and another was already waiting and growing more and more impatient. You would not want to wound the one by thrusting him out, nor to wound the other by seeming indifferent to his desire. No, loveling, it is better that each man knows his proper time and that there is as much time as he desires. Besides—" Magdalene grinned broadly "—you would not want Sir Bellamy to believe I was all his and demand that I leave the Old Priory Guesthouse."

"Oh, you would not, would you?" Tears suddenly stood in Ella's eyes, which were now round with fright, and the color faded from her cheeks.

"No, love, I would not," Magdalene assured her, rising to her feet and hugging her. "I like my freedom and having my own money to spend far too well to yield it to any man ever again, even if I must take clients."

At that point, Letice, who had followed Ella into the common room, touched Magdalene's arm and pointed to the door beyond her own, which had been Sabina's chamber. It was still closed. Letice sighed, shook her head, gestured at Ella, Magdalene, and herself, showed a closed fist, and then made a sharp slicing motion.

"We are tight together, and Hagar is not one of us?" Magdalene said, interpreting what Letice wished to say.

The dark beauty nodded, then shrugged and sighed again.

"Well, I agree with you, although I am grateful to you for finding her for us. Without her we would have had to turn many away, and some, like William's men, were delighted to have a less gentle play-fellow than Sabina. Still—"

She stopped as Letice began to gesture again, then stamped her foot and ran quickly back to her room. When she came out with a piece of slate and a stick of chalk, Magdalene nodded approval vigorously.

Several weeks before, a papal messenger had been murdered in the church of St. Mary Overy, just the other side of the wall behind the Old Priory Guesthouse. Magdalene and her women had been accused simply because they were whores and close by. To save them all, Magdalene had become involved in solving the crime, and Letice had had information they had almost failed to obtain because she could not speak. Both the agony of frustration Letice suffered and the danger of her being unable to tell a crucial fact decided Magdalene that Letice must learn to read and write. Magdalene herself had these skills, most uncommon for any woman and unheard of for a whore, because of a parsimonious archdeacon, who had taught her in lieu of payment for her services. Letice was a quick learner because of her desperate need to communicate and fingers nimble enough to move fragile wax seals from one document to another. In a few weeks' time she had at least absorbed the rudiments.

On the slate was "no sta tu culd."

Magdalene stared at Letice's production, wondering for a moment whether interpreting what she wrote would be any easier than trying to make out her gestures, and then light dawned. "Hagar does not wish to stay because it is too cold."

Letice beamed with joy, her huge dark eyes bright with satisfaction, with relief at having an outlet for the ideas locked within her. She embraced Magdalene with abandon. Magdalene returned the embrace heartily, but her throat was tight with sadness. Writing might help Letice, but reading the few words slowly inscribed on a slate could not really take the place of talking out a problem as she had done with Sabina. Sabina had been blind, but her ears and ability to feel emotion had been keen, and she was calm and sensible. Magdalene missed her more and more. And now she had probably driven Bell away, too. She bent her head to hide the misting of tears in her eyes and kissed Letice's forehead.

Watching them, Ella smiled, pleased by the satisfaction Magdalene and Letice seemed to feel, even though she did not understand it. Then the little frown returned to mar the perfect smoothness of her brow. Slowly she walked to one of the stools grouped near the hearth, sat down, and reached into the basket beside it for a piece of embroidery.

"Hagar annoyed the man," she said suddenly, then looked anxiously from Letice to Magdalene. "Is that telling tales?"

"Not about anything that annoys our clients," Magdalene said firmly. "You know I do not want to hear about what you think Letice or Hagar do wrong about their dress or cleaning their chambers or that they handle knives or eat what you do not like, but anything that troubles a man she has lain with, you must tell me at once."

"I do not mean to speak ill of Hagar, nor did she steal or be rude or unwelcoming," Ella said, naming the greatest sins she knew. "It was only that he wanted her to do something I would gladly have done, and she did not."

Since Hagar was accustomed to satisfying tastes far more exotic than any Magdalene permitted her clients, she doubted the refusal had been deliberate. She sighed. "Probably she did not understand him. She speaks barely ten words in French and no English at all and has not the smallest desire to learn." She sighed again. "I will have to go out to comb the stews again and see if I can discover a girl who is pretty and not too hardened."

Magdalene was not the only person who had come to the conclusion that a new whore must be found for the Old Priory Guesthouse. Sir Bellamy had been in too much of a fury when he left to think of anything, but by the time he had made his way across the bridge to London, weaving around tradesmen's stalls, dodging chapmen selling wares from packs on their backs, and avoiding customers, who kept stopping suddenly right in front of him to examine some item that attracted them, Bell's first fine rage had worn off.

The press of merchants, the nearly desperate enthusiasm with which all cried their wares, the devices they used to attract customers' attention, all reminded Bell of Magdalene's statement of need. He knew, in fact, how much rent she paid on the large stone house that had once been the guesthouse for a very strict order of nuns, so strict that they would not permit any man except the priest into their priory. The order had withered away, and the priory of St. Mary Overy with its church had been taken over by monks who were far less rigid. They had built a fine new guesthouse within the grounds and allowed the old guesthouse to fall back into the bishop of Winchester's hands.

The house was not suitable for many purposes, divided into many small cells except for the large front room, but it was too good to pull down or use for cheap storage. So when an offer was made to rent it for use as a bathhouse (which it was understood would be a whorehouse also) for which it was admirably arranged, that offer was accepted. It was, after all, only one of many such places the Church owned.

Having got that far in his thoughts, Bell recalled that many, many whores worked out of houses paying rent to his master, the bishop of Winchester. Since it was his business to deal with secular problems for the bishop, and most stews had or caused problems, he was well known to all the whoremasters and whoremistresses. Surely among all the women who plied their trade in those houses, he could find one who had not sunk to the very bottom, who was still young and attractive and able to be weaned from the worst ways.

Bell stopped abruptly, causing a man behind him to curse him as roundly as he had previously cursed the erratic progress of people in front of him. If he could bring Magdalene a new recruit and she would return to her practice of never taking a client herself, then he would know she was sincere about not wanting to be a whore.

He suddenly felt much lighter, smiled at the colorful chaos on the bridge, and started to turn around to go back to Southwark and start looking for an appropriate girl only to bump into an oncoming stranger. The check removed the smile from his face, but it was neither the physical contact nor the delay that made his well-shaped lips thin to grimness. He was appalled that he had been ready to put aside— no, worse, had *forgotten*—his duty because of a . . . whore. Yes, she was! She called herself a whore, and who should know better.

He stood rigid, causing several more people to shout curses at him, then started on his way again, his jaw set. Maybe he would look for a new woman for her, maybe he would not, but he had first to deal with a tradesman who had taken the bishop's money and not delivered the goods.

In a hurry now, he pushed past a man hawking candles, another thrusting a tray of hot pies at him, and almost banged into a plank set on two barrels and draped with strips of embroidered cloth. A single glance told him these were nothing compared with Magdalene's fine work, and he muttered several obscenities under his breath as he passed the obstacle and started down the slope that led off the bridge because it seemed he could not shut her out of his thoughts for two moments together.

He turned right at the bottom into Thames Street. That might have been a dangerous route for a man as well dressed as Bell, because all kinds of ill-doers bred among the docks and cheap drinking houses that catered to the sailors. However, the long sword and long knife with their well-worn hilts that hung at his broad leather belt gave warning that he would not be easy prey, and he passed without even a catcall flung after him.

Bell was not unaware of the danger but preferred it to making his way up Fish Street where he was too likely to be splashed with filthy water from the gutter or spattered with offal flung from stalls by busy fishmongers. A short walk past a narrow, nameless alley brought him to a wider street with a fresher smell. Lime Street did not, of course, provide shops only for dealers in limes but for many grocers with diverse but better-smelling stock than fish. Turning left into Lime, Bell passed another nameless alley, which separated the yards of the dwellings and warehouses on Thames Street from those attached to the grander houses of the merchants who had businesses in the East Chepe.

A right turn took him past a pepperer's shop and a large, double counter displaying staples. Before the open door to the next shop was a long trestle, invitingly heaped with bolts of cloth and hanks of yarn, a mercer. Beyond that was a closed door and a narrow, heavily barred goldsmith's window. Bell stopped by the mercer's counter.

"William Dockett?" he asked the man at the counter.

To his surprise, the young man's eyes widened and then filled with tears. "He is dead, sir, this six months." Then he swallowed and added, "Can I help you?"

"My business would be with your new master, then," Bell said, relaxing the severity of his tone. "Would you tell him that the bishop of Winchester's man has come to talk about an order that was paid for but never delivered."

He kept all threat from voice and manner. It seemed there was adequate excuse for the delayed delivery. If Docket had died after the order was made and paid for, there might well have been confusion. He was thus surprised again when the journeyman looked rather frightened and, instead of calling into the shop for his master, began a rambling defense of being sure all goods had been shipped as ordered.

"Then you had better carefully examine your deliverymen because the goods did *not* arrive, either at the bishop of Winchester's London residence or at Winchester. Now, why do you not call your new master? I have with me the original order and the tally stick showing payment. We can examine these and your master's records together and see when this order was made up, by whom, who carried it . . ."

"I cannot leave the stall now, good sir," the journeyman said, his voice quavering a little. "And I am not sure that my master is within. Perhaps you could come back at some later time—"

"I will come back with the sheriff in a quarter of a candlemark," Bell said, his voice rising. "I have more important things to do than to return over and over to suit the convenience of a merchant who is months late in fulfilling—"

"Now just a moment!"

The voice was loud and angry. Bell's hand dropped to his sword hilt, but he did not begin to draw. The new arrival was unarmed and dressed in a long gown that was not meant for action. In addition, he had seen that the man's glance flicked to the threat and dismissed it, instead fixing on his clothes. As the merchant took in Bell's short, emerald green overtunic, lavishly embroidered around the neck and hem with Magdalene's most fanciful work, the rich brown chausses with cross-garters to match the tunic, and elegant knee-high leather boots, his expression grew more and more bland.

When he spoke again, having also absorbed the excellent quality not only of Bell's outer garments but even of his lemon-yellow undertunic and fine white linen shirt, his voice and words were far more civil. And, when he heard Bell's complaint, he invited him in at once and waved him ahead toward the left side of the shop where a steep flight of stairs went up to a second story. Two doors opened at right angles to each other on the small landing. He opened the door facing the stairs to show an office full of boxes of parchments and tally sticks. Toward the back, where a window gave good light, was a table with a stool behind it and two in front.

As he selected one box from a neat pile to the left of the table, he introduced himself as Lintun Mercer, who had taken over William Dockett's business when he had died, very suddenly, the previous November. He quickly found the order, of which Bell had a copy, and then the other half of the tally stick Bell also carried, which proved payment had been made. He frowned then and bit his lip, but then shrugged and drew a deep breath.

Bell was agreeably surprised when, instead of beginning an argument about the difference in price at the time of the order and now or trying to shift the blame, Master Mercer acknowledged that the order had been made, paid for, and not delivered. He apologized profusely, excusing himself by mentioning the grief and confusion caused by William Dockett's sudden and unexpected death. Then he offered to deliver the bolts of cloth to the Southwark house within the week or to Winchester within a month.

Without the smallest hesitation, Bell accepted the apology and settled for delivery to the Southwark house. Carts constantly travelled between Winchester and Southwark on the bishop's business, and he felt the merchant should be rewarded by saving the cost of cartage for his quick offer of restitution. Bell had expected an extended argument about whose fault the loss of the cloth had been and had expected to be occupied at least until dinnertime before he obtained an admission of culpability from the merchant. He was delighted at the quick solution that allowed him almost a whole free day.

He wondered briefly whether he should mention the obvious unease of the young journeyman over the undelivered order. Could it have been diverted from its rightful goal rather than never leaving Dockett's shop? But there could be other causes than theft for the journeyman's behavior, and Bell was reluctant to get him into trouble.

Later, as he walked quickly toward the bridge and the stews of Southwark, Bell asked himself whether he had wished to save the journeyman or to avoid spending the time talking about the subject. A twinge of guilt assailed him, but he told himself that if the young man had taken advantage of the chaos following William Dockett's sudden death, it was not the kind of situation that was likely to be repeated. Likely, too, he had been so frightened by the discovery that the cloth had gone astray that any temptation to help himself again would be cured. And, finally, Bell thought, his duty was to protect the bishop, not to worry about merchants who were too trusting. The ten bolts of fustian would be delivered. He had fulfilled his duty.

Unfortunately, finding a new woman for Magdalene was not so easily accomplished. He managed to visit four stews before hunger drove him to a cookshop, where he sat scowling at the food and thinking how much better he would have enjoyed dining at the Old Priory Guesthouse. He was still not willing to yield to the necessity that Magdalene should take men to her bed, but he had to admit that not one of the raddled, broken, filthy, foul-mouthed creatures he had seen could possibly be presented to the clients of the Old Priory Guesthouse.

Nonetheless, he continued his search through the afternoon, telling himself that there must be one, at least one, who was new enough to the trade to be salvaged. He had repeated that to himself for perhaps the tenth time when he opened the door to a place he knew too well. At least five times in the past half year he had been sent to wrench from the whoremaster rent he had not paid, to seek for stolen items, to investigate complaints about women beaten or not paid, and once to question the whores and the whoremaster about a body pulled from the river (just across the road) who someone swore had been seen entering that place.

Taking a deep breath, Bell stepped into what he always thought must look like the entrance to hell. It was dark and the air was hot and moist from the constant splashing out and refilling of the two huge tubs, the token baths. Someone was always screaming, sometimes with laughter and sometimes with pain, and the sound echoed off the water and the slimy ceiling, while along the walls and in the corners, dark figures humped and squirmed, moaning with lust (or, for the whores, groaning with boredom).

The whoremaster was not at his usual place, half athwart the door where he could trip or seize any customer who had not paid. Bell had just opened his mouth to shout for him when a door to one of the back rooms slammed open and a woman's voice, rich and musical despite the fact that it was loud enough to override all other sounds, began to revile some spluttering male in language that opened Bell's eyes but in an accent that was purer than that of his own mother or sisters.

There was the sound of a slap followed by a male howl of pain, and a woman darted between the two tubs and then turned to stand at bay, having picked up a heavy, long-handled metal ladle, which she gripped with grim determination to defend herself. The man who followed her, gasping and limping, was the whoremaster himself. Bell grinned, guessing he had tried to sample the merchandise without offering to pay.

The whore backed away toward Bell; the whoremaster followed, waving his fists and angling around to drive the woman into a space where she could be trapped. The movement brought her hair and then her face into the light of a dirt-smeared window, and Bell drew a deep breath.

"That's enough!" Bell roared as the whoremaster gestured to two men emerging from the shadows and the whore raised the ladle, but with a sob of terror.

"Who the hell—" the whoremaster began, turning his head just enough to see Bell, whereupon he uttered an obscenity and waved off his bully boys. He had tried once to have Bell overpowered and gained nothing but two crippled servants, a visit from the sheriff, and a huge fine. "I paid my rent," he snarled. "You got no right to interfere—"

"The bishop has a right to do anything he wants," Bell snapped, "including to put you out of this place, so do not tell me what I have and have not a right to do. Who is this woman? I have not seen her before."

"They come and go. Who? She says her name's Diot."

"Come here, Diot," Bell said, gesturing her toward a place where the light would fall more fully on her.

She hesitated a moment, then lowered the ladle and came. Bell drew another deep breath. She was not as beautiful as Magdalene; her mouth was wider and its shape not so perfect, her nose broader, not so fine and delicate, but her eyes were a clear green, large and well lashed, and her hair, even though now it was dirty and stringy, when clean would be the rich color of oak leaves in the autumn. She was wearing little more than filthy rags and sported a number of dark bruises that showed through rents in the fabric, but the skin would be very white, Bell thought, once the grime was gone. He took a farthing from his purse and put it in her hand. Without a word, she turned and led him back into the room from which she had erupted.

There was a torch burning to the right of the door, and the resinous, smoky smell battled with the miasma of stale sweat, stale sex, old vomit, and overused bodies. Worse, the torch cast enough light to expose the thin, filthy pallet near the back wall. A crumpled blanket lay in a heap on it; what color either had been was impossible to guess—both were dark gray and shiny with filth now—but Bell could see a darting movement here and there on pallet and blanket that showed how many six-legged pests inhabited the bed.

Although he closed the door, Bell did not move farther into the room. "Well, Diot," he said, "what was the cause of that altercation?"

"He'll say I stole from him. It isn't true. He wanted to use me without payment. I had given him his tithe when I came. If he wants more, he must pay just like any other."

Bell let his breath out, only realizing then that he had been holding it. The voice was lovely and the speech as good clear French as was spoken in the household of any nobleman of England.

"Perhaps you should not have been quite so forceful," he remarked, smiling. "Men do not readily forgive having their nuts cracked. I do not think this stew will be a safe place for you to work." He saw her nostrils flare, her lips tighten; the sheen of tears that dimmed her green eyes.

"Then I will go elsewhere. There are stews enough in Southwark."

The words were bold, but there was the faintest unsteadiness in the voice. Bell smiled more broadly when he took in her increased anxiety. Likely she had stood up for her "rights" in other places and been cast out; this was not one of the more desirable houses. He shook his head.

"I do not think so. I think you have already made yourself unwelcome in too many places. I think you had better come away with me. I know of a very special house where you might do well and be happy."

"Oh, no!" she exclaimed. "I will take my chances in the ditches and alleys before I go to such a place. At least I will die quick and clean in the streets."

Bell laughed aloud. "Not that kind of special. This is a place that serves only the rich, and the woman who keeps the place does not allow her whores to be mistreated. She might be willing to accept you as a replacement for one of her women who has gone to live with a client. You are very beautiful, and you speak a fine French. Do you speak English too?"

"You want me to speak English while we couple?" she asked in that language. "Good enough. I will not even charge you extra for it."

Bell shuddered visibly. "Couple in this place? It is worse than a sty. I would sooner be celibate forever. Well, Diot, will you come with me? I swear you will be safe and free to leave if Magdalene will not accept you."

When she did not answer, he opened the door and went out, loosening his knife from its scabbard as he came into the main room. Leaning on each of the baths, watching the door, the whoremaster's brutes were waiting. Diot must have peered out of the door behind him and seen them too.

"Wait," she called. "I am coming."

Two

Master Mainard Saddler raised his eyes and his knife from his
work at the same moment. His lifted head exposed a monstrous
countenance. One third of his face, from midforehead to just below
the right jaw, was raised and puckered, a shiny deep red blotched with
purple. The dreadful birthmark ran right up over almost half his scalp
and, where it lay, he was bald. That made the luxuriant growth of
russet curls on the rest of his head look like a travesty of a wig set
askew. His nose was oddly flattened, with too-wide nostrils, and his
mouth was horribly distorted, a harelip having been inexpertly sewn
together in infancy.

The very thin man in a tattered tunic who had spoken his name
did not flinch away from the raised knife or Master Mainard's face
and knew he need not be afraid although Mainard was a good foot
taller and half a man of hard, solid muscle wider than he. He looked
only at Mainard's one beautiful feature, a pair of meltingly warm
brown eyes.

"Mistress Bertrild wants you home," he said.

The voice could have reflected the arrogance of the words, but it
did not. There was only resignation in it. Master Mainard nodded and
drew an oiled cloth over the piece of leather into which he had been
carving an elaborate and very beautiful design. He did not answer
directly but looked across at his journeyman who was using a very

strong, sharp, wickedly hooked knife to cut the seat of a saddle from thick, stiff horsehide.

"Codi, see what is left from your dinner and give it to Jean to eat on his way home." He looked back at the servant, who had murmured thanks with real gratitude. "Tell your mistress that I will come as soon as I have put away my tools," he said, and began to clean the knife with which he had been working.

As soon as Codi had handed Jean a packet done up in a clean rag, the servant left the workroom and went out of the shop, nearly trotting. Mainard quickly finished wiping the knife and tucked it away into an iron-banded box that stood under the table. Having closed the box and slipped a lock through the hasp, he also went into the shop, but he did not go out of the door. Instead, he climbed the steep stair, which was guarded on its open side by a new-looking railing.

At the door at the top of the stair, he paused and called, "Sabina."

"Come in," a sweet voice replied at once.

He opened the door, stepped inside, and caught his breath, then uttered a low chuckle. She had been with him almost a month; he saw her at least once a day, often three or four times—as often as he could find an excuse to go up to her chamber—but he still was not accustomed to the delighted smile with which she greeted him or to her beauty. He looked at the mass of dark hair, the deep red-brown of a well-polished chestnut falling to her hips in deep waves, at the oval face with its short, slightly broad nose and wide, deep-rose mouth. Even the closed, sunken eyes, their dark lashes lying on her creamy skin, added to the beauty by giving an air of mystery to her smiling face.

"Haesel," he said, addressing the girl child who was wrapping up a heel of a loaf of bread to put on one of the shelves to the left of the hearth. "Do not bother to save what is left of our meal. Take it over to the church and give it to whoever is feeding the beggars there. Here is a penny. Buy some pottage and half a roasted chicken and a sweet— less sweet and more food," he told her, shaking a finger at her, "for your evening meal."

The child grinned at him, took the penny, and pushed it through the opening in her gown into the pocket tied around her waist. If she had been afraid of his ugliness when he first took her from the church-yard where she had been left when her parents abandoned her, she was accustomed to it now and was as lively and saucy as any well-fed child of ten should be. She promptly dumped odds and ends of meat, the soaked trenchers off which they had eaten, some rinds of cheese, and the broken remains of a pasty into a basket, and skipped out of the room.

When the door closed behind her, Sabina said, "You will not have the evening meal with us, my love?"

"Are you bored and lonely, Sabina?" he asked.

A sweet smile made her face even more beautiful, and she held out her hand. He hurried forward and took it. "I am always lonely when you are not with me, Mainard."

He sighed heavily. "That was what I feared. You are accustomed to the company of the other women of the Old Priory Guesthouse. There is no one to talk to here —"

"Oh, you silly man." Her laughter was sweet and low, an invitation to intimacy. "Can you not recognize a compliment when you hear one? It is your company I crave, love, not that of my 'sisters,' fond as I am of them. I am not bored or lonely. I have songs to make up and Haesel to teach. You chose well, when you chose her. She is very clever and already speaks a little French."

He kissed her hand and then, when she raised her head invitingly, her lips.

She clung for a moment, then said hesitantly, "Would it be easier for you, dearling, if I went back? At first I thought your wife would not care since she did not want you, but now I know she is angry at my being here. . . ."

"Don't!" Mainard fell to his knees and buried his face in her lap. "Do not leave me!" He drew a sobbing breath. "If you want other men, have them. I will look the other way. Only do not leave me."

She bent over him, kissing his hair and the bald, purple scalp. When she did that, he gasped and shivered. "I will never leave you of my own will, Mainard. I do not want or need other men. You give me such joy that I do not believe I will ever desire another man. I did not ask for my own sake, beloved. I served in a common brothel for years. You know that. I do not care what people shout at me or throw at me or even for blows. I only care that I may be making your life harder." She kissed him again. "It is hard enough already, I know."

"No longer." He looked up at her almost as if he were worshipping at a shrine. "Every day is a joy to me now. I wake up each morning knowing you are here, that I may see you and speak to you whenever I wish. She can say what she likes to me now. I am a man again, which you gave back to me, and I know my own worth. It is for you that I fear."

Sabina shook her head. "It is nothing to me. I know what I am also. If you and only you come to my bed, I am no whore. I am your woman, as good and chaste as any married wife." A frown formed between her high-arched brows. "Except, and I am very sorry for it, that I cannot sew your clothes or cook your meals—"

Mainard laughed aloud. "Neither does Bertrild. Nor did she ever, and never regretted it." He got to his feet but bent to kiss her once more. "You will not be insulted again, beloved. I swear it. I have spoken to the justiciar and the sheriff, and the Watch are warned— and well paid—to guard you. If I can come back before the shop closes, I will, and eat with you. We can always send out to the cookshop for another dish if what Haesel brings back is not enough."

"If you can—" She held out her arms, and he bent and touched her so she could embrace him. "I will be waiting. Whenever you can come to me, I will be waiting. God bless you, Mainard."

She kissed his cheek and let him go. He looked toward the door. "Where is that little devil? You treat her too gently, Sabina. She is doubtless playing games in the Chepe. I do not like to leave you alone. . . ."

"Why not?" Now she laughed. "I have my staff and I promise not to fall into the fire or do anything else silly. I can always call for Codi or the boys if I need help. Go. She will be even angrier if you are slow in arriving."

Although Mainard knew it would make no difference at all if he had flown directly home the moment he heard Bertrild's message, he did not say so to Sabina. When he had first married Bertrild, he had done everything within his power to please her. She had not been willing to live above the shop, so he had bought a fine house on Lime Street and allowed her to furnish it all anew. She was noble born, she told him, and could not cook and clean like other merchants' wives; so he had allowed her to buy four slaves, whom she mistreated shamefully. She had always acted as if she were doing him a favor by taking what he gave, and when he could give no more, she turned on him.

It was better for Sabina to believe that Bertrild would be less unpleasant if he arrived quickly. She, sweet soul that she was, would fret herself less, he thought, as he strode east past Perekin FitzRevery's mercery. He bought much of the fabric he used for decoration and padding from Master FitzRevery, and he raised a hand to the man, who was standing in the door of his shop. FitzRevery also raised a hand and took a half-step forward, as if he would have liked to speak.

Ordinarily Mainard would have stopped gladly; FitzRevery was a good friend and had done him the greatest favor any man ever had. He had told Mainard there was a meeting of the guild involved in building the new stone bridge across the Thames, but either by his mistaken directions or Mainard's misunderstanding, Mainard had ended up in the Old Priory Guesthouse. By then, Bertrild's cruelty had rendered him virtually impotent, and he was backing out faster than he had come in, when Sabina had come forward and taken his hand.

He had realized that she was blind, that she could not see the horror of his face, and just for the need to talk to someone who would not have to look away he went with her. In half an hour she had restored him, and he stayed the night, proving himself a full man over and over. And when he had apologized for taking advantage, she had laughed and urged him on, calling him ... "beautiful" ... as she stroked his broad shoulders, his heavily muscled arms, and his strong thighs.

There was no favor FitzRevery could not ask in return, although he said it had all been a mistake. This time, however, Mainard did not respond, thinking what FitzRevery had to say could not be important or he would have come to Mainard's shop to talk, so he just hurried down the street. He was not hurrying to pacify his wife, but because he hoped to hear what she had to say and still have time to claim he had work to finish or a client to see so he could return to Sabina.

His long legs took him swiftly across the mouth of Fish Street and eventually to a goldsmith's heavily barred window, from which a golden flash caught his eye. Mainard hesitated, tempted to go in and buy a new trinket for Sabina; she got so deliciously angry with him when he brought her jewelry—and frequently made him promise to return the piece, which he never did. Then his twisted mouth thinned. Not on his way to Lime Street. If Bertrild sensed he had anything of value on him, she would begin to scream for possession.

The thought of her sent an odd hot/cold sensation up Mainard's back, a double kind of hatred which he had never experienced before. His hands clenched, and he backed away from the goldsmith's door, setting off again at an even faster pace. Thus, he was a little breathless when he walked in the door of the Lime Street house, and Bertrild sniffed with disdain. Knowing that she was contemptuous because she believed he had hurried to appease her, Mainard grinned as broadly as he could. Bertrild shuddered.

"Freak!" she exclaimed. "You should be dragged along in a player's troupe so you could be shown off as a monster."

"I make more money as a saddler," he said, and laughed.

Bertrild sprang to her feet. "I am glad to hear you say that," she spat. "I need fifty marks."

"I do not make so much money as that," Mainard replied indifferently. "I am a saddler, not an earl. I do not have fifty marks."

"Because you spent it on buying that woman!" Bertrild shrieked. "You would not pay the debts on my father's land, but you paid God-knows-what for that blind whore."

Mainard did not wish to discuss Sabina. He had done his best to hide their liaison to salve Bertrild's pride and had failed. Now he simply ignored that part of her accusation.

"I could not pay the debt on your father's land," he said, and added truthfully, "and had I had enough, I still would not have bought it free. The estate was ruined. I have never held land. I could not have restored it."

"Return the woman to the pesthouse from which you bought her and give me the money, or I will tell the world what you have done."

She would not let the subject go. "I did not buy Sabina," he said flatly. "She was never a slave or bound. I paid nothing and will give you nothing."

"I will find out what you paid, and I will get it!"

Mainard shrugged. "You will only find proof that Sabina is a free woman, lodging above my shop. She pays rent—"

"She lodges in your bed!" Bertrild's voice rose to a shriek again.

He could not deny that but neither could he bear daily recrimination on the subject. With his heart beating like a hammer in his throat, Mainard made an offer it would kill him to keep. "If you will take me back into your bed and serve me as a wife, I will tell Sabina to find other lodging when her lease is ended."

"Lie with a deformed monster and breed more monsters!"

Impervious to all her other taunts and insults since Sabina had restored his sense of worth, he still flinched at those words. It was a fear he had not yet had courage to mention to Sabina. While she had been a whore, he knew she had taken potions to clean out her womb; he did not know whether she was still doing so. He must talk to Sabina, and soon. . . . And the thought brought home the knowledge that Bertrild had refused the bargain he offered, no matter how cruelly. Suppressing his relief lest she see how glad he was and change her mind just to torment him, he shrugged again.

"I am a man. I have my needs. If you will not satisfy them, I must seek elsewhere for my relief."

"You may spend a farthing in the stews then, if you can find a whore filthy enough to accept you. You cannot shame me by establishing a mistress in my house."

"This is your house. You wanted no part of the rooms above my shop, so they are mine to do with what I will."

"You will not keep your whore there! I will go to the alderman, to the justiciar if I must."

"Do not trouble yourself or waste your time. I have already spoken to both alderman and justiciar, and to the sheriff and the Watch also. All know that Sabina is a blind musician. They know the rent she pays, and they know she was once a whore but did not like the life and left it. No men ever visit her. She goes out only to sing and play."

Bertrild gobbled with rage. None of those men would fault another man for keeping a mistress, and she was known to them for so-called false complaints, too. Her hatred was so fierce that, strong as he was, Mainard felt uneasy.

"I will destroy her . . . and you too!" she hissed.

"Unless I finish you first," he said, rage and bitterness over-
whelming him, and turned and left the house.

———•◦•———

Bell was very pleased with the woman he had found until they had
almost reached the Old Priory Guesthouse and, turning a corner, he
noticed the position of the sun in the sky. Until then he had been so
busy watching to make sure the whoremaster had not sent his men to
attack him and take revenge on the woman, that he had not realized
it was midafternoon and the clients who came to Magdalene's soon
after dinner would already have arrived. He glanced at the woman
beside him and shuddered. No way could he bring this filthy creature
where any client could see her.

The full daylight showed how far she had fallen. Now that the
light of battle was gone, her eyes were like the dull green slime on
stagnant water, and her mouth looked hard. Bell moved a little farther
away from her. There were lice and fleas crawling on her. Likely he
had a few of his own, but not so many one could see them walking
about.

He thought of putting Diot in the stable, but he was afraid that
William of Ypres, one of the king's favorites and leader of all his mercenary troops, might suddenly appear. He was very rich, very powerful,
an old friend and patron of Magdalene's, and he tended to arrive when
he liked without warning. He would not be amused by finding something like Diot in Magdalene's stable — or maybe he *would* be amused;
one could never tell with Lord William — but he would tease
Magdalene about it, and *she* would not be amused.

By then they had reached the gate in the high stone wall that
surrounded the Old Priory Guesthouse. When the nuns had it built,
they had arranged adequate protection and isolation for their guests,
although they would not accept them within the priory's walls. The
leather thong of a fairly large bell hung in easy reach. Bell's lips
thinned. If Magdalene was short a woman, all she had to do was pull
the bell cord inside and be less welcoming.

Usually he rang the bell because Magdalene did not favor guests walking in uninvited; this time he did not. He unlatched and opened the gate softly, turned to tell Diot to enter, and just barely caught her as she started to run away. There was terror in her eyes as she looked at the tall stone wall.

"No," she whispered hoarsely, "I will not go in there. God knows what is done to the women kept behind such walls."

"Your name should be Idiot, not Diot," Bell growled. "The walls were built by the nuns who then owned the guesthouse. Did you not see that the gate was open? What matter how high the wall if there is an open gate in it? No one is kept in this house against her will." He pulled her through and shut the gate behind him.

"No!" she cried, pulling back.

Bell seized her and shook her. "Hush!" he hissed. "If you disturb Magdalene's clients, she will murder me. Listen, I swear to you that no harm will come to you here. If you do not wish to stay, you will be free to go. But if you squall and make a stir and trouble Magdalene's clients, I will beat you silly. Now shut up and come with me."

Without further explanation, he dragged her around the side of the house, past the stable and into the garden. There he plumped her down on a bench screened by rose bushes and bade her sit until he returned, threatening to beat her if she ran away. By then the quiet, well-ordered garden, the sheltered bench, the open windows from which no screams could be heard had reduced the terror the walls had wakened in her. Before she could decide whether her fear of this "special" house was greater than her fear of angering a man powerful enough to cow the whoremaster, he was back with a most beautiful, elegantly dressed woman.

"Good God, what is this?" Magdalene asked, stopping short when she saw Diot.

"Never mind the dirt," Bell said hastily. "It will wash away. More important, listen to her speak. I do not know what has befallen her, but if she did not begin in a gentleman's Household, I will kiss her as she is."

"Others have not found it so great a sacrifice," Diot snapped.

Magdalene's lips had parted to make a sharp comment to Bell, but she turned her eyes to the woman. The filthy rags and the bruises that could be seen through them had given the impression of an utterly broken creature, but the tart retort to a dominant male and the faultless accent in the Norman tongue started a new train of ideas.

"You were beaten and cast out of your last place," Magdalene said. "For what?"

"Doubtless for refusing to obey orders," Bell put in, when Diot hesitated. "I saved her another beating, or maybe worse, for refusing to service the whoremaster and doing some damage to his private parts."

"It was a whoremistress who did this to me," Diot said. "I had hoped she would be more understanding, but when I refused to eat a man's dung, she had me beaten, took my clothing and my few farthings, and cast me out like this."

Magdalene sighed. There was, of course, no way to guess whether the woman's statement was true. It was certainly not impossible. And she had now seen through the dirt what Bell's male eyes had more quickly discerned—that the woman was beautiful.

"And you speak good English too?" Magdalene asked.

"English mother, Norman father," Diot replied in that language, "like so many others. But my mother was very beautiful, and my father was fond of her, so he let her speak her own tongue as well as learning his." She stopped speaking abruptly and folded her generous mouth into a thin, hard line.

Magdalene wondered what had happened, but she did not ask. She had no intention of listening to a tragical story that might be pure invention . . . or might not. It did not matter now any more than her own tale, but even if everything the woman said was false and she was not suitable for the Old Priory Guesthouse, Magdalene could well afford to help her a step up out of pure charity.

"From what Bell says, you cannot go back to the place he found you either—"

"It was that house on Dockside opposite Botolph's Warf," Bell said.

Magdalene shrugged. "Well, you would not want to go back there in any case."

"Looking like this, only that kind of place will take me," Diot remarked bitterly.

"Yes, that is true," Magdalene said, "which is why I will offer you a bath and a decent gown."

"How much?" Diot asked, her eyes suddenly brighter with eagerness.

"For *caritas*. I am a woman and a whore also."

Diot caught her breath, one hand clenching on the breast of her tattered garment and started to stand. Then she sank back on the bench and bit her lip. "I will owe you no favor? I will not work in any 'special' house. I do not mind futtering, but I will not be cut or beaten or sodomized or—"

Magdalene turned on Bell. "What in the world did you tell her about this place?" she asked indignantly.

He made an exasperated grimace. "Nothing that could give her such an idea, except that once I did use the word 'special.' I swore you did not allow your women to be misused over and over, but when she saw the walls . . ."

"Those were built by an order of nuns nearly one hundred years ago." Magdalene shrugged. "I will not drag you in. Bell and I will leave you now. The back door is open. If you wish to come in, the first door past the kitchen entrance is the bathing room. If you wish, you may enter there. I believe there is a barrel of cold water and a hearth with a kettle of hot. You may bathe if you like. You may not go anywhere else in the house. If you try to do so, I will have you beaten and taken to the sheriff. You may, of course, leave at any time."

Diot stared after the retreating backs but did not take long to follow them in. She was still afraid, but having heard Magdalene's offer, it now seemed to her that any torture she would experience if she had guessed wrong was a price she was willing to pay to be clean again. Trembling, she entered the open back door, braced against being seized, but only an old woman, who had been sitting in the kitchen doorway, was there. She stood up abruptly and stared at Diot, then pointed wordlessly to the next doorway.

There Diot found exactly what Magdalene had described, including, folded on a stool, a shift, an undertunic, a gown, and stockings. After staring at them for a moment, Diot rushed to close the door and found to her utter delight that it could be locked with a light bar. She dropped that into its slots immediately and hurried to the hearth. Here she carefully removed the twist of cloth that held her three farthings—

two that she had earned and the whoremaster had not yet collected and the one Bell had given her—laid the farthings on the stone and threw the cloth into the fire where, grease-laden as it was, it started to burn at once.

As quickly as she could, she then tore off every scrap of filthy cloth and added it to the fire. Naked, she drew a deep breath of satisfaction. Even if the fine whoremistress had meant to force her back into her old rags if she did not agree to let them do what they wished with her, she could not do so now. If they drove her into the street naked, she could complain—even a whore could complain of that.

Finally, she turned to the bath, dipped water from the barrel until it was half full, added the hot water, and refilled the kettle with fresh water. Then she realized the sides of the tub were too high to climb over and she nearly began to weep before she called herself a fool. Beside the tub there was a second stool and on it lay a clean drying cloth and a brush and a comb, both well used (the comb was missing a few teeth and the bristles of the brush were bent) but perfectly clean, and a pot of soap. Diot drew a deep breath and tears did begin to well over her lower lids.

Diot spent a long time in the tub. She washed twice in the first water, also washing and combing out her hair again and again. Then she got out and dipped out every drop she could into an empty barrel. After that, she hesitated, feeling she might be taking advantage, but the river was only over the road and down the bank. If the whoremistress was angry because she had used too much water, she would gladly fill the barrel again. Humming happily, Diot refilled the tub and began to scrub herself again.

Several times she had been aware of footsteps and voices in the corridor outside the bathing room, but she paid no attention. The door was safely barred. She would be clean again and decently clad before she had to gird her loins to face whatever awaited her.

Eventually and still reluctantly, Diot rose from the nearly cold water and dried herself. Wrapped in the drying cloth, she went slowly about emptying the tub and cleaning it, but she could not make the task last forever and, in fact, she was growing more and more anxious about her fate. Better to know than to fear, she told herself. Still her hair was almost dry before she dressed in the clothing that had been left for her. Now she was listening again, and she realized it had been perfectly quiet for a long time. Stroking the well-worn but clean and whole cloth she wore for courage, she went and unbarred the door.

The old woman was standing in the kitchen doorway again when Diot stepped out, and she pointed up the corridor and said, in a slightly overloud and flat voice, "Go into the common room if you want to speak to Magdalene."

Diot cast a single longing glance toward the back door, but she knew the old woman could tell the whoremistress she had left, and she could be caught before she got out the gate. In addition, clean and decently clad, old patterns were wakening. She had been well treated, even given guesting gifts; she could not escape the obligation of at least returning thanks. She nodded at the old woman and turned to walk up the corridor toward the common room. As she passed a closed door, she heard a woman's delighted giggle. Through the opposite door she heard a man's groan. No screams. No shouts of rage or insults, which usually accompanied the passion of men who needed to hurt women.

At the entrance to the common room, she stopped in shock. It was very large, with two windows on either side of an open door. To the left side of the room was a big, well-polished table flanked on either side with a long bench and at the head and foot with shorter ones. On the other side of the chamber was a substantial stone hearth on which a small but bright fire burned. Around the hearth were four stools, two with sewing baskets beside them. The third held the man who had brought her here, comfortably disposed with one hand on his knee and the other gesturing as he spoke. Before the fourth stool was a large embroidery frame, and behind that sat the whoremistress, working at a pattern which had to be an altar cloth.

Diot stood staring at the central large cross done in thread-of-gold and at the oval beside it which she thought must be a Saint Sebastian. She was speechless. Whatever she imagined, it had not been this chamber, far better suited to a nobleman's London dwelling than a Southwark whorehouse, with a whoremistress embroidering a religious article.

"There!" The man had noticed her. "I told you she would wash up pretty."

The whoremistress — her name was Magdalene, Diot now remembered — turned her head. She smiled. "Pretty is not the word. You are quite beautiful, Diot."

"A curse," Diot said bitterly, and was surprised to see the woman, who was even more beautiful than she, wince.

"So it can be," Magdalene agreed. "Now, would you like to join us?" She glanced at the way the light came in the windows. "I would like to speak to you about whether this house will suit you, but if you do not wish to join us, you may go without let or hindrance."

Diot looked around the room. She ached so to remain in this place, which brought back to her a life she had lost, but she remembered that terrible things could lie under a clean exterior. Her lips parted, but before she could speak, the old woman marched into the room.

"She cleaned up the room real good," she said to Magdalene, "and even remembered to fill the kettle, but the water barrel is near empty."

Diot felt herself blushing, a thing she was sure she had long forgotten how to do. "I took two baths," she confessed in a low voice. "I will gladly fetch water from the river to refill the barrel, if you will show me what to use."

Magdalene smiled at her very warmly. "Thank you. That is a fair and gracious offer, but it is not needful. I have a man who comes in the morning to do such chores."

"Then —" Diot began, still not quite certain what she was going to say, when the old woman made her jump by seizing her hand.

"Here," she said, pressing three farthings into Diot's palm. "You left 'em on the hearth."

Diot stared at the coins. How could she have left them? Yet she knew that she had forgotten because the bath, the soap, the comb and brush, the clean, decent clothing, had pushed her back into a time when she did not need to be much concerned with three farthings. Yet now, they were the difference between starving or selling what she was wearing.

"Th-thank you. Oh, th-thank you," she stammered. "I would not have been able to buy food, and I am so hungry . . ."

The old woman cocked her head but did not reply, and Magdalene said loudly, "She was thanking you, Dulcie. And she is hungry. See if there is some bread and cheese and a cup of ale for her." She turned to Diot as the old woman started briskly back to the kitchen. "She is deaf," she said. "If you want her to understand, you must speak slowly and loudly."

"You have a deaf servant?" Diot blinked. Such people were ordinarily cast away to live or die as they could.

"It has its advantages and its disadvantages in this establishment. Sometimes it is hard to make her understand, but on the other hand, she never hears anything she should not hear, so she cannot blab any client's business—not that she would do so apurpose, but anyone can make a mistake."

Fascinated, Diot took a few steps closer, and Magdalene waved to the empty stools. This time, after a wary glance at the silent man who was watching her, Diot sat down.

"Letice," Magdalene continued, "one of my women, is mute; she cannot say anything she should not either. Ella, the other woman, could not remember or understand, even if she was willing to pay attention to anything other than a man's privates. And that, Diot, is the base and foundation of this house and its prosperity. My clients pay high fees, not so much for futtering a clean, sweet-smelling, beautiful, and enthusiastic woman, although all my women are beautiful, clean, sweet-smelling, and enthusiastic, but for utter security. My clients are mostly rich; some are also important men who cannot afford to have their private pleasures common knowledge. In this house, they are safe, their names, their business, their persons, and their property. No man has ever lost so much as a half-farthing in this house nor had his coming and going remarked if he wished to hide it. No tale has ever come out of this house to discomfit a client."

"You make clear what the women must and must not do," Diot said. "Aside from security, what do the men receive?"

"A good enough counterfeit of affection, admiration, and desire to convince each man that he is handsome, clever, and altogether wonderful; that the woman who served him cannot wait to serve him again. A client also expects a sympathetic ear if he has troubles—but he knows he may not take out those troubles on his woman. That is what you fear, but neither abuse nor unnatural acts are permitted in this house, and I have powerful protectors to enforce my will."

"That is true," the man said with an odd grimace, and got to his feet. "I hope this solves your problem," he added, a touch of anger in his voice.

"I hope so, too," Magdalene said, "but it will make no difference to what I am." Then she sighed and held out her hand. "Will you not stay and eat with us, Bell?"

He shook his head, but took her hand and kissed it. Then turned and went out the door.

Three

On the second Sunday morning after Diot had arrived in the Old Priory Guesthouse, she was occupying one of the four stools near the hearth with a small embroidery frame on her knee. The bells of St. Mary Overy rang out for Tierce and Ella began to sing a hymn in her sweet, little-girl voice. Diot drew in a deep breath and blinked her eyes to drive back the tears that had formed in them. It was as if the whoremaster's men had killed her in that loathesome stew and, having expiated her sins in pain, she had gone to heaven.

Although she had been fearful and doubting a week ago, Diot had not been able to force herself out of that beautiful, quiet house, and when Magdalene again asked if she wished to stay, she had agreed. By that time, the maid had laid a generous portion of bread and cheese and a small cup of ale on the table. Magdalene then secured her needle and gestured Diot to take a seat.

While Diot ate, Magdalene told her that one of her women had gone to live with a lover, and she was in need of someone to take her place. After the clients had left, Diot would be able to meet the permanent residents and decide if she thought she could work with them. Whether or not she wished to do so, she could have an evening meal and a place to sleep. If she thought she would like to stay, she could remain for one week on sufferance. In that time, if she stole, she would be put out penniless; if she was disagreeable to or offended a client, she would be put out with a penny. If she satisfied the clients and did not offend Ella or Letice, she would be paid ten pence for the week's work without charge for room and board, and then she would begin a month's trial.

Diot had not believed a word of it—but it had all been true. The first Sunday had been like a dream. After breaking her fast on a meal she had not seen the like of for two years, she heard Magdalene tell Letice to pay Hagar and take her back to the place where her countrymen stayed. Diot had then been told she would have Hagar's chamber. She had been told where clean linen and cleaning supplies were kept and left to make the room into her own. Wanting to believe the dream, she had scrubbed everything washable and polished everything else until the place smelled like spring and every surface shone.

The next day, replete with good meals and well rested, she was offered her first client. He was a big man and brutal-looking, but soft-spoken and gentle when he touched her. He was also very richly dressed and carried a heavy purse. Diot did not need to feign enthusiasm; she had always enjoyed futtering, and she particularly enjoyed titillating a man until he was so drained he begged for rest.

So after she submitted beneath him, she rose atop to ride him, and after that gallop, she had kissed him softly as he slipped asleep, relaxed and snoring. Diot lay beside him eyeing the jewels twinkling on the collar and sleeves of his surcoat. With a sharp knife, she could lift one or two of those jewels and perhaps she could add a coin from his purse. . . . Would he miss any of those?

Before she moved, however, she had considered the powerful muscles, the hard face, the scarred arms and callused hands. Was that a man who would dress like a popinjay to go to a whorehouse? It was a not-very-subtle trap, she realized, and let her eyes close with relief. She had not really wanted to steal and was relieved to know it was out of her power to do so.

She touched nothing that was not hers all the following week, even running after one merchant to return a shilling he had left on her clothes chest. He had laughed and said it was for her, that she had given him a wilder ride than he had known in years. And then, hardly believing what she was doing, she had gone to ask Magdalene whether she was permitted to keep for herself what had been offered or was required to share with Letice and Ella. A whole shilling! But she had not lost it.

"So long as you never ask nor even give the smallest hint that you desire a present or an extra coin, you may keep what is freely offered," Magdalene had said. "But they are already paying ten times the rate of a common stew and know my women are well paid, so will rarely offer more. Moreover, if any man thinks you are prodding him to give more, he will complain loud and long—and you will have to leave."

"No, no," Diot remembered herself saying, her voice trembling. "I will never ask for more. I will do all I can to please them."

At that point she still did not believe that Magdalene would pay her ten pence for her week's work. Ten pence! Forty farthings. That would have been eighty men where she had been; here it had been twelve, two a day and on two days another man who stayed the whole night, but that was pleasant. They had talked and laughed and played a game of chess and had a little meal in the middle of the night, which Dulcie provided as a matter of course without grumbling.

Then atop that, atop the shilling and the full meals and the clean sheets, this very morning Magdalene *had* given her the same ten pence as she handed to Letice and Ella and told her she would be free to go to the East Chepe to shop, all by herself, any morning before clients came. But best of all, she had what she had been dreaming about for days. Magdalene had said she had done well and could stay for another month.

Diot knew she was still on trial. If she offended a client during that time, she would be put out; if she stole, everything she had would be taken to appease the client and she would be turned over to the sheriff. But she did not care about those strictures. She would never *have* to steal again. She was never hungry or cold now; she was safely lodged in her own clean, well-furnished chamber; and she now believed that no client permitted in the door could tempt her to offend. Diot closed her eyes and swallowed. Surely she was dead and in heaven.

Magdalene had been watching her newest whore from the corners of her eyes as she embroidered one of the final saint medallions of the altar cloth that was due at the mercer's next week. She was far better pleased with Diot than she had expected to be. As the woman's fear of misuse receded, Diot had shown herself to be clever and surprisingly perceptive about the desires of the men to whom she was offered. And she enjoyed her work. Now all that needed to be proven was that she would not revert to her old ways, that she would not tell tales of the clients where she should not, and that familiarity would not breed contempt of her clients.

Just as Magdalene was considering whether she should allow matters to proceed on their own or give Diot a gentle warning, the door, which had been closed against the morning chill, was opened to admit a girl child followed by a blind woman. Magdalene caught her needle into the cloth and smiled, assuming that Sabina had found time to visit.

"Magdalene!"

The voice was so strained, so choked, that the smile was wiped from Magdalene's face, and she jumped to her feet, knocking over her embroidery frame. "Sabina," she cried, starting forward, her arms outstretched. "What is wrong, love? Have you quarrelled with Mainard?"

Orienting on the voice, knowing there would be open arms to receive her, Sabina released her hold on Haesel, dropped her staff, and rushed forward. She flung herself into Magdalene's arms.

"She is dead!" she gasped, bursting into sobs.

"Dead? Who is dead?" Magdalene cried, but she felt suddenly sick.

It must be Mainard's wife who was dead, and if Sabina was so overset, he must have put her out, hoping to find a respectable wife who would bear him untainted children.

"Murdered," Sabina got out between sobs. "Bertrild was all but cut to pieces in the yard of Mainard's shop. Oh, she deserved to die, but now Mainard is suspected."

"Bertrild was murdered?" Magdalene echoed.

She hardly heard the end of what Sabina had said. If Bertrild had been murdered, someone would soon remember the trouble that devil of a woman had tried to make for those of the Old Priory Guesthouse. Would she and her women be accused of taking revenge?

"Mainard did not!" Sabina cried. "I know he did not!"

By now Letice and Ella had put down their embroidery and risen to their feet. Both added their comfort, Letice patting Sabina's shoulder and Ella stroking her head and making soft reassuring murmurs. Diot also put down her work, but she did not move. She watched the scene with wide, frightened eyes. If Sabina's lover was guilty of murder, the blind woman would be forced back into the Old Priory Guesthouse. If she came back, her clients would return to her and there would be none for Diot herself.

"Hush, Sabina, hush," Magdalene was saying. Sabina shuddered convulsively, and Magdalene clutched her closer. "Come, love," she crooned, leading Sabina toward the table and benches. "Come and sit down."

Between them all, Sabina was seated on one of the short benches with Letice and Ella standing beside her and offering comfort. Magdalene sent Haesel off to the kitchen, where Dulcie would keep her busy one way or another. Then she seated herself on the corner of the inner long bench and took one of Sabina's hands in hers.

"Dearling," she said gently, "do you want to come back here to stay? You will be very welcome." She heard a sound, half gasp, half sob, and glanced briefly toward the hearth where Diot still sat, her eyes fixed on them.

"No!" Sabina cried, recoiling. "I will never leave Mainard, never! He did not do it! Oh, help me! Help me to prove that he is innocent. Mainard could never kill a woman, not even such a devil as she was."

"Truthfully, I would not have believed he could," Magdalene said thoughtfully, patting Sabina's hands. "Despite his appearance, I could have sworn Mainard was one of those who tears out his own lungs and liver when he grieves or rages and never allows his bile to spill over on those around him."

"It is true," Sabina breathed.

"Perhaps," Magdalene said. "But I am afraid we will need more than your feeling or mine to keep him from being hanged. I would surely have killed Bertrild if she were my wife." She hesitated momentarily, thinking she was coming too close to her own past truth, and she continued quickly, "Is Mainard taken by the justiciar?"

"No," Sabina gasped. "No. He is gone home to the Lime Street house to wait for the brothers of St. Catherine's Hospital to clean and release the body. He said also he would speak to the priest about the burial."

"If he is suspect, why did the justiciar release him?"

"He did not do it! He was with me the whole time!"

Her hand closed so hard on Magdalene's that the nails bit into the flesh. Magdalene looked down at Sabina's hand. "You told Master Octadenarius that Mainard was with you when Bertrild was murdered, and he allowed Mainard to go home. Then why are you so frightened, love?"

Sabina was shaking so hard that both Letice and Ella squeezed onto the bench with her and embraced her, one on either side. "Because if they cannot find who really killed Bertrild, you know they will discount my testimony. I am a whore!" She burst into tears.

Ella began to cry also, and Magdalene told her to get some wine for Sabina and then to go help Dulcie and Haesel in the kitchen. Ella was easily frightened and should not hear what would prey on her mind becaue she could not understand. As she turned back to Sabina, Magdalene wondered whether what Sabina had said about Mainard being with her was true, and she frowned as she thought of Master Osbert Octadenarius casting around to discover who else might have wanted Bertrild dead. He would surely remember that Bertrild had brought a complaint before him about her and the Old Priory Guesthouse.

When Sabina had sipped the wine and her sobs had quieted, Magdalene said, "I think you had better tell us the whole tale from the very beginning."

"Oh, I am not sure where the beginning is."

"Mainard has been married to Bertrild for some years. He must have known what she was long ago. Why was she killed now? Was there some particular thing that happened, something Octadenarius could discover, that could have driven Mainard to violence?"

"It is my fault. All my fault." Sabina sighed tiredly. "You know when I agreed to go and live with Mainard, both of us believed that Bertrild would not care, that she would be glad to be free of him."

Magdalene's lips thinned and she felt a prick of guilt. She had learned from another client that Bertrild had some spite against her

husband and wanted to make him suffer. If Sabina brought him hap-
piness, Bertrild would do anything to spoil it. She should have warned
them.

"And Mainard did not want gossip to hurt her pride," Sabina was
saying. "He actually charges me rent and finds me work singing so
that I can pay." The sweetest smile erased the fear on her face for a
moment. "I enjoy that so much. My singing is praised. I have been
called back to two of the places to entertain again."

Magdalene smiled. Sabina was blind, but she always knew when
someone smiled at her. Could she "hear" it in the voice? "As soon as
we have a party, I will invite you here to entertain." She patted Sabina's
hand. "But I gather that your pretense was not sufficient to fool her."

"For a while it was, but three weeks ago there was a man waiting
across the road from Mainard's shop, and when I came out, he threw
offal at me and called me a whore."

"Did Mainard drive him away?"

"Oh, no. Thank God he was not there. Codi, the journeyman,
rushed out and chased whoever it was away."

Naturally Magdalene did not bother to ask if Sabina had seen her
attacker. She said, "So far so good. Mainard might never have known
of that."

"Well, he did, but there was worse that everyone in the street
heard about."

Magdalene made a "tchk" of irritation. It would have been better
if Mainard seemed unaware of any insult or attack on Sabina, which
he might well blame on his wife, but he would be worse off if his
friends were ignorant of what his enemies knew. She made an en-
couraging noise.

"Just this last Wednesday," Sabina continued, gulping unhappily
between words, "she came secretly into the shop and came upstairs
and attacked me. Henry would not think to stop her or—"

"Wait," Magdalene said. "Who is Henry?"

"He used to be a saddler, but something terrible happened to his
hands. They are all twisted, and he can hardly hold a spoon or knife
to feed himself. He could not work and had to give up his shop.
Mainard—you know what Mainard is; he cannot bear to see misfor-
tune—he offered Henry the work of selling." Sabina found a wan

smile. "It is true that bread cast upon the waters comes back tenfold. Henry has doubled the profit of Mainard's business. In secret Mainard told me that Henry was never a very good saddler but that he could sell a saddle to a man who had no horse."

"So Henry stands outside the shop at the outdoor counter and must see everyone who enters and leaves. Does he live in Mainard's house?"

"No. He has a wife and children and a house of his own. Well, I think Mainard may actually own it now since he paid Henry's debtors, but Henry does so well between his pay and his commission on what he sells that it is nearly all paid back."

"So Henry let Bertrild pass. Would he not even call out to Mainard to say she had come?"

"He did not," Sabina said softly. "I think he feared her. She used to call him 'cripple' and make cruel jests about his hands, and she said something to him one day—you know how keen my ears are—about knowing the true reason for his crippling and for the loss of his shop."

Magdalene sighed. "Before we are done, we will be hard put to it to find anyone in London who did not wish to kill her. Well, so she came into the shop and upstairs to your chambers. What do you mean she attacked you?"

"First she bade me go back to the pesthouse from which I came and said that if I did not, what had happened to me in the street would grow worse and worse, that she would see to it that the whole Chepe knew I was a whore and unclean."

"No one heard this except you?"

"Not that part. She was speaking very quietly until she ordered me to get up and leave, just as I was, taking nothing, or she would report me to the sheriff as a whore and a thief. But I did not move from my chair, and I said I would not go. I admitted that I had been a whore once but did no longer practice that trade, that I was a singer and player of the lute, and that between my earnings as a musician and my savings I had enough to live without selling my body."

"Were you also speaking quietly?"

"Not as quietly as she. I was a little frightened and hoped Mainard would hear. . . ." Her voice trailed away and she shuddered. "I did not know then that she would be . . ."

Magdalene squeezed her hand, and she swallowed and went on.

"He did not hear. The pounding of the hammers is so loud. But then she seized me and started to try to pull me from my chair, and when Haesel tried to get her loose, she hit the child and knocked her down. Haesel screamed, and I screamed, too, because she had hold of my hair and knocked my staff out of my reach. Then she slapped me, shouting that I was a filthy whore and had caused her father's death." Sabina stopped speaking abruptly and looked pitifully anxious. "That could not be true, could it?"

"Certainly not, love. Do you not remember that drunken sot Gervase de Genlis? Even Ella would not serve him after the first few times, but he came to a nighttime party with some mercers and a goldsmith . . . oh, a little less than two years ago. On his way home he stopped in an alehouse, got into a brawl, and was killed. I remember because Bertrild came here not long after and threatened all kinds of evil. She accused me of murder and wanted me to pay to keep her quiet. I told William, who spoke to the sheriff of London—and that was the end of it, of course. There was no doubt that we had no part in how the unlamented Gervase died."

Sabina sighed. "I am glad. I did not need another death on my conscience."

"Why should Bertrild's death be on your conscience?"

"Because I wished her dead! Oh, how I wished her dead. I prayed for it. . . ." She shuddered again, and Letice hugged her tight.

"But you did her no harm. You said she had knocked down your staff." Magdalene knew that Sabina could wield that staff to protect herself, and a very unpleasant idea had come into her head.

"No," Sabina said. "I was so shocked that I did not even fight back or try to shield my face. Mainard came. He must have heard us screaming. Haesel said later that she thought he would kill the nasty lady— that was what she always called Bertrild, even though she knew her name. She said his face was all one color red, he was so angry." Sabina uttered a sob. "But he did not! He did not do her the smallest hurt, even when he was in a terrible rage. He only picked her up, as if she were a doll of straw, Haesel said—you know how strong he is—and carried her away."

"I do not suppose she took that quietly."

"Oh, no. She screamed and Haesel said she struggled and scratched him and struck him." Sabina sighed. "That was how the whole Chepe knew what had happened. Mainard carried her outside the shop, she screaming and cursing him and me, so everyone heard. But he only set her on her feet and told her to go home and calm herself. Everyone saw that too."

"Was that the last time you saw her?"

Silently Sabina shook her head. Then she said, "She came back again yesterday. It was midmorning, after Mainard had left to bring the week's takings to his goldsmith. He had left early because his friend Pers Newelyne had invited him to his new son's christening party at noon, and I was going, too, to sing."

"So Mainard did not see her?"

"No."

"Did she attack you again?"

Sabina drew in a deep breath. "No. I heard her screaming in the shop, and I thought she was angry because Codi would not let her come up, but I did not think he could stand against her for long. Codi is afraid of her also."

Magdalene watched Sabina's soft lips thin into a cruel line and remembered that this seemingly gentle blind woman had survived some years in an ordinary stew. It was one of the better ones, not like the place Diot had come from, but anyone who had survived life as a common whore had learned self-defense.

"I took my staff and went to open the door." Sabina's nostrils flared wider. "If she came up, I was going to put my staff into her throat and try to break the Adam's apple. And if I could not, I was going to push her off the landing, down into the shop!"

"Did you?" Magdalene asked, almost grinning.

Sabina shook her head again and then started to sob. "Oh, I wish I had. I wish I had. Then Mainard would not be in any danger. And I thought I would get off scot-free. I did not believe anyone would blame a poor blind woman who had lifted her staff to defend herself and overset her attacker by accident." She bent her head and covered her face with her hand, sobbing bitterly for a moment, then said, "I did not even care if they did hang me for it. At least poor Mainard would have been free."

"I do not think he would have been glad of it if he lost you," Magdalene said. "But if you say you wish you had, then you did not. Did you think better of killing her?"

"Not for a moment!" Sabina exclaimed, wiping tears off her cheeks. "She was not trying to get at me. When I had the door open, I could hear what she was saying. She wanted money, and when Codi said Mainard had taken it, she demanded he make her a belt out of some special leather. He told her the leather did not belong to Mainard. It belonged to a customer who wanted it decorated for his wife's saddle. She would not listen. She said if he did not make her the belt she desired that she would report him as a runaway serf and see that he was returned to his old master. Codi would rather be dead. Mainard told me he is all scarred from whipping and burning."

"What! Another who wanted Bertrild dead?"

"I do not think Codi could have killed her, although—" Sabina bit her lip, then said, "You must promise not to tell anyone this, but it was Codi's knife that killed her. Mainard found it when he went to look at the body, and he brought it in and cleaned it—"

"Does the man have a death wish?" Magdalene cried. "Is he trying to make himself look guilty?"

"No," Sabina said indignantly. "He simply does not believe Codi could have done it." She sighed. "You must know Codi before you understand."

"Very well, love. For now I will take your trust and Mainard's for truth. So, from what you have said, Bertrild left the shop making threats to Codi, but she was alive and well. How did she come to be dead?"

"I do not know," Sabina breathed. "I told you that Mainard and I went to Pers Newelyne's son's christening. We were there all day. It was a very happy party. Poor Pers had three daughters before this son came, and the babe is large and strong. His wife is well also. Thus we were all very merry, and I was called to sing and play many times, which I did gladly. We did not leave, Mainard and I, until it was dusk. Indeed, Pers gave Mainard a torch to light our way."

"He will remember that. Good. The house was quiet when you returned to it?"

"Yes, it was full dark by then. Pers's house is all the way north in the West Chepe, and we were very full of food, and Mainard had, perhaps, a cup or two of wine too many. We had to sit down for a while on a bench outside an alehouse, and we were stopped twice by the Watch in different wards and had to explain ourselves. Fortunately the first knew about Pers's christening party, and the second recognized Mainard. But we were very late coming home."

"That is all to the good. The Watchmen will remember you also. And that will be proof of what time you came home. No one was waiting up for you?"

"No, they would not. Codi closes the door to the workroom where he and the boys sleep whenever Mainard stays the night so that, if Bertrild should ask—" she hesitated, swallowed, and went on, "they could say truthfully that Mainard slept on the pallet behind the counter in the shop, where they would find him in the morning."

Magdalene sighed. "That is not so good, but I suppose he did not really sleep there."

"No." Sabina smiled. "He came up with me, of course, and slept in my bed. We were awake for some time longer. What with all the wine he had taken, he was a little slow to rouse and that frightens him because—well, you know Bertrild had virtually gelded him. I had to work to make him ready." She stopped and her lips set suddenly. "That is how I know he could not have killed Bertrild," she added angrily. "He was with me from before noon until near dawn."

"He left you then?"

"Yes, but he could not have killed Bertrild after he left me," Sabina protested.

"Why not?"

"Because the blood on her was all brown and dry."

"How could you know that?" Magdalene asked, astonished.

Sabina licked her lips. "Because the blood on the knife was dry and hard." She hesitated, but continued, her voice soft and steady. "It was not Mainard who cleaned the knife. I had come down when I heard what Gisel was yelling to wake Mainard, and when he came back from the yard, Codi was weeping and Mainard was at his wit's end. When I understood why they were so overset, I said to give me the knife, and I cleaned it."

There was a moment of silence, then Magdalene asked, "He did not leave you at any other time? After all that drinking, surely he needed to piss."

Sabina's head reared up. "He used the chamber pot, as did I. Are you trying to find him guilty, too?"

"Do not be silly. These are questions that will be asked by less friendly folk than I. I must know what is marshalled against your man before I can think how to order my own troops—"

Magdalene stopped and considered what she had said. It was a phrase borrowed from William of Ypres, the leader of the king's mercenary forces and her oldest and most powerful patron. Lord William was the man to whom she would ordinarily go for help, but William was not at Rochester taking his ease and spoiling for amusement. If he was not already in Oxford, he was preparing to meet the king there. Friendship or no friendship, William was not going to be late in attending on the king to help her save a whore's lover from a charge of murder. But she needed—Ah! Before he had lost his temper and called her "whore," Bell had mentioned that the bishop of Winchester was not going to Oxford, which meant that Bell would not go either. She drew in a deep breath.

"Yes," she said, "that is what we need, troops. Sit still, love." She patted Sabina's hand and stood up. "I am going to send Dulcie to get Bell."

Four

21 MAY
OLD PRIORY GUESTHOUSE

Fortunately, Sir Bellamy had little enough to do on a Sunday after he had attended Mass. Dulcie found him at the bishop's house, idling among the clerks and men-at-arms, and he was immediately ready to come back with her. He was a little troubled, thinking that Diot had transgressed in some fatal way, and he would be asked either to expel her from the house or to have her punished.

Dulcie was able to remove that anxiety, but she had no idea about why he was wanted, which allowed him to indulge himself in believing that Magdalene had missed him enough to summon him. At least he could indulge himself for as long as it took to walk past the priory gate into the priory grounds, across the length of St. Mary Overy Church, to the gate in the wall (always invitingly open so those who sinned in the Old Priory Guesthouse could come to the church and confess), through Magdalene's garden, and in the back door.

As soon as he came down the corridor into the common room, he saw Sabina, her face blotched and her nose reddened with tears, which somehow squeezed themselves out under her sealed eyelids. Although he had never touched any of Magdalene's whores (he was holding out for Magdalene herself), he was fond of them all, particularly of the soft-spoken and gentle Sabina, who had done what he wanted Magdalene to do—given up whoring for love of a man. Sabina's present condition could scarcely be an inducement for Magdalene to follow her example, however, and Bell strode forward, furious with Mainard who, he believed, had caused the gentle whore's distress.

"What has happened, Sabina, love?" he asked, trying to keep anger out of his voice.

"Mainard's wife is dead. . . . Murdered," she said.

"Oh, good Lord!" Bell exclaimed, dropping down on the bench beside Magdalene. After another moment, he said, "She surely wanted killing, and with the evidence he can bring it may be that he can escape with 'justifiable homicide,' but I am not sure what I can do to help him."

Magdalene turned her head to stare at him, but he did not notice. She thought bitterly that if a woman nags at and berates a man, and he kills her—that is justifiable homicide. But if a man berates a woman, abuses her, beats her, threatens to mutilate her, and she kills him—that is murder.

Bell might have noticed the fixed, angry eyes had not Sabina cried, "He did not do it!"

His attention fixed on her, and Magdalene, having controlled a feeling she could not explain without breaking open a long-hidden grave, nodded and said calmly, "You had better listen to what she says."

After the tale was retold and he had made almost the same comments as Magdalene about Pers Newelyne and the Watch, he looked from Sabina to Magdalene and lifted a questioning brow. Magdalene gave a barely perceptible shrug, indicating that she was no surer than he that Sabina was not lying for love about the blood being hard on the knife and that Mainard had never left her bed until dawn.

"I can do no more with hearsay," he said. "I must go look at the body, if it is not yet washed and shrouded, or speak to the brothers if it is. I must look at the place where the body was found. . . ."

Sabina stood up immediately. "Haesel!" she called.

The child came from the kitchen at once, chewing on a piece of unbaked pastry and giggling, probably at something Ella had said or done. Magdalene smiled at her, recalling the pathetic scrap of skin and bones, shivering with terror, that Sabina had brought to show them only a month ago. Bell had got up when Haesel appeared and Sabina took in hand the staff Letice had fetched for her. Now Magdalene got to her feet also.

"I think I will go along with you," she said thoughtfully. "If you tell me what questions you want asked, Bell, I will try to get answers from the apprentices and possibly from Codi, too. They will be less frightened of me than of you, and Sunday is quiet here." She turned toward the hearth. "Diot—"

The new woman rose nervously to her feet, clasping her hands before her. Magdalene smiled at her.

"As you know, we have no regular appointments on Sunday, but sometimes a client finds himself with some free hours and wishes to spend them here, or someone passing through might stop. If the man is known to Dulcie, take his money and let him go with Ella or take him yourself, unless he is Letice's client. If she is still here, and he asks specially for her, ask if she will see him. Usually she goes to where her countryfolk gather on Sunday. If it is someone new, you may use your judgment as to whether it is safe to let him in . . . and make sure he pays ahead of time."

Diot flushed a little—her white skin readily showed her emotions. She was aware that she was being given this chance to show whether she could manage, partly because of the other women's disabilities and partly because she could do little damage on Sunday. Nonetheless, she was delighted and grateful. Sabina was as disabled as the others.

"I will do my best, Magdalene."

"Thank you," Magdalene said, and went to get her veil, which she draped over her head to cover her hair and raised one end to hold across her face.

Haesel led Sabina, and Bell fell in behind with Magdalene. "Diot seems to have jumped high in your estimation," he said.

"So far I am better pleased than I expected to be," she agreed. "If she continues as she has begun, you will have brought me a treasure."

"Now that she does not look so gaunt and haunted, she is even more beautiful."

"Yes, but that is less important than her honesty and her manner. Leaving her in charge was something of another test, to see how she behaves when I am gone. Letice and Dulcie will watch her. Of course, she is still very new and the memory of Stav's stew is still clear in her mind. I am concerned mostly about the future, about whether she will grow abusive or try to swindle or steal from the clients when that memory dims."

"The men like her?"

"Yes, they do. She is very clever and seems able to judge just what will please them best, sometimes in despite of what they say they desire. One man, and he is not the most generous of souls, left her a whole shilling! He said she had given him the wildest ride he had ever had, yet he had chosen Sabina, he said for her gentleness."

Bell shrugged. "Different night. Different desires." He looked sidelong at her. "If Diot is satisfactory, I hope you will find no other excuses for—"

"I do not need excuses. Whoring is my business." Her voice was sharp, but she caught his hand as his jaw set. "You must believe me, Bell. I swear it is for your own good. If you think of me as 'your' woman, disaster *must* follow."

"Why?" he asked stubbornly.

She sighed. "Because I have been a whore for ten years. I cannot wipe that out. You cannot wipe that out. I am an honest woman and a good and loyal friend—William will tell you that." She laughed. "Many men will tell you that."

He winced, and she laughed again. She squeezed the hand she held.

"That is why it would be a disaster. Think about it, Bell. Think about accepting me as I am for what I am."

"Master Mainard seems content with a retired whore," he snapped back. Then his lips twisted. "Perhaps content enough to want to be rid of his wife."

Since they had arrived at the bridge, neither said any more until they had passed through the crush generated by the shops, the customers, and the peddlers. When they had turned up Gracechurch Street, Bell, who had not forgotten what he had said, increased his pace until he could walk beside Sabina.

"Have you been happy with Master Mainard?" he asked.

"Oh, yes!" she exclaimed softly. "He is so good to me. He is so good a man! You cannot imagine the good he has done." Her mouth hardened. "That stupid Bertrild! She threatened Codi that she would

send him back to his master, but he knew she could not. Because
Mainard did not want Codi to feel trapped, he had explained to him
that once he lived as a free man for a year and a day, his bonding as
a serf was ended. He could live free anywhere and take any employ-
ment he wished."

"Then Codi had no reason to kill her. You know, Sabina, it *is*
Mainard who had the best reasons to wish her dead."

"And I," Sabina said stoutly. "I told you I wanted to kill her."

"Because you expected Master Mainard to marry you?"

"Marry me?" She turned her face toward him, astonishment showing in her voice and every line of her body, even though her eyes
could not open in amazement. "Why would Mainard want to marry
me? I was a whore."

Bell winced, but he was not touching Sabina and she remained
unaware that she had pricked him in a sore spot.

"I think he loves me and will keep me," she continued, "but that
has nothing to do with marriage. I am sure that if he marries again, it
will be to a woman of fine reputation about whose children no jests
will be made."

"You will not mind if he marries again?" Bell asked.

Sabina was silent for a long moment, turning her face forward as
if she could see where she was going. Then she sighed. "Yes, I will
care," she said very softly. "I love him, and it will grieve me that he
beds another woman, even if it be only to make children." She sighed
again. "And it will not be only that. If she will welcome him, Mainard
will love her. He is gentle and needs love and so returns it readily.
And it is his right to have children." She squared her shoulders. "I can
always go back to Magdalene."

"Then perhaps you did not really want Bertrild dead?"

"Oh yes I did!" Bell was surprised at the vicious tone. "She hurt
Mainard. I would gladly have killed her. Gladly!"

"With a knife?"

He was grinning, and she heard it in his voice and turned her
head in his direction again, making an impatient gesture. "With anything I had in my hand, and I *could* have gone down to the privy in
the yard."

Bell laughed aloud. "Yes. Without your staff so that you bumped into all the furniture and tripped over the sleeping apprentices, through a back door, which you could not find, carrying a knife, which you have no idea of how to use, just in case. . . ." He put an arm around her shoulders and gave her an affectionate squeeze.

"Who said I did not have my staff!" she said, trying for indignation.

"Because if you had your staff, love, you would have hit her with that. I remember how neatly you cracked Waleran de Meulan's man on the head. If Bertrild had been dead of a crushed head or a broken neck . . ."

"Just a moment," Magdalene said, coming up on Bell's other side as the street widened. "In all the excitement about finding Bertrild dead, no one has asked the first question that needed to be asked. What the devil was she doing in Mainard's yard at God-knows-what time of night?"

"That is a fine point," Bell said, all laughter gone from his voice and manner. "Sabina, you said you were at Newelyne's until dusk and that the Watch will confirm you and Mainard were still abroad when it was full dark. You say also that the house was dark and quiet, the journeyman and apprentices asleep when you came home."

"Yes."

"If that is true, can either of you believe that Bertrild was dead out in the yard before dark?" Magdalene asked. "Is not a visit to the privy the last thing most people do before going to bed? Could her body have been overlooked?"

"I do not know," Sabina said. "I was not taken out." She smiled a little sheepishly. "To speak the truth, I was never in the yard. But I will swear that Codi and the two boys are not the kind to see a dead body and go quietly to bed and to sleep."

Bell chuckled. "I cannot say I am surprised. That takes more *sang froid* than most people have."

"Yes, yes," Magdalene said impatiently, "but then what was Bertrild doing prowling about Mainard's yard when she should have been at home and safely in bed?"

"Spying?" Sabina asked faintly. "There is a window in my bed-chamber in the back, and in this weather I open it. There is a hedge and a fence, an alley and another yard between us and the house behind, so I have never worried about anyone looking in. Could she have been watching for Mainard to pass before the window?"

Magdalene made a dissatisfied noise. "Yes," she said. "Unfortunately, Bertrild was just the kind to spy. I had hoped that there was no reason for her to be there and that she might have been killed elsewhere and dumped in the yard. If that were so, it would be nearly impossible for Mainard to have killed her."

"Oh, is that possible?" Sabina cried. "I am sure Bertrild did not know the back entrance to the yard. She never lived in the rooms above the shop. She insisted that Mainard buy the Lime Street house before they were married."

Magdalene and Bell glanced at each other and grinned. "Enough, love," Magdalene said. "Please do not tell anyone else. It says a little too much of how much you care for Mainard and how little you care for the truth and will only cast a bad light on your saying he was with you until dawn."

"But he was!" Sabina exclaimed.

The growing noise ahead of them relieved Magdalene and Bell from needing to comment and indicated that they were coming into the market. Sunday might be quiet in the whorehouse, most men being unwilling to so soon soil the cleansing of attending Mass, but it was a favorite day for buying and selling. Bell dropped back, frowning a little as he thought over what Magdalene had said and what Sabina had said also. He thought their warning to Sabina would keep her from suggesting Bertrild had been killed elsewhere, but that *was* a definite possibility.

Why should Bertrild bother to spy on Mainard? Establishing a whore in the rooms above his shop might be grounds for complaint. But seeing him in the woman's bedchamber would not make anyone more willing to listen to that complaint. There was no law against a man keeping a mistress; such behavior was between him and God, a sin, not a crime.

That she had been killed elsewhere and put in Mainard's yard was more likely, actually, than that someone had come out of the house carrying a knife just when she was there and stabbed her—unless she had made a noise and the journeyman had gone out intending to drive off a thief. Or Mainard had heard something through the open bedchamber window and recognized Bertrild? Had his patience broken? Had he rushed out with a knife and killed her? And just left her lying there and gone in again to futter Sabina? Nonsense! Could Mainard have got out of the house without waking his journeyman or apprentices? Probably not. Would they lie for him? Bell sighed. From what everyone said about him, probably yes.

Other questions: Was there anything of enough value in the yard to make worthwhile the danger of needing to drive off a thief? Had Bertrild brought someone with her? Or had she agreed to meet someone? In the middle of the night in the yard of Mainard's shop rather than in comfort in her own house in Lime Street? Ridiculous. But say there was a reason for a meeting there, why should the person she agreed to meet at such a time and place—which must mean she did not fear that person—suddenly pull a knife and stab her?

Bell could think of any number of people who might have stuck a knife into Bertrild in a rage, but it was impossible for any argument to have taken place in Mainard's yard without waking someone in the house. That meant that whoever had come with Bertrild or agreed to meet her intended to stab her. Possible, but it was still more likely that she had been killed elsewhere and dumped in Mainard's yard. After dark it would only take moderate care to avoid the Watch and no one would have seen the body moved.

While Bell's mind was busy, they had turned right at Gracechurch, passed the cordwainer's shop on the corner, and come to the front of Mainard's saddlery. The counter was missing, the door closed. Bell was about to pound on the door, when Haesel came alongside, simply lifted the latch, and led Sabina in. Magdalene followed with Bell on her heels.

"The shop is closed—" Henry began and then sighed. "Oh, Mistress Sabina, we wondered where you had gone."

There was something in his voice that made Sabina bristle. "You mean you thought I had deserted Master Mainard as soon as he was in trouble. Well, I did not. Since I have more brains than an overcooked pease porridge, even if I cannot see, I went to get help. I have brought Mistress Magdalene, who has powerful friends, and Sir Bellamy of Itchen, who is the bishop of Winchester's knight and is accustomed to unraveling mysteries."

"I thought no such thing," Codi said, getting to his feet.

To right and left a boy rose with him, clinging to him. The younger had a tear-smeared face, and the elder still looked pale and sick. Codi himself was a hulking young man, almost as tall and thick as his master but without Mainard's grace of movement. He had a shock of brown curls and a thick, neatly trimmed brown beard. His eyes, which were small and deeply set, were also brown and, had his expression been less lugubrious, he would have looked like a friendly bear.

"Well, whatever you thought," Bell said firmly, "Mistress Magdalene and I are here to discover what we can to help Master Mainard. Now, who found the body?"

The older apprentice grew even paler, but he swallowed hard and said, "I did, sir."

"And you are?

"Gisel, sir."

"Now I see that you are still very upset, Gisel, but do you think you can show me the exact place where Mistress Bertrild was lying?"

The boy began to tremble, and Codi put an arm around him. "I saw it, too, sir," he said. "In fact, it will be easier for me, because when Gisel ran in screaming that Mistress Bertrild was lying in the yard covered with blood, I told him to go wake Master Mainard, and I went myself to see if she had perhaps fallen and hurt herself and I could help."

"Then Mistress Bertrild was often in the yard?"

"Oh, no, sir. I never saw her in the yard before. She often came into the workroom. She liked to snoop around and pick out specially fine pieces of leather and insist we give them to her for shoes. But she never went out back. I really thought that Gisel was mistaken, that some other poor woman had been hurt and wandered in from the alley. But Master Mainard would have had to be wakened in any case, so I didn't ask any questions, only ran out to look myself."

"Good enough," Bell said. "Let us go out."

He cast a glance at Magdalene, and she reached out and took Gisel by the arm. "Sit down, child," she said, backing him toward the stool from which he had risen with Codi. "You have had a terrible shock." She looked around at Henry, the other apprentice, Haesel, and Sabina. "Have any of you eaten?"

There was a concerted shaking of heads, except for Henry, who said he had broken his fast at home. Gisel swallowed convulsively, and Magdalene smiled at him, realized he could not see that through her veil, and patted his shoulder. "I know that even thinking of food makes you feel sick, but part of that is actually hunger." She reached into the purse hanging from her belt and took out two pennies. "Haesel, I know you buy Sabina's meals. It is near dinnertime. Suppose you run across to the cookshop and bring back whatever you think will be best for everyone. Would you like to go with her, Gisel? How about you?" she asked the second child.

"My name is Stoc," the younger boy said. "I will go. Haesel will only bring back a pot of slops. I want some ham and bacon and some pasty as well as soup or stew, and—"

"Very well," Magdalene said, grinning behind her veil at the boy's resiliancy, "but we will also need bread and cheese and some ale—"

"There is ale," Gisel said. His color was somewhat better already because of having something else to think about besides a dead woman covered in blood. "Master Mainard buys it by the barrel, and it is good ale. It is in the cellar. There is wine, too, if Mistress Sabina prefers."

Before Sabina could protest that she could not eat a bite or drink, Magdalene touched her hand, and she said only, "No, for a first meal I think ale is better."

"Very well, Haesel," Magdalene said. "See what the boys would prefer, but do not let them overrule your good sense. And they must help you carry." When they were gone, she said to Henry, "What was happening here when you arrived?"

"Nothing!" he exclaimed with a scowl. "Usually when I come at Prime, the counter is out and what Master Mainard wants to be sold is on it." He thrust out his crippled hands. "I cannot carry, so Codi sets up, but he could not sell gold for rotten eggs. As soon as I come, he goes into the shop, but today they were all there," he waved at the three stools, "sitting on those stools where you found them, holding each other and shivering. As if it were not the best night's work I ever heard of that she is dead!"

"You did not love Mistress Bertrild, I gather?" Magdalene asked.

"If prayers could kill, she would have been dead of mine a long time ago, but—" he lifted the crippled hands again "—I could not have held a knife firm enough to kill her, aside from being at home with my wife and four children. I live by the Walbrook, south of Watling Street. For that matter, wanting Mistress Bertrild dead can be no strong indication of who did kill her. There cannot have been ten among all those who knew her who did not want her dead."

Magdalene shrugged. "That many disliked her, I know. She was an unpleasant woman. But dislike and stabbing someone are different matters altogether. I disliked Mistress Bertrild myself, but I had other methods of dealing with her than to need to kill her."

"Need to kill her?" Henry repeated. He was silent for a while, searching as if to find her expression behind the veil; then he turned away. "You know that as well as I," he said, looking out of the window instead of at her. "But I cannot believe he did it. He knows how to suffer, that one. What has his life been but one long suffering? In all that time, I do not believe he once, even once, struck out at anyone to ease himself."

Only that made it worse, Magdalene thought. When a person who knew so much pain had been provided with a perfect anodyne and then threatened that that relief would be snatched away, a terrible desperation could be engendered, a desperation strong enough to result in murder. Except that the threat of losing Sabina was not really so immediate or so strong. Still, Mainard was probably the only one who could have got Bertrild into that yard. If he had told her he would be at a party with Sabina and that afterward he intended to stay at the shop, she could have counted on seeing him in Sabina's bedchamber. He could have been watching for her from the window. . . .

Magdalene did not like the trend her thoughts had taken, but before she needed to pursue them further, Haesel and the boys were back. "That was quick," Magdalene said.

"It is between times," Haesel replied, "after the morning meal and before dinnertime, so he served us right away."

She set several packets and a loaf of bread down on the counter. Gisel and Stoc added their burdens and began to pull off covers. Just then Bell came in again with Codi, who looked much less frightened.

Before anyone could speak, Bell bade Gisel to come with him and went out the back door again. The cheerfulness disappeared from Codi's face.

"He does not believe me," he said.

"I am sure he does," Magdalene said, not sure at all but wishing to keep Codi from becoming too wary and frightened to talk to her. "What he wants is to be able to say he had two witnesses who told him the same thing. And you had better have something to eat at once before you begin mixing up the hollowness of hunger with the hollowness of fear."

Stoc was already helping himself liberally. Haesel, Magdalene was glad to see, ran up the stairs and brought down two bowls and spoons, one of which she filled and set into Sabina's hands. She filled a second, too, but wrenched a piece off the bread and took slices of ham and bacon, which she began to eat. They were hardly started when Gisel was back. He was, perhaps, a little paler but not really sick looking, and he went at once to the counter and began to help himself to food. Bell appeared at the workroom door and gestured for Magdalene to come.

"I do not believe she was killed here," he said softly, drawing her through the workroom and out through the back door into the yard. "Both Codi and Gisel pointed out the same spot, and I could find no sign of blood there or anywhere else near. But from what Codi said of the body and the knife he showed me—the one they found beside her—she must have been soaked with blood from a huge wound in the throat. She was lying on her back so some blood would have run down her neck. Now, even if most of that was absorbed by her cloak, some should have marked the grass."

Magdalene had been looking around the yard as Bell spoke. It was neat enough, but there was no garden. Three small sheds lined the west side of a man-high wooden fence; beyond them were two well-pruned apple trees, blossoms gone and young fruit too small to see yet. Then came a sturdy gate, its latch firmly closed and the leather latchstring pulled in from the latchhole and hanging down. Past the gate were two other fruit trees and then a tall hedge which screened all but the slanted roof of what must be the privy. Extending past the hedge and along the east side of the fence was a good patch of bramble showing plenty of white flowers and promising succulent berries in June and July. The center of the yard, instead of being planted with vegetables, was covered with grass and in the middle a rough table with stools around it—a pleasant place, Magdalene thought, for the journeyman and apprentices to eat on a summer afternoon or evening.

"Where?" she asked.

Bell pointed to a spot to the right of the table, and Magdalene could see the grass was somewhat crushed there. But if Bertrild had come to spy on Mainard, that was the wrong place. To see the window clearly, she would have needed to be on the other side of the table, perhaps even farther west behind the trees. And watching from the side of the table where she had been lying, she could not have been seen from Sabina's window either, although she could have easily been seen from the door of the workroom.

Her eyes scanned the yard again, seeking for a place where Bertrild might have hidden and yet seen Sabina's window, the place where she might have been killed. It would have been impossible to hide behind the hedge or the brambles; one could see nothing. Magdalene looked left along the fence, glancing at the house now and then to see where a good angle to spy would have been. Her eyes came to the gate, and fixed.

"The latchstring is in," she said.

"Yes, I noticed," Bell said. "But it would be no great feat to put a wire or even a twig with a bump on the end through the latchhole and pull the string out. See how the heavy knot in the leather makes the string stand up. Also, the gate is not that well fitted. A man could run a long knife between it and the post and lift the latch that way."

Magdalene shrugged. "I see it has no lock. Clearly they did not fear thieves, so no one would have rushed out with a knife to drive a thief away."

Bell nodded. "Your thoughts run with mine. The woman cannot have been mistaken for a thief and stabbed to death by accident. If she was killed here, it was done apurpose. A thief is unlikely anyway. Codi said that the sheds were well locked and hold only scraps of wood or leather. He does not think there is anything worth stealing. Finally, no one would have gone out to drive a thief away because

Mainard always said that if anyone needed scraps of wood and leather so desperately, he would not stand in the way of their need."

"That sounds like Mainard," Magdalene said.

"An unlikely murderer," Bell agreed. "And, as I said, I do not believe she was killed here. There is relatively fresh horse dung right outside the gate. Do you know whether Mainard has a horse?"

"I do not believe so. He always walked when he came to see Sabina, but Codi would know that."

"He says not, but horses are often brought here to try out saddles so a frame can be planned to fit, especially if the animal is unusually large or small or must not be galled, like a destrier. But Codi said no horse was here yesterday because Mainard was away from before noon to after dark."

"You think the horse was used to bring Bertrild's body here?"

"Yes. The alley is not paved, so the hooves would not be heard if the beast were kept to a walk. But it would have had to be done after dark by someone who knew the alley well enough not to bump into things—it is not clear of hazards. It would be too chancy, I think, to try to bring a body, even well wrapped, through the Chepe while it was still light."

"Yes, indeed. And the person would have to know about the gate being only on the latch, not locked, and ill-fitting enough to be opened easily. Most shops lock the back gate to discourage thieves, but—" Magdalene grinned "—I suppose Mainard never did because a saddle is a very awkward thing to steal and presupposes owning a horse. Beside that, the chance of waking saddlery journeymen and apprentices who are all too accustomed to wielding heavy hammers and large knives might also make a thief think twice."

Bell laughed. "It would make me think twice, and Codi might make me think twice anyway. He is strong as a bear!" The smile changed to a frown. "He is also very uneasy about something—not only that his knife was used as the murder weapon, but something else. See what you can find out about that." He cast a last glance around the yard and shrugged. "I can do no more here. I will go on to St. Catherine's."

"Do you not want something to eat? It is nearly dinnertime and Haesel brought back enough for all."

He shook his head firmly. "First to St. Catherine's to see the body if I can. After that I will stop at a cookshop." He grimaced. "I do not want my meal coming back into my mouth."

Magdalene raised her brows. He had not shown any such sensitivity over the bodies he had examined the previous month in St. Mary Overy Church.

Bell looked a touch self-conscious. "A woman . . . I have heard what she was, but still . . ." He shrugged, then continued briskly, "When I have spoken to the brothers to learn if there was anything about the body I should know, I will go and talk to Mainard at Lime Street. If you need me, you can send one of the boys. They must know the way well."

Five

21 MAY
MAINARD'S SHOP

As soon as Bell went out through the back gate, Magdalene hurried to the area in which she thought Bertrild must have hidden if she came to spy on her husband. Apparently Bell had not thought about Mainard seeing her from the window, rushing down in a rage, and killing her where she was, and Magdalene had no intention of putting the idea into his head. If Bell could prove to the justiciar that Bertrild had been killed elsewhere and that Mainard could not have done it, Magdalene would be quite content—even if it was not true.

Nonetheless, she had not quite made up her mind whether she would destroy or report any evidence that Bertrild had been killed in the yard. What she could find, others could. Thus, she was relieved, after she had examined the ground carefully, to find the grass unstained and undisturbed in the whole area from which one could see into Sabina's window. Magdalene drew a deep, satisfied breath. Well, then, since Mainard was innocent and Sabina would be happy, it would be a pleasure to find the killer and clear Mainard completely.

With a light step, she reentered the door to the workroom and paused to look about curiously. The chamber was lit by windows in each side wall, and there was a clear walkway from the back door to the door into the shop. To the left of the walkway was a storage area that extended under the steep stairway. In the center of the room, there were three large, sturdy worktables, one just ahead of her near the entrance to the shop, a second to the right of that, and closer to the back wall, to her right beyond the hearth, a third.

On the table near the entrance and the one near the hearth were several cloth-covered forms. Magdalene thought she could make out the shape of the seat of a saddle and beyond it a roll of uncut hide. Some pieces, those on the table closest to the hearth, were covered more carefully with oily looking cloth, and she could not tell what those were. On the last table there were pieces of wood, some mere blocks, others partially carved.

Then Magdalene realized there were no tools at all, no knives, no saws, no hammers, no punches, no chisels. Work without tools was impossible. She looked at the walls. A big, two-man saw and several very large mallets hung behind the table near the hearth, but no tools suitable for the work she saw. She stepped briskly into the shop.

"Codi—"

Three gasps interrupted her. Magdalene's lips thinned. She was accustomed to the reaction when men first saw her face, but she was annoyed with herself for forgetting to raise her veil again. Not that it mattered; she would have had to remove it to eat anyway. Haesel and Sabina had also turned to face at her, but they just seemed puzzled. She looked severely at Henry.

"You are too old and too well married for that," she snapped. Her eyes went to Gisel. "And you—" but she could not help smiling at his blush "—are too young or should be." Then she laughed. "And Codi, I suspect, is too poor. Besides which, I no longer take clients. So let us just put any thoughts of my work away and concentrate on what can be done to save your master from being suspected of murder."

There were soft, embarrassed murmurs of agreement, and Magdalene continued, "I saw no tools in the workroom. Where is the knife that was found near Bertrild?"

"Locked in my chest," Codi replied. "All the tools are locked up every night. They are costly and over time become fitted to one's own hand." He started to stand up. "Do you wish to see them?"

"No. Bell looked and that is enough, since I would not know one knife from another."

She waved at him to resume his seat and sighed. More evidence that Bertrild's death was no accident, not even a killing in a moment of furious passion. If the death had taken place after dark on Saturday night, all the tools would have been locked away already. But then . . .

"But then," Magdalene's voice echoed her thought, "how could anyone have got your knife to use on Bertrild?"

"I lost it on Friday," Codi said, very low, his eyes staring at a piece of cheese he was holding as if he had no idea what it was doing in his hand.

"You lost it on Friday!" Magdalene echoed. "Sabina, why did you not mention that?"

"She didn't know," Codi muttered. "I hadn't told anyone. I thought I had mislaid it. I have done so before. Master Mainard . . . he spoke quite sharply to me the last time it happened. I looked all over. . . ." His voice faded to nothing and then rose. "Even in the yard. I swear I looked all over the yard. In the sheds. Under the table . . ."

"We looked, too, Gisel and me," Stoc said suddenly. "We guessed Codi had lost a tool again because he was all upset when he locked up his toolbox on Friday night, and all day Saturday we looked all over the shop and the workroom and the yard. It wasn't here. Really it wasn't."

"That is very interesting. Very."

Magdalene looked around and Codi got up and brought her a stool from the workroom. She thanked him, drew her eating knife, and sliced off a piece of cheese and bit into it. The ham and bacon were gone, but there was a piece of pasty left and she took that and sliced a trencher out of the bread. When she had settled herself on the stool, she put the bread on her lap and set the cheese and pasty on top. Gisel got a cup from someplace in the workroom and brought it back filled with ale.

"So," she said when she had swallowed the bite of cheese. "When did you miss the knife, Codi?"

"Not until I put the tools away just after we heard the bells for Vespers. I had used it in the morning to shape the heavy leather for a seat and a broad pommel. After that, I was using the smaller knives for trimming and a punch for holing. I think I had laid it inside the curve that fits over the pommel frame, but I had some trouble with the holing and had to sharpen the punch."

"Then the knife was lying out on the table and anyone who came into the workroom could have taken it." She turned her head toward Sabina and Haesel. "Have you ever been in the workroom, Sabina?"

"I do not think so." Sabina smiled very faintly, then sighed. "I asked Mainard once. I wanted to know as well as I could what he and the others did, but he said it was too dangerous for me with all those knives and hammers."

"You had better tell Mainard that you may be blind but you are not a fool or a cripple," Magdalene said sharply. "You managed well enough in places where people cared less for you than here. If you do not clear his mind of that silliness soon, he will wrap you completely in fleece and hardly let you breathe."

"I know," Sabina said, smiling, "but it is hard. It makes him so happy to take care of me."

Magdalene "tchked" with irritation. "We have no time for that now. Haesel, what about you? Are you often in the workroom?"

"Often enough," the child said. "When Mistress Sabina does not need me, I go to talk to the boys. But I did not take Codi's knife. For what would I want a great heavy knife?"

"I do not think you took it, Haesel. I just want you to think back carefully and try to remember whether you were in the workroom on Friday afternoon. You might have seen something, even seen the knife so we would know at what time it was still there."

"Not Friday afternoon," Sabina said. "After dinner on Friday, Haesel took me to buy a new veil and ribbons for Master Newelyne's christening party and then she helped me choose a gown to wear, clean a few spots from it, and change the laces. She did not go down at all until Mainard came up to share my evening meal."

"Besides, there were men in the workroom that afternoon," Haesel said.

"Were there?" Magdalene said with bright interest.

"Yes," Sabina agreed. "I remember now. I heard their voices and I was a little annoyed because I thought they might take Mainard out with them. I wanted to show him how Haesel and I had fixed my gown."

"You feared they would take Mainard out, so you knew the voices?" Magdalene asked eagerly.

"Yes. Some. Master FitzRevery from the mercer's shop next door.

I know his voice. There were two others I knew, too, but I do not know their names. They are all members of one of the Bridge Guilds. You know, Magdalene, they are groups that have formed to raise money and to oversee the labor of building the new bridge."

"Yes," Magdalene said slowly. "I do know. Remember, several of the guilds hired the Old Priory Guesthouse for meetings. After all, where else could they get the privacy we offer as well as lively company and a good meal? Dulcie's years in the cookshop have not gone to waste. Besides, we are so close to the works of the new bridge."

Her mind was not on what she was saying, however. It was unlikely that Sabina had recognized voices from the meeting of any Bridge Guild, although she had sung at several. What Sabina had meant, but would never say except in total privacy to Magdalene alone, was that she recognized the voices of clients of the Old Priory Guesthouse.

That sparked a further memory. It had been Master Perekin FitzRevery who had arranged for Mainard to lie with Sabina and had paid for a whole night of her service. Only Mainard had not come for that purpose. FitzRevery had summoned him to Magdalene's house with a tale of a meeting of the guild and had instructed Sabina to do her best to seduce Mainard into sexual congress once he came. It was a gift from their guild to Mainard, FitzRevery had said, but with such a wry twist to his lips that Magdalene knew there was a special purpose to that "gift." A Bridge Guild buys a gold chain or a fine brooch or a silver candlestick to honor a member; it does not pay for a whore's services.

Suddenly Magdalene took her lower lip between her teeth. It was to spite Mainard's wife, she realized. Master FitzRevery had warned her that Sabina would have difficulty convincing Mainard she was willing to lie with him because Bertrild had scorned him and diminished him. But why should a Bridge Guild or even Master FitzRevery alone care about Mainard's troubles with Bertrild?

No, not FitzRevery alone. Surely he would have wished to claim the "gift" for his own if he had paid the entire sum. If it was accepted, Mainard would be deeply in his debt; even if it were refused, Fitz-Revery was already identified with it so he could gain nothing by the claim that others had contributed to that first night with Sabina. And those others as a group must all have wished to do Bertrild some harm.

More harm than merely making her husband unfaithful, if one of them had stolen Codi's knife. Interesting.

Which others? Ah! Sabina had already told her that. They were members of a Bridge Guild that had hired the Old Priory Guesthouse and also clients. Magdalene began to rack her brains for the members of the Bridge Guild to which Mainard belonged, but her thoughts were interrupted.

"If you don't want me no more," Henry said, "I might as well go home. Codi and the boys never work on Sunday, but it'll be a real treat for me to be off."

"I am not the master here," Magdalene said, "but I cannot believe Master Mainard would object. What do you think, Codi?"

"Who will tell those who come to the shop why it is closed?" Codi asked, his voice trembling slightly.

"No need to answer questions," Henry said. "Just drape the door in black cloth and everyone will know there's been a death."

Codi hit himself in the head gently. "I am all to bits and pieces," he said more firmly. "I should have thought of that myself. What kind of cloth should we buy, Henry?"

"I would go to the ragpickers for it myself," Henry replied with twisted lips, "but Master Mainard will not wish to be niggardly. Send Gisel next door to Master FitzRevery. He will give him a decent cloth at a good price."

"Yes." Codi sighed with relief. "Of course. I did not think of that either. And Master FitzRevery will put the cost onto Master Mainard's tally, so no one will need to find the coin to pay."

"Then I will be gone," Henry said, nodding at Codi and the boys and getting to his feet.

"Just a moment." Magdalene laid a hand on his arm. "I have a question. You must have seen the men who came in on Friday. Can you name them?"

"Of course. Master FitzRevery, Master John Herlyond, Master Ulf-maer FitzIsabelle, Master Lintun Mercer, and Master Jokel de Josne. They are the main members of the Bridge Guild to which Master Mainard belongs, and they meet with the other members of the guild once a month. But at odd times those five also meet without the other members of the guild to dine together or—" he cast a knowing glance at Magdalene "—to seek other amusement. Master Mainard used to go with them, but after Mistress Sabina came to live here, he most often refused. Friday they came to invite him to dine with them. . . ." He hesitated and then said, "Today, yes. It would have been this afternoon they were to meet at Master Ulfmaer FitzIsabelle's house."

"You heard the invitation?"

"Yes, they were in the shop right behind me then. Master Mainard refused. He said he had another appointment. This time they did not wish to take no for an answer. They followed him back into the workroom. I could hear them arguing with him, but not the exact words."

"He didn't want to go with them," Sabina put in. "We had talked about going on the river because I had never been . . ." Her voice faded and her brows knit in a frown. Magdalene waited. Those were sure signs that Sabina was trying to find words for what she had "heard" when someone was speaking of something else. "But it was not only that," Sabina continued as Magdalene had expected. "We could have gone on the river any Sunday. I do not think he liked those men . . . or some of them. There was something in his voice when he spoke of them and also . . ."

"Yes?" Magdalene urged. "This is no time to worry over telling tales."

"But I do not see that what Mainard said to me can have anything to do with Bertrild."

Magdalene was suddenly aware that Henry, Codi, and the boys were all listening with deep interest. "Then let it go," she said easily, knowing she could get Sabina alone either in her own rooms above or back at the Old Priory Guesthouse and discover what Mainard had said.

"So those five went into the workroom," she said turning toward Henry and Codi. "Did anyone else do so?"

"Lord Baltom and his wife were there earlier in the morning," Codi said. "He was on his way to Oxford and stopped in to bring a special blue-dyed leather to be decorated and used for the cantle and pommel of a saddle he has ordered for his wife's mare—a lovely animal, but small."

"They came on horseback?"

"Yes, but the horses remained in the Chepe." Obviously Codi

remembered Bell asking about the horse dung near the back gate. "There were grooms to hold them. The lord and lady came into the workroom to see the saddle frame and then we all came out into the shop. They are both in love with that mare and wanted to choose padding for the saddletree of soft-enough leather. They even had Stoc and Gisel out there to warn them to stitch carefully. Master Mainard warned that the soft leather would wear out, but the lord laughed. He said he would replace it, as with his wife's present saddle. But he could have had nothing to do with Mistress Bertrild's death. They were leaving London on Saturday morning."

Magdalene swallowed a sigh of impatience, but made no reprimand. She *had* asked who had come with no qualification. She corrected herself. "I meant who could have taken the knife and used it on Bertrild."

Codi shook his head. "No one. There were two—"

"No, three," Gisel interrupted.

"Yes." Codi nodded. "Three other customers who came into the workroom, but they, too, were on their way out of the city. Master Snelling lives in Greenwich. He only comes to London on Wednesday to do business and goes home on Friday. And Shipmaster Peter and his factor were sailing back to Spain. They came to ask whether Master Mainard had any special orders for them."

"Are you sure?" Magdalene asked.

Henry shrugged. "I suppose someone could have sneaked from the shop to the workroom while I was busy with a customer at the counter outside, but I do not think so."

Codi and the two boys consulted one another with their eyes. Magdalene watched keenly, but under half-lowered lids. Nothing appeared in any expression to give her reason to think they were hiding anything. Finally, Codi said there had been no one in the workroom except those he had named.

"And you can ask Master Mainard. He was there all day, except for dinnertime, and we had the door closed then."

Magdalene nodded slowly and with considerable satisfaction. "Then it was one of those five who took the knife. Well, we are progressing."

21 MAY
ST. CATHERINE'S HOSPITAL

Bell had made several interesting discoveries too. When he left Mainard's shop, he had gone across the Chepe and north a little way along Gracechurch Street to a narrow road that held a stable. There he had rented a stolid gelding that would carry him safely, if not quickly, through the chaos of the market to the Postern Gate, from where he could ride south through East Smithfield to the Hospital of St. Catherine.

He was already known to the brothers, having done various kinds of business with them for the bishop. The infirmarian was a little surprised when he asked to see Bertrild's body because the death had taken place in London, but made no objection, summoning one of the lay brothers to lead him to the small chamber where she lay.

"We did not put her into the mortuary," the brother said chattily, "because we are waiting for her husband to send her coffin and her shroud so she can be taken home for the funeral. But you need not fear. She is decently covered."

"I am reasonably well acquainted with dead bodies," Bell replied dryly, "and I have come to examine this one, so I will have to uncover it. She was sent here by Master Octadenarius because her death was not natural. Can you tell me who looked at her to determine the cause of death?"

"Oh, that would be Brother Samuel. Here is the chamber where she lies. Do you desire that I fetch Brother Samuel to you?"

"Very much, if he is free. It would be best if we could look at this body together."

As the young lay brother hurried out, plainly not eager to be in the same room as a corpse, Bell almost called him back. He did not want to be kept waiting while a monk unhurriedly finished meditating or praying or attending to another dead body. However, he was not kept waiting long. Before he was even much tempted to uncover Bertrild's body, a long, thin monk with wisps of gray hair and kind, tired eyes, came into the chamber. He had an odd gait, lifting his knees like a wading crane.

"Sir Bellamy? Is the bishop in Southwark?"

"No. Nor has he any interest in Mistress Bertrild. I was asked by the friend of a friend of her husband's to learn what I could, this friend fearing Master Mainard would be blamed for her death."

"They were not a happy couple?"

"I fear not."

Brother Samuel sighed. "She was killed with great hatred. Not only that, but it is possible that more than one person attacked her."

"More than one person?" Bell echoed, thinking of Sabina saying how much she wanted Bertrild dead.

She and Mainard had come back late to the house in the Chepe and could prove that, but Sabina had admitted it had taken them a long time to get from Master Newelyne's house to theirs. Instead of sitting on an alehouse bench, could they have made a detour to the house on Lime Street, got into some quarrel with Bertrild, and killed her there? That was very possible, but why then should they bring the body to the yard behind Mainard's shop? That would be insane. And where had they found a horse at that hour?

The monk had not responded directly to Bell's astonished echo of his suspicion, instead stalking over to the trestle on which the body lay and pulling away the stained and threadbare blanket that covered her. Bell followed, right on his heels, all concern for a female victim of violence lost in his sharp interest.

"You see?" Brother Samuel said, pointing to the wound in Bertrild's throat. "And then look here," he added, one long finger just not touching a bruise and dent that almost certainly marked a broken collarbone. His finger moved then to indicate several other wounds in her chest, belly, and side.

The knife wound that had killed her was not nearly as large as Bell had expected it to be, and its edges were smooth, although the bruising of the flesh around it gave silent testimony to the force with which the blow had been delivered. On the other hand, the wounds in her chest, belly, and side were not only wider but showed a telltale tearing of the flesh at the top of each.

"She was stabbed in the neck by one knife and then several times more by a different weapon—one with a curved tip," Bell said.

"That is what I see also," the monk agreed.

"But it was the wound in the throat that killed her?"

"Oh, yes. The knife went right through the Adam's apple, the windpipe, and one of those big veins. She must have been dead before she could cry out."

"Then why were the other wounds inflicted?"

The monk looked very distressed. "Hatred?"

"Possibly." Bell's voice was redolent with doubt.

That kind of hatred simply did not fit with Mainard's character, nor with Sabina's either. That Mainard, drunk, had come to wring some concession from his wife, might have been prodded into a rage sufficient to stab Bertrild was possible. That he should then take *Codi's* knife and stab her dead body several times. . . . No. And why would he have been carrying Codi's knife?

Bell could easily have accepted a crushed head or crushed throat as Sabina's work, but not stab wounds . . . unless the randomness of where the blows went could be a result of her blindness. A shocking notion leapt into Bell's mind. If Bertrild had come to the shop in the Chepe and been hiding inside, and then had attacked Sabina in the workroom, the broken collarbone could have been Sabina's work, even the aimless stab wounds, if Sabina had dropped her staff and picked up whatever was closest to her hand with which to defend herself. Then Mainard might well have killed his wife to save Sabina from punishment.

"Could the other stab wounds have been made first and the one in the neck last?" Bell asked the monk.

"No." Brother Samuel shook his head sadly. "Come. I will show you why."

Beyond the trestle on a stool by the wall was the clothing that had been removed from the body. The monk said that he had ordered it not be washed because he was sure the justiciar should see it. First, he picked up the cloak. Bell noticed at once that the fronts were both stained and stiff with blood, more nearer the neck than the hem.

"She was standing when she was stabbed," Bell said, frowning.

The blow that broke her collarbone should surely have knocked her down. And would she not have screamed her head off from the pain? Unless—was not the bruising fainter than it should be for such a blow? Could Bertrild's collarbone have been broken *after* she was stabbed? If Sabina thrust at her at the same moment that Mainard used a knife. . . . Yes, that was possible: Bertrild rushed toward Sabina to attack her; Sabina thrust at her with her staff; and Mainard struck out with his belt knife. And Brother Samuel's next remark did nothing to cause him to dismiss his thought.

"Yes, she was standing or possibly even coming toward her attacker. The front of her overtunic is also stained."

Brother Samuel laid aside the cloak and shook out the overtunic. The front was also bloodied, but not as much as Bell would have expected. However, that was not nearly as surprising as the tears where the knife with the curved tip had gone in. Those tears were hardly bloodstained at all; maybe a slight smear right along the edge but even that was hard to see. Bell fingered two of the cuts.

"Did her shift and undertunic soak up the blood?" But even as he said the words, Bell shook his head.

The flesh had been torn by the curved tip of the knife. Had Bertrild been alive when those wounds were made, they would have bled freely, especially as the knife had been ripped from the flesh and used a second and a third time. And who would stand close and allow a second and third wound to be inflicted?

"Those wounds were made after she was dead," the monk said, and sighed.

"But why?" Bell protested. "That is quite mad."

Brother Samuel slowly shook his head. "Hatred," he said again. "Hatred can amount to possession by the devil."

There could be no doubt that Sabina had hated Bertrild, but Bell found it very difficult to believe that her hatred could be so strong she would stab a corpse. And what he had been imagining would have required the complicity of Codi and the two boys. Well, Codi had been terribly distraught and the elder apprentice, Gisel, had been sick and shaken, but the younger one seemed to be only frightened by the distress of his companions. Bell could not really believe that those three had been witness to a violent murder. Unless they had been sent out into the shop to be away from Bertrild's and Mainard's quarrel and were not witness to it . . . Mainard was surely strong enough to carry his wife's body out into the yard.

Could he have missed bloodstains on the floor of the workroom? Bell wondered. He might have done, thinking them stains of dye or oil. Or had the floor been covered with rushes? Had the rushes been fresh? Bell's lips tightened against an obscenity. He had been so busy looking at the yard, at the place where Gisel found the body, that he had hardly taken in the workroom at all, except to notice that there was no disorder. Could that have been the reason that the body was carried out to the yard? To delude a careful examiner that Bertrild had *not* been killed there?

Fresh rushes or not, there would be no scrubbing bloodstains out of a wooden floor, Bell told himself grimly. The marks would be there when he returned.

While he was thinking, he had examined the remainder of Bertrild's clothing, determined not to be careless again, but he had only assured himself that the monk had not misread any signs. He then asked Brother Samuel when he thought Bertrild had been killed.

"She was hard as a rock when she was brought here," Brother Samuel said, turning back toward the corpse. "That was closer to Tierce than to Prime. I would guess she must have died before Vespers."

"Before Vespers?" If Bertrild had been killed before Vespers, Mainard and Sabina were out of it. At that time they had been at Pers Newelyne's house in the West Chepe. "Not nearer to Matins?" he asked anxiously.

"Well, sometimes the hardening comes faster, sometimes slower, but when the weather is mild or warm it is more likely to be slower than faster. It is barely possible that she died near Matins, but see?" He touched Bertrild's index finger, and the flesh dented ever so slightly; also the tip flattened. "Of course, it is never possible to be sure, but I think the stiffness is beginning to pass off, so I would say it is more likely that she was killed well before Vespers, maybe even near Nones rather than near Matins."

"If that is so, Brother, I will be well pleased," Bell said cheerfully. "Her husband, whom my friend wants to be innocent, was in the West

Chepe at the christening feast of a friend's child between noon and Compline and could not be responsible for his wife's death before Vespers."

"But someone was," the monk sighed. "Someone, or perhaps two, contrived to wrest this woman's life from her."

She well deserved it, Bell thought, but did not voice his judgment. Instead he thanked Brother Samuel for his help and assured him that he would consider it a duty to seek out the murderer. Bertrild was doubtless an unpleasant woman who would be no loss, he thought as he collected his horse and rode back through the gate and then north to Fenchurch Street. Nonetheless, one could not have a person who killed, even for good reason, running about loose. The next killing might be for a less-good reason.

Six

21 MAY
MAINARD'S HOUSE, LIME STREET

The road Bell had chosen was longer than the straight route he had taken to get to St. Catherine's, but it was much more peaceful. On Sunday the shops along Fenchurch were closed to avoid the strictures of the Church. Trading in the licensed markets having grudging permission, those merchants who felt the need for extra sales rented stalls or found partners with shops along the Chepe.

Bell tried as he rode along to make sense of what he had learned. If Brother Samuel was right, Mainard was innocent, but who else had a good enough reason to kill Bertrild? Being a public nuisance does not really invite murder. What he needed was information about who besides Mainard would profit from her death.

He turned right on Lime Street where the second house in from the corner belonged to Mainard. It was a handsome place, clearly a gentleman's residence in the past because it was set well back from the street with no provision for a sales counter at the front. A gravelled path led from the street to the front door and then divided right and left to go around the house, which was separated from its neighbors. Along the right-hand path were well-made wrought-iron hitches; Bell dismounted and tied his horse to the first, stepped up onto the thick flagstone slab, and pulled the bell rope.

The door opened even while the bell was still sounding, but the thin servant looked shocked when he saw Bell. He said accusingly that

Bell was not the coffinmaker and that the master of the house was not receiving guests because his wife had died.

"I am not exactly a guest," Bell replied. "Tell your master that Sir Bellamy of Itchen, knight of the bishop of Winchester and friend of Magdalene of the Old Priory Guesthouse" (Bell never minded identifying the whorehouse by that name because it sounded eminently respectable to anyone who did not actually know) "has come to ask him some questions."

To Bell's surprise, fear and rage flicked across the servant's face, and he slammed the door in Bell's face. The reaction was so unexpected and inexplicable — although it was clear evidence that the man knew there was something strange about his mistress's death — that Bell just stood staring. However, in moments the door opened again and Mainard himself stood in the doorway.

"Come in. Come in," he said. "I remember meeting you once at Magdalene's. You were at the evening meal. Do forgive Jean. What has happened has completely overset Bertrild's servants. But how did you know Bertrild had been murdered?"

As he spoke, Mainard led Bell into a sizeable chamber that had a window and a hearth on the left-hand wall and a wide wardrobe with handsome dishes on the right. The back wall was plastered and hung with painted cloths and in the far corner, surprisingly, a pallet covered with a worn quilt. The floor had a carpet of clean rushes in good condition for the time of year, and a wooden frame holding three oil lamps was suspended from the ceiling. To either side of the hearth were benches. Mainard moved toward one, gesturing Bell toward the other.

"As to how I knew of your wife's death," Bell said as he sat down, "Sabina came to ask Magdalene's help." He saw the look of pain on Mainard's face and hastened to add, "Because she had been a whore, she feared the justiciar would not believe her assurances that you were with her. Since she knew you to be innocent—" unless you and she are in it neck deep together, Bell thought "—and she remembered how Magdalene had sought out the murderer of Messer Baldassare last month, she hoped Magdalene could find the real killer to absolve you beyond doubt. Magdalene felt she might need a strong arm to help and sent for me."

"You are both very good to trouble yourselves," Mainard said, his voice not quite steady. "I was not afraid at first, but when the coffinmaker and the priest and the others I had to speak to about Bertrild's burial left, I began to wonder who else in the whole world would wish to kill her? God knows, she was not a kind or considerate person, but one does not kill because of a harsh word or rudeness. I had good reason to want her dead, but I cannot think of anyone else who had."

"I am afraid you will have to think about that again, and more seriously, Master Mainard. You must not let your good nature interfere with the truth. If what Brother Samuel of St. Catherine's Hospital says is true, and he has a wide experience and no reason at all to tell lies, Mistress Bertrild was killed before Vespers. And if my own careful examination is not at fault, then she was not killed in the yard of your shop."

"Not killed in the yard?" Mainard repeated. "But that would mean that someone . . . someone *brought* her to my yard and left her there apurpose."

"Yes."

The saddler's misshapen lips trembled. "Who hates me so?" he whispered. His beautiful eyes were full of tears. "Have I unknowingly hurt someone so much? I have striven to be a good man—to belie this horror." He passed his hand over his face. "Oh, heaven, do not tell me that Bertrild's death is my fault, that someone killed her just to gain some revenge on me."

"No, I do not believe you need to fear that. Whoever struck at your wife struck with a terrible rage. She was killed by someone who hated her."

"That I can believe," Mainard said softly. "But—but then why move her from wherever she died to my shop?" His expression of distress hardened to anger. "Never mind that blame was cast on me. If Bertrild had done so much harm, the blame for it might spread to me. I was her husband and should have controlled her and did not. But who could be so heartless, so careless, as to wish to cast such a shadow on my poor apprentices and journeyman?" His eyes mirrored rage. "Who used Codi's knife to kill her?"

"Codi's knife did not kill her."

"But it was beside the body, all bloody—" His hand came up to cover his mouth. "Oh, God, I did not mean that. I—"

Bell almost laughed. The man was certainly not a natural liar or accustomed to lying. "Do not bother to try to shield Codi. I cannot say he is innocent, because someone did kill your wife, but it was not done with Codi's knife."

Mainard now stared at Bell, utterly speechless, and Bell recounted his visit to St. Catherine's and what he had learned there.

"I see," Mainard said at last. "Bertrild was killed with an ordinary belt knife. That and the force with which the blow was delivered make it unlikely she was killed by a woman. But then she could have been killed anywhere, if she angered someone enough to pull a knife and stab her. And she—God forgive me for speaking ill of the dead—she had a vicious tongue and took some pleasure in tormenting others."

It was interesting, Bell thought, that Mainard ignored totally the mention of the blow that had broken Bertrild's collarbone. Clearly, Mainard did fear that Sabina had killed his wife. If he had not, would he have made such a point of the belt knife and the force of the blow, which could incriminate him? But if Sabina had done it, she would have had to meet Bertrild before noon, when she was ready to go with Mainard to Master Newelyne's son's christening.

That was not impossible from what Brother Samuel had said. Sabina could have set Haesel a task and caught Bertrild in the Chepe after she had threatened Codi. Would the woman have gone with her to the yard behind Mainard's shop? And if Sabina had struck her down and then stabbed her, why had Bertrild not screamed? And where could Sabina have hidden the body? When could she have dragged it from concealment to the place beside the table without Codi and the boys knowing? No, the whole thing was too unlikely.

Thought is swifter than speech, but Mainard had stirred restlessly before Bell said, "You are right. Your wife could have been killed anywhere by someone who was driven to desperation. She was wearing a cloak and must have been outside the house, just leaving, or newly returned. But then that person somehow got the body into your yard after dark, got into your workroom and stole Codi's knife, went back to the yard and stabbed the corpse several times."

As soon as Bell got to 'into your workroom,' Mainard began to shake his head. "That is not possible," he said. "Whoever it was could have got into the yard. I have no lock on my back gate and it is possible to open it, even when the latchcord is in, but the tools are all locked away in boxes, and the back door to the workroom is also locked and Codi keeps the key. There is often money in the box I keep in the workroom and the boys—well, Gisel, at least—are of an age when roaming the city at night seems an adventure."

Codi kept the key to the door. Codi's knife was locked in his box so only he could get it. Bertrild might well have come to Mainard's house to meet Codi or obtain something from him. But could Codi have killed Bertrild without the boys knowing? Reluctantly, Bell came to the conclusion he could have done so. Apprentices work hard and sleep hard. It would not have been impossible for Codi to go out after the boys were asleep. But then, why stab the woman with your own knife and leave it beside her when you had already killed her with a knife no one could identify?

Moreover, Bertrild had *not* been killed in the yard. Blood had run down her neck—Bell had noticed it along the lobe of her ear where it had not been washed away completely when the monks prepared her for burial. Doubtless that had happened when she fell or was laid down after she had been killed. Nor had the blood been caught in the hood of her cloak, though there was some on the back of the neckpiece, so it would have stained the grass. So Codi, if he killed her, must have done so in the workroom. Could Gisel and Stoc have slept through that or not betrayed any consciousness of such a horror? And there was the fresh horse dung.

There must be another solution, Bell thought, and said to Mainard, "Then it becomes important to know what your wife did after quarreling with Codi on Saturday morning."

"She quarreled with Codi? But . . ." He took a deep breath and the normal skin on the left side of his face reddened with rage. "Did she attack Sabina again?" And then his eyes widened with realization of what he had betrayed.

"No, she did not," Bell said. "Sabina heard her demanding that Codi make a belt out of some blue-dyed leather, which Codi refused to do. Mistress Bertrild did not go up to Sabina's rooms, and she was seen to leave your shop alive and in good health." He shrugged. "Master Mainard, you need not lie to protect Sabina or anyone else. Sabina trusts Magdalene utterly and me because she knows Magdalene would murder me if I betrayed her. We know everything Sabina knows."

If anything, Mainard looked relieved, but he shook his head. "I cannot tell you where Bertrild went or what she did. To speak the truth, Bertrild and I were not on such terms that we talked about anything. Our only exchange of words was for her to demand money and, mostly, for me to refuse to give her more. I have no idea what she did all day—or even at night."

"Would the servants know?"

"I have no idea. They are slaves, not free, and she treated them very badly. I did what I could, but if I tried to ease their circumstances, she inflicted new torments on them. She did not confide in them, of course, but doubtless they would know when she was in the house and when she was gone. Shall I call them?"

"One at a time, please."

Jean was the first. Mainard brought him in, patted his shoulder gently, and went to sit down again on the bench near the hearth, leaving Bell facing the man. Bell remembered the hostile look, the slammed door, but the servant was already trembling with fear, and he could see no point in increasing his terror, which could easily lead to his insisting he knew and remembered nothing.

"I am Sir Bellamy of Itchen, the bishop of Winchester's knight," he said quietly, "and I have come here to discover, if I can, who killed Mistress Bertrild."

"I don't know," Jean cried. "I didn't."

"I did not think you did know," Bell replied soothingly, but did not comment on the terrified denial.

He took in the man's starved look, the clothing worn to shreds— most unusual in household servants, even slaves. Normally what held household servants to their work, even for unpleasant masters, was the expectation of warmth and shelter and full bellies. Could the mistreated household slaves have been tried too far? Did Jean and the others know Mainard's shop and its yard? To voice any suspicion, however, was to silence his witness.

"What I would like you to tell me, if you can," Bell went on calmly, "is nothing immediately to do with the murder. I want to know what Mistress Bertrild usually did every day. Of course, if you know what she did on Saturday, that would be specially helpful."

Jean's eyes went past Bell to Mainard, and the saddler nodded encouragingly. "Just tell Sir Bellamy anything you know, Jean," he said. "You need not be concerned about me. I am out of it. I was at a christening from noon until Compline."

To Bell's pleasure, Jean turned back to him almost eagerly. "Well, mistress was alive long after noon. I can swear to that and so can cook and the maid and Hamo, for she sent us all out on errands maybe a candlemark past Nones."

"All of you? All at once?" Bell asked.

Jean nodded. "Yes."

"And had she done that before? Was it usual?"

"No, master, not usual. Can't remember her ever doing it before. Belike it was to do with that messenger that came and waited for her."

"Messenger?" Bell repeated eagerly. "From whom? What did he look like?"

"From her uncle, he were. Least that's what he said to me. 'From Druerie de Genlis to see Mistress Bertrild, at once. The matter is urgent.' I told him she weren't here and he seemed angry, but then he said he'd wait and I took him in here."

"Can you describe him?"

Jean shook his head, looking disappointed. He was clever enough to recognize Bell's interest and that it was safer engaged on a stranger than on himself. "Never saw his face," he admitted. "He was coughing and sneezing and wheezing and had his hood pulled way down to his nose. Don't think his voice was like it usually was either. He was sort of croaking and choking."

"Interesting," Bell said, and turned to look at Mainard, who stared back, wide-eyed with surprise. "Did Bertrild's uncle often send her messengers?" he asked, including both men in the question.

"I cannot remember him ever having done so before," Mainard replied at once, "although he did send a message back with her courier that she would be welcome when she asked if she could stay with him for some months last winter. But since then, if one came during the day, I might not know."

"No, master," Jean said promptly. "None came that I ever knew of. But he must have come from her uncle because she knew him. As I closed the door, the mistress said 'So eager, Saeger? You are early.' "

"Saeger?"

Bell turned to Mainard again, who shook his head. "I know no Saeger—not that I know Sir Druerie's servants—and I never heard Bertrild say that name before."

"Bertrild was childless so whatever she brought to the marriage would go back to her next of kin if she died. . . . No, wait. I think I know Sir Druerie. Of Swythling, is he not? That is just upriver from Itchen. How strange that he should be Bertrild's uncle. He seemed like a decent man—but then, I only met him once or twice, and that was years ago."

Before Bell finished, Mainard had begun to laugh. "I never met Sir Druerie, but decent man or not, he would not have wanted what Bertrild brought to our marriage. Believe me, that would be no reason for him to do away with her. She brought nothing but debts. There might be other reasons. She lived in Swythling from November until February. Who knows what happened there. Could she have made an enemy of this Saeger?"

Bell turned his attention back to Jean. "When she said 'So eager, Saeger? You are early,' did she sound angry? Frightened? Surprised?"

Jean's mouth turned down. "She sounded like always. Like she was lookin' down her nose, talkin' to a worm."

"He must have put back his hood if she recognized him," Bell said thoughtfully. "Was he still coughing and sneezing then?"

"No." Jean's eyes brightened. "No, nor when I opened the door for the mistress to go in. It was quiet in the room. And I'll tell you somethin' else. His boots weren't right."

"Weren't right?" Bell urged.

"They were city boots—polished leather with thin soles. No countryman wears boots like that, specially not a servant carryin' a message."

"Do you remember anything else . . ." Bell began, and then held up his hand. "No. This is no way to go about this. Start at the beginning of the day, Jean, and tell me everything you remember that your mistress did and said."

The man looked puzzled, but began at once. "She got up usual time. Nell can tell you that better than me, and cook will tell you what she ate. She left the house a little before Tierce, like always—"

"Yes," Mainard put in. "That would be right. She came to the shop Saturday mornings for money for the week. I left that for her with Codi. I had to go early to Basynges to deposit the week's earnings because I had to take Sabina to Newelyne's house by noon."

"She came back in a real fury. Slapped me when I opened the door and kicked me too. Then she went up to the solar. She sent for dinner just before Sext."

"Did you bring it up?" Bell interrupted.

"No, sir. Never allowed onto the upper floor, not Hamo nor me. We cleaned, tended garden, carried water and such but all down here. Nell did the cleanin' in the solar and bedchamber. She or cook carried up the mistress's dinner. I'm not sure which."

Bell nodded. "I'll speak to them later. Go on."

"Came down maybe near two candlemarks after Sext carryin' the usual bundle of tally sticks—"

"Tally sticks?" Mainard echoed. "Are you sure? For what did Bertrild need tally sticks?"

The servant naturally could not answer the last question and assumed, correctly, that it was just an expression of astonishment. "Knew they was tally sticks because once she tripped on the stairs and dropped them. Wrapping came open, and they fell out all over the floor. Know what tally sticks are. Me dad had them afore we lost the farm and I got sold."

"Do you know where she took the tally sticks?"

"No, sir."

"Did she have them with her when she came back?"

"Yes, she did. When I said there was a messenger from her uncle in here, she . . . she bit her lip and went through to the kitchen. Didn' have the bundle when she came back. Then she pointed for me to open the door, and she went through. Like I said, it was quiet until she asked this Saeger if he was eager."

"Did you hear anything else?" Bell asked.

Jean pursed his lips, then pulled them back. "A squeak?" he said uncertainly. "I was just goin' away to sit on the stair, but he couldn't of killed her then because a little while later she opened the door and told me she had several errands that must be done at once. The only thing . . ." Jean hesitated.

"Yes, go on. Even if you don't think it's important, tell me anyway."

"It's just . . . those errands, they weren't nothing special. She sent the cook off to market for extra food, as if the messenger was going to stay, and she sent Nell off to the laundress, like more sheets and tablecloths was needed. And she sent me and Hamo all the way over to the West Chepe to buy candles, like we didn't have a candlemaker just beyond Master Josne's house on the corner of the East Chepe."

"Well, it is clear enough that she wanted you all out of the house. The question is why. No, never mind that, Jean. There is no way you could know the answer to that. So you all left. And when you came back?"

"There weren't no one here. House were empty—and not locked up neither, only the bell rope and the latchstrings they was all pushed inside. Had a time fishin' out the one for the back door."

"You all came back at the same time?"

"No, acourse not. Cook was back first. She was mad as fire, the fish havin' dripped all over her basket, and Nell was there, too, when me and Hamo came. But cook and Nell couldn't think of how to get the latchstring out, so they just sat down to wait. We saw the horse were gone, and we didn' know how to feel about that. Mistress would be glad to save what he would have eat, but if she wanted him to stay and he wouldn', we'd all get beaten."

If anyone had good reason to kill Bertrild, those four servants did, but Bell did not think—if Jean was any example of what the others were—that they had sufficient spirit. And if they had, there would be time enough to question all of them more straitly. So far, Jean was talking freely and easily, and Bell did not want to dry up the source by implying suspicion.

"Did you look through the house when you got in?" he asked.

"No, sir. Thought the mistress and the messenger would be back any minute. Cook was ravin' 'cause she didn' know whether to make extra for the evenin' meal—if she made more and didn' need it, mistress would whip her. And Nell were cryin' 'cause she didn' know what kind of bed to get ready and whether it should be down here or up in the solar. She'd get whipped too for not bein' ready. Hamo and me just sat down on the stair—me to open the door and carry whatever needed bringing in and Hamo to take the horse to the shed." He paused and then a beatific smile lit his thin, haggard face. "But she never come, and now she never will."

Such open delight in Bertrild's death almost precluded Jean being a cause of it. "You did not think to send a message to Master Mainard when his wife did not return home?"

Horror filled Jean's eyes. "Send a message without the mistress's order? How could we know if she went somewhere with the messenger and didn' want master to know? She'd of tortured us to death!"

"Very well," Bell said. He had experience with mistreated servants, who would do nothing without specific directions, and he thought that for the moment he had drained Jean dry. "Send in Hamo, please."

The second man was even more pitiful than Jean, dull and terrified. It took Bell and Mainard a little while to calm him enough to answer at all. He had been outside when the messenger came and had seen and heard nothing, but then Bell struck the right note and asked about the horse. Dull, Hamo was, but he loved horses and knew them. When he and Jean had come around the front of the house to go to the West Chepe, he had seen the horse. The messenger's horse, he reported eagerly, glad at last to have something to tell his master, did not look as if it had come a long way, not unless the rider had travelled very slowly. Moreover, he said, the horse and the saddle were like Bell's, and then, wringing his hands, that he didn't know how to say it better.

"But I am not riding my destrier, or my palfrey," Bell said to Mainard. "I rented a horse from a local stable because I did not wish to walk all the way to St. Catherine's."

"That's what I saw," Hamo whimpered, trembling.

"We believe you," Mainard soothed. "Do not worry about it. I know you are good with horses. Was there anything else you saw that was strange?"

"Not then." Hamo swallowed hard. "When we come back, after we waited a while for mistress, I remember that I left the wheelbarrow out, and I run out back to put it away in the shed . . . but it weren't

where I left it. I near to died of fright. I didn't dare tell no one." He
began to shake with recalled terror, and tears ran down his face. "I
thought maybe if I run to the master before light the next day, he'd
let me say he wanted it. But when I got up to sneak out of the house,
the wheelbarrow *was* there—"

"It was exactly where you left it?" Bell asked eagerly.

Hamo's face wrinkled with anxiety. "Not perfect sure, maybe it
was more to back of the tree. Thought maybe I just missed seein' it
last night."

"Do you do the rushes on this floor, Hamo?"

"Yes, sir."

"Is there anything different about them today from how they were
Saturday morning?"

"Rushes get moved by walkin'," Hamo said uncertainly. Then he
frowned. "Put the rushes down Wednesday. Maybe they should be
flatter in the middle? If mistress expected company after Mass on Sunday, she'd tell me to rake up the rushes on Saturday. Not yesterday
though, so I didn'."

"Anything else, Hamo? You have done very well." The man shook
his head. "Good enough. If you think of something later, tell your
master. We will not blame you for having forgotten. That often happens when a man is excited. Master Mainard will be pleased by anything you recall. You can go now. And send in Nell."

The maid had not much to tell them. She had seen and heard
little of the messenger. He had been standing behind Mistress Bertrild,
quite close, when she sent Nell to the laundress and bade her tell the
cook to buy fish and some other things in the market, but he was in
the shadow and did not speak, and Nell had been concentrating on
what her mistress told her. Making any mistake or failing to carry out
Mistress Bertrild's orders exactly brought painful retribution. And,
though she had carried up Mistress Bertrild's dinner, she had seen
nothing at all unusual. The mistress was examining her tally sticks, as
she often did on Saturday afternoon. Mainard shook his head over this
second mention of the tally sticks, but did not interrupt.

The cook, who was the only emaciated cook Bell had ever seen,
had even less to say. She had received her orders from Nell and had
not been near mistress or messenger. The one thing she told them

that was of real interest was that part of her distress over Bertrild's absence was that all except the small paring knives were kept locked up, and she could not clean the fish she had bought. Mainard dismissed her with an order to make a good evening meal for the whole household, while Bell stood looking down at the rushes under his feet.

When the cook had left the chamber, sobbing with joy, Bell turned to Mainard and said quickly, "I am sorry if it troubles you, but I think Mistress Bertrild was killed here, likely right in this chamber."

"By the servants?" Mainard's voice trembled.

"They had cause enough, but I do not think so. None of them was frightened about Mistress Bertrild's death, and all expressed their joy in it quite openly. All except Jean are dull, but not stupid enough to do that if they thought they might be suspect."

"No one would have believed them if they expressed grief," Mainard remarked dryly.

"No, nor even if they expressed concern, but they could have acted indifferent, as if they did not know what would become of them. Also, I do not think any has the spirit." He paused to smile. "And of one thing I am sure, Master Mainard, none of them would involve you in any way."

The saddler shook his head. "None has cause to love me. There was little I could do for them. I sneaked them a little food when I could, but. . . ." He shrugged.

Bell's lips turned down with distaste. Servants and slaves needed lessoning and he had no quarrel with that, but slow starvation and constant punishment were beyond what he could approve.

"What little you could do must have seemed like manna from heaven to them, but that was not what I meant. They are slaves. If Mistress Bertrild was dead and you accused of it, they would be sold again, perhaps into even worse circumstances. Beside that, why in the world should they carry your wife all the way to your shop, struggle to open the back gate, and harm a man they know would be kind to them when they would need to take her no farther to dump her in the river? And, the body was not carried to your shop in a wheelbarrow. The wheel would have bit deep in the soft border when it was stopped near your back gate and I saw no sign of that, only nearly fresh horse dung."

"Horse dung? The messenger? No, I cannot believe that a messenger from her uncle would kill Bertrild."

"He said he was a messenger from her uncle, but there is no proof of that. Perhaps you should ask Sir Druerie about it. You must tell him of his niece's death, after all."

Master Mainard put a hand to his head. "Of course I must. I had forgotten. Now who can I send as messenger? Jean and Hamo are useless. I cannot spare Codi, Henry cannot manage a horse because of his hands, and the boys are too young. I suppose I could hire . . . wait. I know. I could—" He stopped abruptly, his brain finally having taken in what his eyes were watching. "What are you doing, Sir Bellamy?"

While Mainard was speaking, Bell had been using his feet to sweep aside the rushes in a broad swathe from near the benches toward the door. He was utterly amazed to see the planks of the floor scrubbed nearly white, but even with that bleaching of the wood he was not sure he would find anything. Even if blood had spattered when Bertrild was stabbed, the drops might have been caught solely in the rushes. Those could have been removed and, even if not, the drops might by now easily be confused with natural spotting as the rushes dried.

Nonetheless, Bell felt it was worth the small effort he was expending, and, about two-thirds of the way to the door, he was rewarded. Several dark spots appeared on the planks. Bell knelt, wet a finger, put it to the spots, smelled it, and then tasted it.

"I was looking for blood," he said, in answer to Mainard's question, sitting back on his heels, "and I think I have found it. I am almost certain now that your wife was killed right here, not lured out to the yard behind your shop."

"Killed by the man who said he was a messenger? But then where was her body? The servants were all back in the house before Vespers."

"I would suspect it was hidden in the shed, and that the wheelbarrow that disappeared had been used to move it." He grimaced. "What a pity wheelbarrows and garden sheds are covered with stains and soil."

Upon which words, Mainard burst out laughing. "Not Bertrild's," he said. "See this floor? Scrubbed white? That was what she had the servants doing every minute they were not employed in some other task. It was her favorite punishment for them. They had to remove the rushes, scrub the floor, and replace the rushes. Upstairs and down, the kitchen, the shed, the wheelbarrow, the ladders, even the privy, are all scrubbed white."

Bell raised his brows. "Well, if the soul knows what passes here on earth and can have feelings about it, Mistress Bertrild must be feeling considerable satisfaction because having the servants scrub everything white may well help catch her murderer."

Leaving Mainard staring after him, Bell went out through the door into the kitchen—where the servants gasped and huddled together and then slowly relaxed as he paid them no attention—and then into the garden. This was remarkably well cared for but without the smallest grace, the flowers in circumscribed clumps and the vegetables in rigid rows.

In the shed, Bell found his supposition proved right. There were spots of blood on the back of the wheelbarrow and, behind a pile of old laths, several smears that might have come from the stained cloak. So the body had been moved from the house to the shed in the wheelbarrow and then, perhaps after dark, from the shed to the horse. The gate at the back of the garden was locked, but Bell did not consider that a check to his theory. There had been no keys among the possessions piled up on the stool in St. Catherine's Hospital, so likely the murderer had Bertrild's keys.

As Bell returned to the house to warn Mainard about that fact, he heard voices and heavy tramping. When he came in, he saw that the coffinmaker had returned with the body from St. Catherine's. He waited politely while Mainard sent Jean out to bring the priest back, and then told him about what he thought had happened and that Bertrild's keys seemed to be missing.

"The house doors have bars as well as locks, and I will warn the servants to be sure the bars are set firmly," Mainard said with only the most cursory interest. Then he frowned and asked, "Will you be going back to my shop at all today?"

"Yes. I must return my horse to the stable off Gracechurch Street."

"Would you be so good—I do not mean to use you as a servant, but these poor souls here will have all they can do to help me make ready to receive visitors—would you be so good as to tell Codi and the boys to come here to Lime Street? As part of my 'family' they should be here as mourners." He hesitated, biting his lip and looking uncomfortable, but then he added, "Would you also ask Sabina if she would go to Magdalene's for the night? I do not like to think of her in the shop with no one but little Haesel."

Feeling a little guilty about sending the whore back to the whore-house? Bell wondered. But the man was now free to make a decent marriage, and Bell could not really blame him. A twinge of doubt went through him. Would he treat Magdalene the same way if a good marriage tempted him? The flicker of guilt he felt in himself made him keep his voice and expression bland.

"Gladly," he said. "And if you like, I will take her to the Old Priory Guesthouse myself, as I want to speak to Magdalene."

"Thank you very much," Mainard said, as Bell turned away, then uttered a "tchk" and followed him. "And another imposition, if I may," he said, opening the door. "Would you be good enough to step next door into FitzRevery's shop and ask him if he would call on me here at Lime Street?"

"Will he not be coming to the funeral?" Bell asked, surprised.

Mainard looked down for a moment, then sighed. "Bertrild had been very offensive to him about an utter stupidity. She once came to FitzRevery's shop and accused him of being the cause of her father's death by introducing Gervase to the Old Priory Guesthouse and thus corrupting him. I will be grateful if FitzRevery comes to the funeral, of course, but I cannot expect it. But when you spoke of notifying Sir Druerie, I recalled that FitzRevery has a farm and storehouse for fleece at Hamble, which is not far from Swythling. In fact, one can pass right by Swythling on the way to Hamble. I can send a message to Sir Druerie by one of FitzRevery's men."

"A good thought, but please do not tell Sir Druerie any more than that his niece has been murdered. No details, except that you have been exonerated. You should ask, of course, what message Sir Druerie sent to your wife, saying that your servants told you of the messenger but that Mistress Bertrild was killed before she could inform you what he desired of her—or of you."

"Do you think he will send the same messenger back?"

"He might, and that would be convenient, but it does not matter.

Your question would not imply any suspicion on your part and should cause no alarm. If Sir Druerie does not send the same messenger, I can easily ride to Swythling when I return to Winchester to question the man."

With that, he raised a hand in farewell, and Mainard closed the door behind him.

Seven

B ell returned his hired horse with a sense of relief. The beast did not demand the same kind of attention that his destrier or even his riding palfrey did in the crowded Chepe, but it was so sluggish that he found himself expending almost as much energy in grinding his teeth with impatience. Once dismounted and walking toward Mainard's shop, Bell wondered why he should have been impatient. He had not been in any special hurry . . . and then his lips turned down with a new irritation as he realized his impatience arose from his desire to come the sooner to where Magdalene might be.

Nonetheless, when the door of the shop was opened by Codi and he saw Magdalene looking at an array of leather and woodworking tools laid out on the counter, a sense of pleasure suffused him. She looked up and smiled, and he could not help feeling that there was a special warmth in her expression and that it was particularly addressed to him.

"I agree with you that Bertrild was not killed in the yard," she said. "I have been in every place a person could hide and another come upon her and kill her, and there was no sign of any disturbance or any blood. I have also examined the floor of the shop—"

Bell could not help laughing aloud. There could be no doubt now that Magdalene's warm smile had been exclusively for him, but as a help in her investigation, unfortunately, not as a man she desired.

She raised her brows at the laughter. "Well, I admit that no real proof can be drawn from the floor, which has some thirty years of stains on it, but it is not that funny to have looked. There might have been a sticky place that smelled different from leather polish or a new-washed spot."

"No, not funny for that reason. I thought of it myself after I left and was annoyed by my carelessness in having forgotten to look. Still, I hope you did not waste much time on it. Mistress Bertrild was not killed here at all. She was almost certainly killed in her house on Lime Street, and the murder weapon was not Codi's knife."

"But it must have been Codi's knife," Magdalene said. "Why else should the knife have been stolen on Friday?"

"Stolen on Friday?" Bell echoed. "That is impossible."

"What do you mean, impossible? Did Master Mainard say Codi was using that knife on Saturday?"

"No, no. Wait, we are talking at cross-purposes. Let me tell you what I discovered at St. Catherine's and by questioning Mistress Bertrild's servants."

He could not have had a more attentive audience. Codi all but held his breath when Bell described the wound that had killed Bertrild and cried out in protest against the idea that, no matter how much he hated the woman, he would be so insane as to stab her corpse and with his own knife. And, although she did not interrupt his story, Magdalene shook her head over the evidence that Bertrild had been struck a blow by a weapon like Sabina's staff. She was diverted from any protest, however, when Bell suggested Bertrild had been killed by the messenger sent by her uncle.

"Why should the uncle want her dead?" she asked as soon as Bell stopped speaking. "According to Sabina, Bertrild brought nothing to the marriage except debts, so there would be no profit to him in her death. And why not kill her when she was with him? Surely in Swythling an accident could have been arranged. And why wait four months?"

"I thought the messenger himself might be the killer. There is, after all, no proof that the man did come from her uncle, only his tale to the servants. And she knew him. She called him Saeger—a name Mainard said he did not recognize."

"Yeeesss." Magdalene drew out the word as she considered what

Bell said. "But you had better hear what I learned from Codi and the boys." She then recounted the evidence that only the five men who had visited the workroom on Friday could have got Codi's knife. "And, even if it was not the murder weapon, it *was* used to stab Bertrild," she concluded. "Unless . . . could she have been stabbed with Codi's knife after the killer brought her body here?"

Bell gnawed gently on his lower lip as he considered that. "I am not sure," he said slowly. "Brother Samuel said she was hard as a rock when he received the body, and he felt that she had died well before Vespers, perhaps not very long after Nones. Still, the stiffness that comes after death might not have been so great when she was brought here. Indeed, I wonder how the body could have been carried on the horse if it were rock hard." He bit his lip a moment longer, then suddenly his expression cleared and he shook his head. "No, the wounds inflicted with Codi's knife could not have been made long after death because there was some oozing of blood from them, and if she had been hours dead, I doubt there would have been any."

"But what if the messenger brought her some information she had desired from her uncle, then he left, and she used that information in such a way that whomever she used it against killed her? Maybe she did not send the servants out to prevent them from seeing the messenger or learning what he said but to keep them from seeing the person who came next?"

"That is certainly possible. The errands Mistress Bertrild set the servants would have taken some time—sending the men to the West Chepe, for example. And even when the cook and the maid got back, the latchcords were all pulled in, and they had to wait for the men to hook them out." He sighed. "I will speak to Master Octadenarius as soon as I can and ask him to have the neighbors questioned."

Magdalene nodded. "And if you can convince him that Bertrild was killed before Vespers in the Lime Street house, then no guilt could attach to Mainard. I will just run up and tell Sabina—"

"Wait just a moment before you do that," Bell said to her, then turned to Codi. "Master Mainard would like you to take the boys and go to the Lime Street house. He said that as you were part of his family you must appear there as mourners."

"Yes, of course," Codi said at once, beginning to gather the tools

Magdalene had been looking at from the counter and replace them in his box. "It is not right for him to keep vigil with the dead all alone, and I cannot believe *she* had any friends who would sit with him. I will get the boys washed up and dressed in their best."

Closing the box, he hurried through the door into the workroom. Magdalene cocked her head inquiringly at Bell.

He shrugged. "After you tell Sabina that Mainard is cleared of suspicion in his wife's death, you had better tell her to go back to the Old Priory Guesthouse with you, too. Mainard told me to ask her to do that."

A flicker of intense pain passed over Magdalene's exquisite features. "Poor child," she whispered. "I believe she truly loves him, and she never liked whoring." Her eyes rose and her glance fixed his.

"I wouldn't!" Bell exclaimed, defensively.

Magdalene laughed, raised herself on tiptoe, and kissed him on the nose. "You will never have the chance, love. You will never have the chance. I admit I do not like whoring either, but I *adore* being my own mistress — and managing the Old Priory Guesthouse gives me that."

She stood for a moment, smiling a challenge, and Bell's fair skin reddened, but there really was nothing he could say. Naturally, if he took Magdalene into his keeping, he would expect to be master of the household. Her smile broadened and with a gurgle of laughter she turned away to climb the stair to Sabina's chamber. Seething, Bell started to follow her, but he knew if he did, he would say something quite unforgivable, considering Mainard's message. Fortunately at that point he remembered the second message Mainard had asked him to deliver, and with a sigh of relief, he walked out of the shop to the mercery next door.

The din and crowding in the market had abated somewhat in the late afternoon lull. Nonetheless, the young man who stood beside the display of cloth, yarn, and rough, sheared wool was alert. A single glance at Bell made him step to the door of the shop and call for his master.

A man just entering his fourth decade walked through the door, bowed slightly to Bell, and gestured him to come in. He had light brown hair, showing a few glints of gray, round muddy-colored eyes, and an indeterminate nose.

"Is it true?" he asked Bell as soon as he was inside. "Is Mistress Bertrild dead?"

"Dead, but not of natural causes," Bell replied, somewhat repelled by the man's eagerness even though he knew no one would miss Bertrild. "To whom am I speaking?"

"Oh, I beg your pardon. I am Master Perekin FitzRevery. I forgot to say because I know who you are, Sir Bellamy. Is the bishop—"

"No," Bell said. "My lord of Winchester is not involved. I am looking into the matter for a friend of a friend."

"Ah." A faint knowing smile touched Master FitzRevery's lips, but he did not mention Magdalene's house or Mainard's whore. "Yes, it was rumored that Mistress Bertrild was murdered. I do not know what to say. I have not seen Mainard all day. Do not tell me that he is suspect? Oh, he had reason to want to be rid of her, but he is not that kind."

"You need have no fear of suspicion attaching to him," Bell said, with some satisfaction, wondering whether Master FitzRevery was defending or subtly accusing Mainard. "Master Mainard has most excellent witnesses that he could not have possibly killed his wife."

"That is a great relief," FitzRevery said, but Bell was not certain whether it was relief or surprise, even a touch of alarm, that showed on his face.

"I have just come from Master Mainard, who is holding vigil for his wife in the house on Lime Street. You know where that is?"

"Yes." The answer was short and hard.

"Master Mainard asks if you would do him the favor of stopping by the house. He needs to inform Sir Druerie de Genlis, Mistress Bertrild's uncle, that his niece has died and would like, if it is possible, for one of your men to carry a message."

"Oh, of course." Now there was no mistaking the expression of relief on FitzRevery's face. "Indeed, I will have a man starting for Hamble tomorrow. Is there anything else I can do? We have been friends a long time, Mainard and I. I would like to help in any way I can."

"He did not say anything else to me, but he was uneasy about using me as a messenger for fear my pride would be hurt. I am sure, as you are friends, that he will speak more freely to you."

"Yes, of course." To Bell's surprise, FitzRevery's face actually paled, and his mouth twitched briefly into angry and bitter lines. His eyes shifted from Bell's, and he added hurriedly, "If you will excuse me, Sir Bellamy, I will go at once and see what I can do for Master Mainard."

Considerably bemused, Bell returned to Mainard's shop, just in time to hear Codi say, "The boys and I are leaving now. Do you have your keys, Sabina?"

"We are leaving now also," the young woman said softly. "Please wait and lock up after us. There is no need for me to take keys. I will not be returning without Master Mainard."

Her simple dignity made Bell furious with Mainard and gave him the sinking feeling that the saddler had used her to help him murder his wife. Then he called himself a fool. Mainard might be innocent in some ways, but he ran a successful business, which warranted some shrewdness. No man who had used a woman to help him commit murder would then set her aside. But perhaps she knew he had not. Her serene face, her steady voice, the fact that she was taking nothing from the house, except her lute, all spoke her confidence that she would return.

Nonetheless, Bell felt a sudden determination to make sure that Mainard had been at Master Newelyne's house from Sext until Vespers, so he asked Magdalene if she needed his escort. She grinned at him; he knew it even though the veil swathed her face; he could hear it in her voice, see the amusement in those lovely, misty gray-blue eyes as she thanked him, very gravely, and said she was sure they would be quite safe walking home.

She did not need him. He knew it, but it was a bitter potion to swallow each time she reminded him of it. And after this betrayal of Sabina by Mainard, it was less likely than ever that Magdalene would consider coming into his protection. With an ill-natured snort, Bell preceded the women out of the house and set off back to the stable where he demanded a less-sluggish mount.

He realized when he reached the West Chepe that he had no idea where Master Newelyne's house was. However, he did know the man was a cordwainer, another leatherworker like Mainard, and a single question at the corner of Cordwainer Street brought him sure directions. A decent, contented-looking servant opened the door for him and led him into a well-appointed shop with displays of boots and shoes on shelves behind a broad counter. There were benches along the wall, likely for the trying on of shoes, on which the servant invited him to be seated while he went to "find" his master, but Bell found himself too restless to sit, and there was no need. Master Newelyne opened the door in a wall that closed off about one-third of the area into an office and entered the shop.

"Sir Bellamy? How may I serve you, sir?"

"I am the bishop of Winchester's knight, and I have been asked by a tenant of my lord's to look into the death of Mistress Bertrild, Master Mainard's wife."

"Bertrild is dead?" Newelyne gasped, and then grinned broadly. "Well, thank God for that! I cannot think when a man has brought me better news—except that my wife had birthed a strong son after three daughters, only it was a woman who carried that happy word. Come in. Come in to my private chamber. Have a glass of wine."

He gestured expansively toward the door, then hesitated and frowned. " 'To look into the death,' " he repeated. "That sounds as if there is some doubt about the manner of it?"

"Yes, there is, Master Newelyne."

"I see," he said, more soberly, but gestured again toward the door.

Behind it was a very pleasant chamber with a small window looking out into Cordwainer Street, and a small hearth on the far wall, vented through the side wall of the house. Facing the door and at right angles to the window was a sturdy table with a chair behind it so the best warmth of the fire would fall on the seated person's back. There was no fire in the hearth on this mild spring day, of course, but a flask of wine and several well-polished pewter cups stood to one side of the table.

"Sit. Sit." Master Newelyne gestured to the several stools, one at each end of the table and two along its length. He poured a cup full of wine and set it in front of the stool Bell had chosen, poured another for himself, and went around the table to take his place in his chair. "How is his lordship of Winchester interested in this matter?"

"Not at all," Bell answered promptly. "He is in Winchester and will know nothing about it until he receives my report. At the moment I am acting for Mistress Magdalene of the Old Priory Guesthouse—"

"Sabina's whoremistress?" Newelyne's cup hung suspended halfway to his mouth. "Just a moment. How did Bertrild die?"

"She was murdered."

"How? When? Where?"

When Bell had answered those questions, Master Newelyne sighed with relief, drank deeply from his cup, and set it down on the table. "Then Mainard cannot be accused of her death, thank God. He was here, in my house, on Saturday at the celebration after the christening of my son, from a little before Sext until after Vespers."

"You are sure of that?"

"Yes, indeed," he said positively, then shrugged. "Well, I did not have my eye upon him every minute, and Mainard always found a dark corner in which to hide himself so he would not shock or frighten anyone, but he brought Sabina to sing. I greeted him myself and showed the girl where to sit. But the question is ridiculous."

"How so?" Bell asked blandly. "He had the best reasons."

"It does not matter," Newelyne said. "Mainard would not have committed murder, no matter the provocation." Then he sighed. "I know that, but she was a devil and it might seem to others, who do not know Mainard as well as I do, that he had reason enough to have killed her ten times over. Well, he did have reason, but Mainard would not hurt anyone, not even Bertrild, so I am glad to be able to assure you that he was here."

"All the time? You are certain? There might have been circumstances—"

"Not under which Mainard would harm another living soul," Newelyne said positively. "I have known Mainard all my life. My father had a cordwainer's shop in the East Chepe when I was young, and Mainard and I played together as children and attended the same school. He saved my life some two or three times." Newelyne laughed fondly, remembering. "As a boy, I was somewhat more daring than sensible, and even then Mainard was very strong. He pulled me out of several scrapes—once literally, when I had gone into a deserted house that then collapsed around me."

"You might feel a sense of obligation toward him, then, and wish to protect him."

"No, no. We were always even. I saved him many more times, sometimes just from a drubbing—" the smile Newelyne had been wearing changed to a grimace "—but once or twice he might have been killed by fanatic fools who claimed he had been marked by the devil. Killed because he would not defend himself."

Bell nodded. "I can believe that. I know Master Mainard a little. But perhaps if it were not himself he needed to defend?"

Newelyne laughed. "That would be no trouble for Mainard. He looks strong, but you do not know the half. It is as if his body should make up to him for his face. He is much stronger even than he looks. He simply steps up to the attacker, pins his arms to his body, and carries him away."

"An attacker with a knife?"

The cordwainer shook his head. "That makes no difference to Mainard. I saw him do it only a few months since. The Bridge Guild was meeting in the Salters Hall that is north of Candlewick Street. Most of the contributors to the building of the new bridge were there, but the largest donors were up front on the dais. Someone, I do not remember who now, moved that the names of those who gave more than ten pounds should be engraved on a plaque to be fastened to the stones at the bridge entrance. This was so agreed without argument, and the men gave their names. That was when the trouble began. When one of them, Lintun Mercer, spoke, a young man suddenly sprang to his feet and cried out that Master Lintun's name must not appear but that of his father, Master William Dockett—"

"Lintun Mercer? William Dockett? Why do I know those names?" Bell muttered.

Newelyne realized that Bell did not expect him to make any answer to those questions but took his remark as a desire for more information and continued, "This younger William Dockett claimed half the business still belonged to his father, also William Dockett, who had been the original member of the guild, and said he wished to give permission to have the guild dues and contributions deducted from his share. At that point, Master Lintun protested that the business was solely his, that young William had seen his father's name and seal on the document that reserved a half share to William Dockett only during his life."

"What has this to do with Master Mainard?"

"The dispute over the inheritance, very little, except that Mainard was a witness in the case. But I was telling you of Mainard's strength and at that point the young man drew a knife and leapt at Lintun. I think he would have killed him had not Mainard been there. He grasped young Dockett's wrist, shook the knife free from his hand, pinned his arms, lifted him right off the floor, and carried him out of the hall. And all this before anyone could raise a cry."

Bell had been giving only a divided attention to this tale, which seemed to have nothing to do with Bertrild's death. He had heard of Mainard's strength before, and he was increasingly annoyed by the familiarity of the names of Lintun and Dockett when he was sure he did not know any such people. Unless, he thought, with an unpleasant sinking sensation, he had heard the names at Magdalene's? The notion made him uneasy, but a moment later he remembered with relief that the familiarity had nothing to do with the Old Priory Guesthouse.

The memory of the cloth that had gone astray sparked a mild interest in him. "Was that just general benevolence on Mainard's part or did he have some interest in young Dockett?"

"Well, he had known the older Dockett through his neighbor, Perekin FitzRevery, and wanted to save the son trouble. As I said, Mainard stood witness for young Dockett. He said that at the time Lintun bought a half share of the business he had heard the father assure the son that he and his sister would still share half the business when he died. Old Dockett said that perhaps one of his grandchildren would wish to be a mercer."

"But if he and the son had quarreled, could he not have changed his mind?"

"According to Mainard, there was no quarrel. The son wished to be an apothecary, and he is. The daughter married a goldsmith, a match greatly desired by both young people, not so much by the fathers, who would have preferred marriages within their own trade. But Dockett was very indulgent." Newelyne shrugged. "Mainard thought it strange that he had cut them out."

Bell thought it strange too — if Newelyne's tale was near the truth.

It brought to mind the frightened journeyman at Master Lintun's counter, but he could not guess what had caused the fear and it was none of his business, as long as the bishop's cloth was delivered as promised. He also shrugged. "If the case was settled—"

"It is not," Newelyne said. "Mainard told me it was put aside by Andrew Buchuinte when he retired from office, and Octadenarius has not yet completed his investigation." The cordwainer grimaced. "It seems that there were questions raised as to the probity of the witness to the documents, but—" He stopped abruptly, looked uneasy, then smiled. "I see the crease is gone from between your eyes. Have you remembered where you heard the names?

Bell laughed aloud. "Oh, yes. I went to see Master Mercer on the bishop's behalf. He had not delivered an order of fustian cloth."

"Oh?" Newelyne raised his brows and cocked his head as if Bell had said something that was not altogether a surprise to him.

"He promised to make good without any argument," Bell hastened to say. "And the order had been given just about the time that Dockett died, so some confusion was almost inevitable."

"Hmmm, yes. Dockett's death was very sudden, a surprise to all of us and something of a grief to Perekin FitzRevery, Mainard's friend next door. A shock, too, when he found that Dockett had sold the business entire to Lintun. Master FitzRevery did some special trading with Dockett and had believed that would continue through Dockett's son and daughter, who were to inherit Master William's half share of the business. FitzRevery also stood witness that the father did not intend to give up the whole business."

Bell nodded. "I met FitzRevery. He, too, gives Mainard a good name."

"There is no one who will not give him a good name," Newelyne said.

Except Sabina, Bell thought, as he thanked Newelyne for his assistance and obtained the names of several others of his guests who knew Mainard. She, poor creature, has been set aside without even the courtesy of a farewell. Not that Sabina would ever complain. The whores of the Old Priory Guesthouse did not speak ill of a client, except possibly among themselves. Clients who displeased the women or Magdalene were simply not accommodated again. Bell moodily kicked a stone as he walked farther down Cordwainer Street. There were always plenty of clients waiting. No hope that Magdalene's business would fail and she would come to him.

By the time Bell returned to Newelyne's house to retrieve his horse, he was thoroughly annoyed. Every man to whom he had spoken barely managed to hide a grin—or did not bother to try hiding it—when he mentioned Bertrild's death. Every man had nothing but praise for the saddler, for his skill in his profession, for his honesty, for his kindness. Not one even looked speculative before denying that Mainard would kill Bertrild. A few showed barely veiled contempt for a man who would not even beat so shrewish a wife into submission. And, unfortunately, all together they could not assure Bell that Mainard had been in Newelyne's house all the time from Sext to Vespers.

One remembered seeing him soon after he came in and speaking to him just before he left. Another recalled Mainard taking food and drink to Sabina and standing by her to see that she ate and drank without interruption from demands for another song. A third had deliberately sought him out to ask whether he had a ready-made saddle that he could buy. He remembered it had been hard to find Mainard, who betook himself to shadowed corners. And none could speak firmly about when they had seen him; the celebration had been too crowded, too lively, too enjoyable for anyone to make a note of the time.

What it all amounted to, Bell thought as he rode toward the bishop's house, was that Sabina was cleared of all suspicion. Everyone remembered her. She had remained pretty much glued to her stool all day, partly because of the frequent demands for her singing and partly because of the crowd and her unfamiliarity with the house. On the other hand, Mainard could easily have slipped out of Newelyne's house not long after noon and returned up to about a candlemark before Vespers without anyone being the wiser. Of course, that was true for everyone, but not everyone had Mainard's reasons for wanting Bertrild dead.

Eight

21 MAY
OLD PRIORY GUESTHOUSE

Diot's look of distress when Magdalene brought Sabina back did not escape Magdalene's notice, but she said nothing about it, asking instead whether all had been quiet. Ella burbled that Letice had gone out, as usual, and that she had finished another row of flowers on the ribbon she was embroidering. She jumped up and proffered the work as she spoke.

"That is lovely," Magdalene said, quite truthfully. Ella's skill with the needle had been improving steadily and, given a design, her embroidery was now excellent. "If you should ever wish to retire, love, your needle will give you another source of income."

"Retire?" Ella echoed, eyes round. "But I cannot take my embroidery to bed. You know how needles are, one moment firmly fixed in the cloth and the next gone. Why it might prick a friend who came to lie with me."

Magdalene's mouth opened, then closed, and she simply hugged Ella. "You are right," she said. "It is better not to take needles to bed. It was silly of me to say that." She took a deep breath, putting aside her concern for what would happen to Ella in the years ahead. At least that concern was many years in the future. "Now, love," she went on briskly, "we need another stool by the fire. Sabina will be with us—" she glanced sidelong at the blind woman's still face and continued without any hesitation "—for a few days, until after Mistress Bertrild's affairs are settled, at least. See if Dulcie can lend us one from the kitchen."

Ella returned her piece of embroidery to her basket and ran off. Magdalene smiled at Diot. "I am afraid you will have to move to the new stool," she said. "It will be easier for Sabina to find her old place." Then she turned to Sabina. "I have taken on a new woman, love. Diot is in your chamber, and I hate to ask her to move."

"Oh, no," Sabina murmured, turning her blind face toward where she knew her stool to have stood. "Of course Diot must stay there. It would be very wrong to change. The clients are used to that chamber. I will do very well in the last room—unless Bell is staying with us?"

Magdalene laughed. "No. Bell is not in charity with me right now. I have offended him mightily by taking your old clients 'the Widower' and 'the Young Maiden, to my bed—"

Sabina giggled. "Did you not tell him that your virtue was not likely to be smirched by either one?"

"Now, now, Sabina. That would be telling tales about a client. Bell is not truly a part of the family, and we must not forget it."

"Oh, is he going to be a friend then?" Ella asked, coming in with the stool. "If you do not want him, Magdalene, I will be glad to have him. He is a very pretty man. Very pretty, and looks to be well furnished below."

"I have no reason to think otherwise," Magdalene said, biting her lip as she thought of Bell's probable reaction to Ella's remarks, "but he is, as usual, on business and not looking for entertainment. And I do not think he can afford our prices." She turned to smile at Diot. "Where would you like the stool placed, Diot?"

When that was settled, she took Sabina to her new room. The bed Bell used when he stayed with them was still there; Dulcie arrived with bedclothes. Magdalene thought about Diot's white-faced silence and wondered whether she should have set her mind at rest about keeping her despite Sabina's return—if it was a return. There was still a possibility that Mainard would want her back, but even if he did not and some of Sabina's old clients would prefer her services, Magdalene had no intention of putting Diot out. For one thing, there would be no real trouble in expanding the number of clients; for another, Magdalene was finding it very convenient to have someone else who could go to the gate and deal with arrivals; for a third, Diot was too intelligent and beautiful to work in a common stew and not yet rich enough to set up for herself.

Moreover, Sabina's arrival provided the opportunity for a final test of Diot's character. If Diot tried subtly to torment the blind girl, her good behavior was too thin a gloss over a too-intense self-interest for deep trust. Pariahs as they were to the whole world around them, the women of this household needed to trust and support each other no matter what their small resentments and jealousies.

As Letice did not return for dinner, Diot cut up Ella's food for her without needing to be asked. She began to reach for Sabina's, Magdalene noted with interest, and then checked herself when she saw how deftly Sabina managed on her own. Then, as if the words were being pulled out of her, she asked about the murder.

Ella looked up. "Murder? Someone was killed?" She shuddered. "Who?"

"A very unkind and unpleasant person. You do not know her," Magdalene replied soothingly.

"But will someone try to blame us? Brother Paulinus?"

"No, love." Magdalene smiled at her. "Brother Paulinus is gone from the priory. You know that. Brother Boniface is now sacristan."

"Oh, I *like* Brother Boniface," Ella said, an enchanting if totally vacuous smile on her face. "Even if he prefers Letice to me, he never says I am damned and cannot pray."

"He does not *prefer* Letice," Diot said. "He likes you very well too. He goes with Letice because she is not a Christian. Thus, when he lies with her, he has only his own sin to answer for and need not worry about corrupting a Christian soul."

That remark left Ella frowning slightly as she tried to understand, but Sabina quickly mentioned that she had learned several new songs and began to speak of how much pleasure it gave her to go about and perform, which permitted her to meet other musicians. Diot's eyes brightened and her expression grew less rigid, particularly when Magdalene asked who Sabina's clients were, and Sabina explained that originally they had all been Mainard's friends but that others had heard her perform and invited her to sing for them also. There were now some who did not even know Mainard, and her clientele was growing.

By common consent, no further mention was made of Bertrild's death even after the remains of the meal had been cleared away and they had gone back to their seats near the hearth. Sabina began to sing, but only songs she knew so well that music and words came from her without thought. It was the murder that was in the forefront of all their minds. Magdalene racked her brains for a way to be rid of Ella, but nothing she suggested caught the simple girl's fancy until, like a special dispensation from heaven, the bell at the outer gate pealed.

Magdalene almost danced out to answer it, and greeted the man leading his horse through the gate with such enthusiasm that he looked at her most suspiciously. Somer de Loo, one of William of Ypres most trusted captains, was a survivor, like his master, and not given to taking anything at face value—not even an unexpectedly warm greeting from Magdalene, at whose house he was a frequent visitor.

"Dear Somer, I am so glad to see you! Is William coming?"

"William is in Oxford, and I have been left behind to defend Rochester—in case Waleran or one of his brothers should get any bright ideas about the keep being without a master. I have come to London, in fact, to make sure that Hugh le Poer has no more men at Montfichet than he should have and does ride to Oxford as Raoul de Samur sent us word he would."

"So Raoul is serving William's purpose," Magdalene said with considerable satisfaction. "I hope William has the means to keep an eye on him. Stupid clod."

Her voice turned hard and cold as she remembered Raoul de Samur, Waleran de Meulan's man, who had come to her house and tried to terrorize her and her women to obtain the pouch of a murdered papal messenger. She had thrown wash water in his face, giving Sabina a chance to stun him with her staff. Then she had carried him to William of Ypres, who had bound him to his own service.

"That was a good night's work you did," Somer de Loo assured her. "Raoul has been very useful. I think Waleran may not have 'appreciated' Raoul enough. William keeps him sweet with a gift—and some pieces of news that can do us no harm—now and then. I think he enjoys working for us now that his fear has somewhat abated."

"Good enough," Magdalene said, accompanying him as he walked toward the stable. "Will you stay the night with us?"

He looked down at her and tilted his head questioningly. "I would rather stay here than at an inn, you know that. And I know you and the women like me well enough, but such a joyous invitation. . . . Are you going to slit my throat for some purpose?"

Magdalene laughed. "No, it is Ella's throat I want slit." And when Somer stopped short, eyes wide and mouth open, she laughed even more loudly. "No, no. I would not harm a hair on her dear, empty head. I just want her out of the way for a while, and if she has you in bed, she will not think of anything else. I know you have been lying with Letice, but she is not here right now, and Ella is damnably in my way."

"Why?" he asked, resuming his walk to the stable, but watching her suspiciously.

"One of our clients took Sabina to be his leman a few weeks ago. Now his wife has been murdered. He cannot have done it because he was with Sabina, but you know what the word of a whore is worth before the law. I would like to find out who really killed the woman, to remove suspicion from Sabina's lover."

"Another murder!" Somer exclaimed. "Maybe I *should* stay at an inn. It is becoming dangerous to be your client."

Magdalene laughed again. "You will keep Ella busy, will you not? I will explain to Letice."

"I will keep Ella busy with the greatest of pleasure," Somer agreed. "But do not try to drag me into this murder. I am just a dogsbody. I do not have William's power."

"No, no, of course not," Magdalene assured him, turning to go into the house and leaving him to settle his horse in the stable.

Ella greeted Somer with cries of joy and almost dragged him out of the common room. Magdalene was about to reprimand her, but Diot, who had also risen and smiled at Somer, asked if he would like something to eat or drink. Magdalene did not smile, although she was tempted. Diot was trying to show she was willing to put in more than was strictly required, since the women were paid a standard wage and usually no clients were scheduled for Sunday.

Her interruption also recalled Ella to her duty, and she too offered

Somer refreshment, adding, "I did not really forget. I was trying to get you into my room before Letice comes back. I *like* you. I remember that you were with me one night last month. That was fun. You are very strong."

Somer grinned and nodded at Diot. "Well, I cannot resist that. Would you please see that Dulcie brings a pitcher of wine to Ella's room? I think I may need its reviving qualities."

It turned out that Ella was just in time in taking hold of her prize. Soon after Diot delivered the flask of wine—drawn from one of the casks that William of Ypres had delivered to the Old Priory Guesthouse for his own and his men's use—Letice returned. Magdalene hastily explained what she had arranged and Letice nodded vigorously, then ran to fetch her slate.

"hoo kil" she wrote on it.

"We do not yet know," Magdalene said, after reading "Who killed" aloud for Sabina and Diot. Then Magdalene gave a brief résumé of what she and Bell had learned and finally said, "It seems to me that the killer must be one of the five men who were in Mainard's work-room on Friday and could have stolen Codi's knife. It is possible, of course, that the messenger from her uncle killed her, but Bell admits that her strange behavior in sending away the servants might well have been because she expected someone to come after the messenger left. And I cannot see how the messenger could have obtained Codi's knife. Can anyone think of anyone else?"

Diot, eyes intent, shook her head. "No, because unless Henry, Codi, and the boys are all lying, no one else could have had the knife, and it was used to stab the woman, even if it did not kill her. So, those five, but how does that help us to decide among them?"

"All except one are clients," Magdalene pointed out. "We do not use clients' true names, but I know them all. I want to hear everything you know or guess about these men. Remember this is within the family and will go no farther, so you may say anything at all. Even if you have been told in confidence and swore to be silent, speak up."

Letice laughed silently and held up her slate, now clean and ready.

"The man we call 'Banker,' " Magdalene said, "is a goldsmith and does not come often. A tall, thin man, mostly bald but with a fringe of brown hair. He wears a long gown, usually black, and complains bitterly about the price."

Diot snorted. "I got stuck with him the last time. He certainly tried to get his money's worth out of me, and he was furious when he couldn't get it up the third time, no matter what I did."

"If he asked more of you than you desired to give, you should have told me," Magdalene said. "This is not a common stew, and 'Banker' would be no great loss if we were 'too busy' for him in the future."

"I had only been with you for four days," Diot said, "but I did not permit him to strike me —"

"Strike you!" Magdalene exclaimed. "You should have told me that at once!"

Diot shrugged. "He said he was sorry, and I think he was —" she smiled wryly "—maybe more over his loss of control than because he tried to hit me. But it was clear to me that he knew it was not permitted, and that made me so happy I forgave him. I even tried again to draw up his standing man and succeeded, so he was happy."

"Well, he will not be happy here again," Magdalene said, thin-lipped.

Letice touched her arm. "must," the slate she held out said, "til kiler fownd."

Magdalene sighed irritably. "Yes, Letice is right. She says we cannot refuse 'Banker' until the killer is found."

Then she "hmmm'd" and added slowly, "And a burst of temper like that . . . Bell said that whoever killed Mistress Bertrild drove the knife in very hard. He said it was a sign of hatred, but it might just as well have been because the killer was furious."

"But why should he kill her?" Sabina asked. "Of course she could infuriate anyone, but why should 'Banker' go to Bertrild's house in the first place and then kill her? He was not close friends with Mainard. In fact, Mainard did not like him. He thought him . . . dishonest."

So even without the name, Sabina knew the man, Magdalene thought, but all she said was, "Why 'Banker' went to Bertrild's house is easy enough. She sent for him."

"But the servants were gone," Sabina said.

"Yes, that is so. Perhaps the messenger fetched him? 'Banker' is a goldsmith, and the servants spoke of Bertrild's tally sticks. Could he have been her banker? Could he have mishandled her funds?"

"How could her uncle, from near Winchester, know that a London goldsmith had diddled his niece's funds?" Diot asked, looking doubtful.

Magdalene shook her head. "I have no idea. We are guessing too wildly. The next man is 'Dealer.' He is a mercer. Black oily hair and beard, short and squat, often wears a leather tunic."

This time it was Letice who wrinkled her nose. A few practiced gestures indicated that he stank and was not much of a lover. A word or two on the slate and more gestures made clear that "Dealer" seemed more interested in discovering whether Letice's compatriots had items for sale than in her sexual skills. And from the way he spoke, she felt he would not mind stolen goods so long as they were cheap.

"Another who is no prize," Magdalene sighed, "but again, I cannot see that he would have any reason to kill Bertrild."

The slate was presented quickly: "fownd owt cels stol stuf?"

Magdalene bit her lip. "Even if Bertrild did find out that 'Dealer' sold stolen goods, it would not be reason enough to *kill* her. Specially if the goods were from foreign places. He could always say he had not known and had bought whatever it was in good faith."

"But it would still be very bad for his business," Sabina put in. "Mainard told me that Bertrild had already caused trouble to all five men. She had chosen a time when each was at his shop with customers and she stood in the street screaming at the top of her lungs that each was dishonest and corrupt and had caused her father's death by introducing him to lechery and drunkenness."

"Introducing him!" Magdalene exclaimed. "That man must have been born a drunk and a lecher to have achieved the state he was in long before he came to this place. He was a nobleman and so I accepted his custom for a time — Ella took him; he was not looking for finesse — but the last time he came with some others, I would not let him stay." She hesitated and then continued slowly. "I think that was the night he was killed in an alehouse in London. Perhaps if I had let him in, he would not have died."

"If not that night, from what you have said of him, then another," Diot said, her voice hard.

Magdalene smiled at her. "Very likely. The next man is 'Humbug,' also a mercer. He is another who wears long gowns, and he is one who goes to the priory and comes through the back gate so that none will know he has been here—except when he comes with all the others for a meeting of the chiefs of the Bridge Guild. Light brown hair, mud-colored eyes—"

Letice held up a hand and thrust out her slate on which were three letters. "ela."

"Oh, yes." Magdalene sighed. "I should have remembered. Well, I will ask her when she is free, but I doubt I will get more from her than the size of his member and the strength and duration of his thrusting." She shrugged and was about to speak, when Letice thrust forward her slate again.

"long ago in oter hows shang seel."

Magdalene read the words and frowned, not undetanding. Letice ran into the kitchen, then darted into Magdalene's chamber, and returned with a knife and a sheet of parchment. She laid the parchment on the table, pretended to heat the knife at the unlit candles, and then slid the knife along the parchment.

"You changed a seal for him!" Magdalene exclaimed, her breath shortened by a terrifying and vivid memory of Letice lifting the seal of a papal letter only a few weeks earlier.

Letice nodded vigorously.

"Oh, that is very important," Magdalene said. "That is a real crime and might be worth killing to conceal." She hesitated again, looking out over her women's heads, then nodded. "Yes, I remember. It was Ella who called him 'Humbug.'" She shrugged. "Sometimes out of the mouths of babes comes real wisdom. I wonder what she means by it . . . or if she knows what she means?"

"Likely she means he boasts or makes promises he does not keep," Sabina said, smiling.

"Very likely," Magdalene agreed, dismissing the subject. "Letice, one of the men is the one you call your 'Cuddle Bear.' What do you know of him?"

Letice nodded, but now she looked very troubled. She held out the slate, which read, "long tiim. nize." Magdalene read the words to the others. By then Letice had wiped the slate and added, "woreed for munth mabee mor." And below that, "hym seel to."

"You lifted a seal for 'Cuddle Bear,' too?" Magdalene echoed in a shocked voice. "And he has been worried for a month or more?"

Letice nodded and immediately shook her head. She wrote, "seel long ago. not woreed wen com heer. only now." Before Magdalene could hand back the slate, she left her stool and paced around with short quick steps; sat down, looked off into the distance, and picked at her clothing. She opened her mouth as if she would speak, closed it, opened it again.

"He has been restless and not really paying attention to you or what you were doing, and several times he acted as if he were about to tell you something, but changed his mind," Magdalene said, putting Letice's actions into words for Sabina, who could not see, and Diot, who was not yet accustomed to interpreting Letice's charades.

"Hmmm," she continued. "It is too bad that he had no appointment with you this last week. Perhaps we would have known whether he was more anxious or less. I wonder if he will celebrate Bertrild's demise by coming to you. . . . Oh, well, there is nothing we can do about that. The last man is John Herlyond, a mercer. He is not a client so I can give his name, but I have no idea what he looks like. Have any of you heard his name, perhaps among the whispers that pass from house to house in this district?"

"I have heard the name, of course," Sabina said. "But I do not remember anything special. Oh, yes. He must also wear a long gown; I have heard it rustle. His voice is pleasant, a light tenor, not deep like Mainard's, so he may be a smaller man or more slender. I do not believe he has ever touched me or I him, so I cannot say more about his size and shape or whether his scent is sour. Of them all, except Letice's 'Cuddle Bear,' who I think I know and is a long-time friend, I believe Mainard likes Master Herlyond best."

There was a short silence during which, in the back of her mind, Diot cursed Master Mainard with every foul word she knew. It seemed now that even if he were not accused of murder, he would not keep Sabina. And that meant that, likely, Diot's dream of joy was over.

It had been so perfect—a life almost as elegant as that she had been driven from by her jealous husband and, added to the comfort and security in which she lived, a variety of men. A few were old and ugly, but many were in their prime. And none could tell her how to live her life, except for what kind of sex he desired. Even the sex was better. None of them was simply using a convenience that lay beside him, as well known and about as well regarded as his chamberpot. Most of the men came primed and ready for laughing and playing, for trying any new little game her fertile mind could devise, eager to escape from proper and dull cohabitation for the purpose of procreation and, since they were sinning already, ready to indulge in any extravagance of lust.

Somehow, Diot told herself, she *would* hold on to what she had. There was hope. Magdalene had allowed her to keep her room; it was Sabina who was lying on a camp bed in the spare chamber. Diot's mind fixed on that bed and her spirits lifted. Sabina could entertain no clients on that bed. So she did not intend to take back her clients; she expected—or hoped—that Master Mainard would take her back whether or not he was free to marry.

If he could! Diot hastily withdrew her curses and imprecations. The best chance to rid the Old Priory Guesthouse of Sabina was to be sure that Master Mainard was not accused of murder and kept his reputation intact so he could afford to keep a mistress. Magdalene wanted gossip. Diot racked her brain, but the descriptions were too general to attach to any man she had seen in the stews, and besides, she did not really believe any of the men who came to Magdalene's house would take a woman in the places she had worked. But there was one name. She bit her lip.

"Yes, Diot?" Magdalene said. "No matter what has come into your mind, tell us."

"It is not about the men," Diot replied. "But I have heard the name Bertrild before. It is not a common name, but there was one woman I once knew who was called Bertrild—she was from an old Saxon family—so when I heard it called aloud in Stav's stew it stuck in my mind. Specially considering who was calling out thanks to Bertrild. It made me laugh. The Bertrild I knew was so high and mighty proud."

"You do not mean to say that Bertrild worked in Stav's stew?"

A Personal Devil   123

Sabina's voice was redolent with disbelief. "She, too, is—I mean was—high and mighty proud. Her father was a lord and had a fine estate, and she blamed Mainard for not buying back the estate from the debts under which it was buried. She said she would have endured him, even borne him children so they could inherit the lands."

"No, no," Diot said. "I did not mean that Borc was exclaiming in pleasure over what a woman named Bertrild did. What happened was that this Borc is so degenerate, so filthy and diseased, that even Stav did not welcome him. However, one day he came to the stew with a handful of farthings. Stav made ready to drive him away, saying he did not want the sheriff in the house looking for a thief, and Borc said that Stav need not worry, that Mistress Bertrild had found a new source of money and had paid him for collecting it for her."

"A new source of money," Magdalene muttered, "and tally sticks of which Mainard knew nothing. Hmmm." She looked at Diot. "Do you remember when this was?"

Diot sighed and shrugged. "Time was one long nightmare in Stav's house. All I can say is that it was colder than it is now but not winter. A month past, perhaps a little more. Do you think it might be the same Bertrild? And if so, can the memory be of any use?"

Magdalene made no immediate reply. She was now staring at the floor biting her lower lip. "Borc," she muttered. "I am sure I have heard that name before . . . or do I just want to remember it? Surely though . . ." She looked up at Diot again. "You sound as if Stav knew this Borc."

"I think he did, but from an earlier time. One of the bath women, her name was Ann and she warned me against Borc, said that Borc used to come to Stav's old house, one that was almost under the bridge. She told me Stav left that place because it came under too-close and too-frequent scrutiny by the sheriff's men, being so close to the main road south."

"That would make it quite close to this house," Magdalene said, her eyes intent. "So if a master came to this house, the man might be sent off or choose to wait at Stav's place. Yes, go on."

"Well, in those days Borc apparently had money to spend, and he always liked to have two or three work on him at once—a tongue in his mouth, fingers up his ass, someone sucking his cock, and another licking his balls. But one night he came in and when he was done, he said he couldn't pay, that his master was dead. Stav was going to have him beaten to a jelly, but he swore he had a new place lined up and would pay the next time."

"So," Magdalene said, sounding satisfied, "my memory was not at fault. Go on, Diot. I think you may have found the end of an important string."

"There is not that much more. Ann said that Borc did come again, a few weeks later, but that time Stav wanted his money first, and Borc had only two farthings. That Stav wrested from him—in part payment of the debt he owed—threw him out, and told him not to come back until he had the full sum—and not to dare to go elsewhere when he had the money or he would be found and broken in parts."

Magdalene nodded. "Yes, indeed, it all fits. I am almost sure the woman who gave Borc the money was Mainard's wife, Bertrild—"

"Would Bertrild know such a person?" Sabina asked. "She holds— held—herself very high."

"She knew Borc because he was her father's servant. I knew I had heard the name when Diot mentioned it. At that time he was not so filthy and ragged, although he was usually drunk. He came with Gervase de Genlis, and I refused to let him wait for his master anywhere in my grounds or go to the priory because the first time de Genlis brought him, one of our clients found Borc going through his saddle-bags when he came out of my house. Borc might well have gone to Stav's place to wait for his master."

"So if Borc collected money for Bertrild," Diot said thoughtfully, "would it not be most likely one of those who paid her—I suppose to be silent—would kill her? Perhaps one was her uncle and his messenger brought death instead of gold."

"True," Magdalene agreed, "although there is still the question of how he got Codi's knife. But, if one of the five who was in Mainard's workshop is also on Borc's list of those from whom he collected money . . . Yes. Now, how do we lay our hands on Borc to ask him? Do you think Stav would know?" she asked Diot.

"Stav always tries to know something about those who come to his house, but Borc . . . I do not see what he could hope to gain from knowledge of Borc."

"Who Bertrild was? From whom she was collecting? Well, well, it is too late now; it is near dark, but I think I will go to Stav's place and also to—" She turned to look at Letice. "For whom did you work when you lifted seals, Letice?"

"not tere now" the slate read.

"I know," Magdalene said, "but the new whoremaster or whore-mistress will probably know what happened to him."

Letice nodded and shrugged, then indicated that she would take Magdalene there the next morning.

Nine

21 MAY
JUSTICIAR'S HOUSE, LONDON

After he had interviewed the last of Newelyne's guests who had known Mainard, and a few more—in case Newelyne had given him only the names of men who would speak well of the saddler—Bell decided he had better take the information he had gathered to a responsible official. He settled on the justiciar because he had worked with Master Octadenarius on a problem the bishop had needed secular authority to settle.

It was nearly sunset when he arrived at the justiciar's large and elegant house, so he was not surprised to find him at home.

"You are zealous, Sir Bellamy," Master Octadenarius said. "My lord of Winchester is well served."

As he spoke, he waved Bell across the large common room to which the servant had admitted him through a doorway and into a private chamber. He preceded Bell to a short, highly polished table and indicated a handsome stool, himself moving around the table to sit down in a large, imposing chair with arms as well as a back. While Bell settled, by habit immediately arranging his sword so that it did not pull his belt and would draw freely from the scabbard, he was aware of Octadenarius's shrewd black eyes rapidly assessing him.

"Not today," Bell said, smiling. "I confess I have been hard at work, but not on the bishop's business. Well, I did straighten out a small matter of some bolts of cloth that had not been delivered, but most of my business today was interfering with your affairs, my lord Justiciar."

"What?"

"You know that the Church, in particular the diocese of Winchester, owns the property adjoining the priory of St. Mary Overy called the Old Priory Guesthouse?"

"I do," Octadenarius said, not quite so cordially.

Aha! Bell thought, he is or has been a client there; however, nothing showed on the experienced soldier's face. "Through collecting rents and suchlike," he continued blandly, "I have become well acquainted with the whoremistress, Magdalene la Bâtarde."

"Was not she involved with the murder of a papal messenger only a few weeks ago?"

"Yes, she helped prevent the murderer from stabbing the bishop, and I was forced to kill the man. It would not have come under your hand anyway, because Guiscard was a clerk in minor orders. The Church would have dealt with him. As to Magdalene, despite her profession, she is a decent woman and treats her whores well. When one wished to leave her, she did not interfere, and soon after the murder was solved, the blind whore from her house was taken into keeping by a master saddler, Mainard—"

"Whose wife was found dead in his backyard. Yes. What is this to do with you?"

"Sabina, the whore, is deeply attached to Master Mainard, who has been most indulgent to her. She came and begged Magdalene to save Mainard from being accused of killing his wife, who, I must admit, richly deserved killing."

"The whore said Master Mainard was with her every moment from noon, when they went to a christening party, until they were wakened by the apprentice's finding the body."

"Yes, and that is likely true."

Bell was shocked as the words came out of his mouth. He had not, until that moment, been sure whether he would tell Octadenarius that the saddler's whereabouts during the party were by no means certain. It seemed he had decided without real thought. Well, he had heard enough over the day to be sure that if Mainard *had* killed his wife, he was not likely to commit another crime.

Bell sighed. If he found real proof of Mainard's guilt, he told himself, he would have to reconsider, but for now there was no sense in casting a shadow over Sabina's lover. If Octadenarius thought he had the killer in hand, he would look no farther, and Bell could use his help. He had spoken right by instinct, Bell decided. He would keep his own counsel about Newelyne's party.

"But—" Octadenarius prodded, having noted the sigh.

"But Sabina," Bell continued, "was terrified that you would discount her word because she had been a whore. And she knows what her word would be worth in a court of law if Master Mainard were tried for the crime."

"So?"

"So Sabina went weeping to Magdalene, and Magdalene, knowing I was in London on the bishop's business, sent for me, and I . . . ah . . . cannot resist Magdalene, so I went to see what I could see. And I discovered that Mistress Bertrild was not killed in the backyard of Master Mainard's shop or anywhere near the shop."

The laughter that had crinkled Master Octadenarius's eyes, although his lips did not twitch, when Bell said that he could not resist Magdalene, promptly disappeared and was replaced by shock. "What?"

"Because none of us could understand what she was doing there in the middle of the night, I carefully examined the entire yard and—"

"She was not killed in the middle of the night," Octadenarius interrupted rather sharply. "Brother Samuel at St. Catherine's Hospital told me he believed she was dead before Vespers, possibly not long after Nones."

"That is true, my lord Justiciar, he told me the same thing. Can you really believe that the body lay in the middle of the yard from before Vespers until dawn the next day without anyone noticing it?"

"No, of course not. I assumed she was killed in the shop, hidden, and then put in the yard at night."

"Killed in front of Codi and the apprentices? By whom? Hidden where?"

"I believe she was killed by the journeyman—she was heard to threaten him earlier that day—and the apprentices were terrified into silence—"

Bell began to laugh. "Did those boys look terrified of Codi? Of Master Mainard?"

Master Octadenarius scowled horribly. He was a busy man. The murder of one unpleasant woman of no particular stature or reputation in the community was not a very important matter, and the solution of the crime had seemed obvious. He had intended to send a man to gather a few more facts and then to arrest Codi.

Now that he had been forced to rethink his quick conclusion that Codi was guilty, he had a vivid image of the two boys clinging to the big journeyman; he heard again the reassuring voice in which Codi had urged them to tell everything they knew. He knew he did not really believe they were afraid. They sported no bruises; they were well fed, well clothed. There had been no shadow on either boy's face when asked about Codi or his master. He sighed gustily.

"As I remember from the time I worked with you to settle the bishop's problem, you are not wont to look for an easy path, Sir Bellamy. So what have you to tell me?"

It was such a sufficiently long and interesting tale that the justiciar invited Bell to take the evening meal with him. And when both were replete and toying with cups of wine, Octadenarius said, "So she was killed in her own house and moved to the shop. In God's name, why?"

Bell shrugged. "Hate for Master Mainard? Although, to speak the truth, I have not found a single person who will say a word against him—except that he should have beaten his wife and did not. Possibly only self-protection, to make it seem Mainard or Codi was guilty, in case he had been seen entering or leaving the Lime Street house. Certainly, to find her by Mainard's shop would muddy the waters for you."

"And he made me look a fool for not examining the place more carefully." Octadenarius's mouth was set in a grim line. "So are you about to leave the matter with me now?"

"If you so order, my lord Justiciar, I must obey, but I beg you will not. Magdalene would be furious with me, and, if the criminal is one of the men who was in Master Mainard's workshop, she must know him because the Bridge Guild often meets in her house. It is convenient, and what they say to each other will be carried no farther. Many find her house useful and comfortable for private meetings. The fee is the same as at any good inn and the security much greater."

Octadenarius nodded. "I am aware. But her mouth is sealed shut, that woman. I have tried to get information from her in the past, and she would tell me nothing. And I had the feeling that if I persisted I would have William of Ypres paying me an unwelcome visit."

A muscle in Bell's jaw jumped, and he saw that Octadenarius had noted it. "Yes," he said, trying to keep his voice indifferent. "Since Lord William commonly uses the Old Priory Guesthouse as a meeting place with people who would rather not be caught consorting with him, he values Magdalene's unwillingness to talk about her clients—except when he cannot get information either. But that is trade or politics, honest or dishonest, not murder. And do not forget that this time she is protecting one of her own. She is fierce as a lioness in defense of her women. She will talk about those five men—at least to me."

Again the crinkles around the justiciar's eyes indicated amusement, but he did not smile and only asked blandly, "So do you wish me to leave this matter in your hands?"

"I would like best if I could continue to examine the crime under your authority as justiciar, Master Octadenarius. The bishop has nothing to do with this, and if I may not act as his hand, I am only a poor, simple knight and no one need answer me or obey me. Also, I am a little short of men, as I came with only four."

At that the justicar laughed aloud. "I see. I am to furnish men and power and you—"

"Privileged information and, I hope, a murderer," Bell said, grinning. "What I need most now, to speak the truth, is men who know the East Chepe and Lime Street to question the neighbors about anything they saw or heard on Saturday afternoon. We know when the messenger from Bertrild's uncle arrived, but not when he departed and if it can be discovered where he went. Also we must learn whether anyone besides the messenger came to the house, whether Mistress Bertrild went out and returned with someone, whether there was any activity noted in her garden or the alley near the back of her house not only that afternoon but also after dark."

"I cannot complain. Those are sensible inquiries. Very well, I will send out some of my people tomorrow."

"Thank you, my lord Justiciar. In turn, I will discover what, if anything, Magdalene has learned, and I will attend the burying of Mistress Bertrild."

"You will report to me anything you discover?"

"Yes, Master Octadenarius. However, there are several cases in which the bishop has an interest that are to be presented tomorrow afternoon, and for me, the bishop's business must come first, of course. Between that and Mistress Bertrild's burying in the morning, I will have little chance tomorrow to discover what Magdalene knows." That was not strictly true; in fact Bell intended to visit Magdalene while her women were all busy and they could talk alone. But that was none of Octadenarius's affair, and Bell continued without any hesitation. "I should be able to catch her on Tuesday morning, before any clients arrive, so I will likely come about this time on Tuesday to tell you what I have learned."

The justiciar bowed his head in acknowledgment, and Bell set down his empty winecup and rose.

"It is full dark," Octadenarius said. "Will you be safe riding . . . ah . . . wherever you are riding?"

Bell patted his sword. "Quite safe," he said, but he was glad when a servant appeared very promptly in response to Octadenarius's bellow, and he left the house with no more than a farewell bow and a half-lifted hand.

He was in no mood to respond to the justiciar's mild teasing or to satisfy his curiosity. In fact, he did not know when he mounted his hired horse where he was going. The temptation to cross the bridge and stop at the Old Priory Guesthouse was very strong; however, Sabina was there, which meant there would be no empty chamber for him. A good excuse to pay for a place in Magdalene's bed? Heat flooded his loins and his instant response made him shift backward in the saddle. The horse jibbed and he relaxed the rein he had unconsciously tightened.

No! He would not be pulled to her house by his rod. Bell tapped the horse's sides with his heels, and when he did pass Magdalene's gate, pushed the beast into a trot. It would be stupid to stop there. At the bishop's house he would find servants to care for the horse and to return it to the livery stable in the morning. At Magdalene's he would have to feed and unsaddle the beast himself. Moreover, he would have to go back to the bishop's house anyway. His clothing was there, and he would need a decent dark gown or at least a more sober tunic for a burying. And finally, he thought as he turned the corner to the road to the bishop's house, if she had another client, Magdalene might refuse him.

---

22 MAY
OLD PRIORY GUESTHOUSE

By late Monday afternoon, after the bishop's business was finished, Bell's doubts were gone — not about the wisdom of buying Magdalene's favors; free of the sudden rush of desire, he knew he was not ready to capitulate to her demand he take her only as a whore. Restored to common sense, however, he accepted the need to see and speak to her. He had attended Bertrild's funeral, which had been interesting and worth discussing in the light of what she might know of the five men under suspicion, but what Mainard had found after Bell had left him on Sunday might be more significant.

For a time after the coffinmaker had set the box on its trestles in the common chamber, Mainard told Bell, he had just sat beside it, still unable to absorb what had happened. At dinnertime, Jean had come in, scratching the doorframe timidly, and when Mainard looked up, had asked his master whether he wanted food brought in or served in the solar and what he preferred to eat.

Mainard had been about to say he was not hungry and send the man away when he realized that Jean was clad in little more than rags. Whatever Bertrild had done, it was not fitting that servants should attend to guests at her burying in such disgraceful condition, he thought. So he had told Jean to have his dinner brought to the solar, above, and when he had eaten it — he found he was hungry as a wolf once he began—he started to look through Bertrild's chest to find garments suitable for the cook and the maid.

Most of the dresses were too richly ornamented, but at the very bottom of the chest were some worn gowns from which the embroidered collars and facings had been removed. And when those were lifted out, Mainard saw the bundles of tally sticks. He told Bell he had stood staring, knowing there was something foul connected with those hidden accounts.

He had given the clothing to the maid and sent her away, weeping with joy. Then he had removed and examined the tally sticks. He had not recognized the banker's mark, but that had been no surprise, he told Bell; if Bertrild had hidden the accounts from him, she would not be likely to use the same banker as he did. That had spurred him to send the now passably clad cook and maid out to the market to buy one decent tunic and chausses apiece for Jean and Hamo, since his old clothing would be much too large. When the women returned with those, Mainard sent Jean to Master Leon Basynges, his own banker, with a note asking him to provide the name of the banker whose mark was on Bertrild's tally sticks. Jean had returned promptly; Bertrild's banker had been Master Johannes Gerlund.

When Bell, who had arrived at the Old Priory Guesthouse as he had planned, shortly after the second set of clients was safely locked away with their women, got that far in retelling the tale to Magdalene, she uttered an exasperated sigh. "Master Mainard will get little help from that man."

"Why? Is he dishonest?"

Her lips quirked. "Only insofar as he is one who enters the priory as if for a religious purpose and then sneaks through the back gate to us." She shrugged. "That might mean he could be dishonest if pressed, but what I was thinking is that Gerlund will never offer an opinion and thus be of no help if Master Mainard needs advice."

"He would not, you think, have a false set of tally sticks that show the account was paid and closed so he could keep whatever she deposited? That would be a good reason for murder."

"Yes, but there is the problem of Codi's knife."

Bell snorted. "Whyever did the murderer steal the knife? God knows it is being more help to us than it is to him. Even if he had killed Mistress Bertrild with it, as he planned, it must limit the number of people who could be guilty."

"Yes, but he intended using Codi's knife to limit the number of suspects to Mainard and Codi. He probably did not know that Mainard would be at Newelyne's christening party and—"

"Where is Sabina?" Bell interrupted suddenly, looking around.

"She had an engagement to sing and play for a betrothal dinner. She was of two minds about going, wondering if she would be thought improper for going to sing when there was a death in her 'family,' but I pointed out that she would be leaving her client with no entertainer if she did not go. I suggested she speak to the client and explain what had happened and leave the decision to him."

"Well, thank God she is not here because I must tell you that Mainard's defense of being at Newelyne's party is very little defense at all."

"What do you mean?"

"He hides in dark corners. I spoke to a dozen people, all well disposed toward him, and even combined with Newelyne's testimony his whereabouts cannot be definitely accounted for much after Sext, when he brought Sabina food and drink, until nearly Vespers, when he went to stand near her in readiness to take her home. All the time between, he could easily have left the house, and no one would have noticed he was gone."

"Do you think him guilty?"

Bell sighed. "The truth is, I do not. If Sabina had been with him, if Bertrild had attacked Sabina—and there is that bruise on Bertrild's body that could have been made by Sabina's staff, only Sabina could not have been there; she was in plain sight all but a few minutes when she was taken to the privy—then it is barely possible that his rage would have been so great that he would have drawn his belt knife and struck at Bertrild."

"But he did not do so only a few days earlier when Bertrild did attack Sabina in her room, above the shop. He only carried that madwoman out, kicking and screaming. And whatever his rage, I cannot imagine Mainard taking Codi's knife and using it to implicate his poor journeyman."

"No, nor can I," Bell said, shrugging. "So let us go back to the five men who could have stolen Codi's knife."

"Wait. Before I tell you what I learned, did you see the tally sticks?" Bell shook his head and Magdalene shrugged. She had not really expected he would be able to examine them while making ready to bury Bertrild. "Well, when you do, see if there are any dates indicated, and if there are, see if the deposits begin about a month or six weeks ago."

"A month or six weeks," Bell repeated. "You have some reason to believe that was when Bertrild's demands for money began?"

"Yes. According to Letice, one of her men became worried and uneasy about that time. And another man, Ella's, suddenly cut the number of his visits from three times a week to one. That looks to me, since he did not ask for a different woman, as if he was being pinched for money."

Bell nodded. "To me also, which implies that she was demanding a substantial sum."

"For a substantial reason—at least for two of the men. You knew that before Letice worked here she served in a house that sold more than sex?" Bell nodded again. "Well, she knew two of the men, recognized them as men for whom she had transferred good seals to new documents."

Bell whistled sharply between his teeth. "Yes, yes, that is more significant than visits to a brothel. Which men?"

He was not pleased when Magdalene shook her head. "What will you tell them when they deny they have ever done such a thing and ask who accused them? The whoremaster for whom Letice did the work is gone from that house now, and I could not induce the whoremistress who runs the house now to tell me anything."

"Induce the—" Bell echoed. He was shocked and angry, but habit kept his voice low. "Do you mean to tell me you were down in the stews looking for information? You fool! Those are dangerous people! You could have been set upon—"

"Do not *you* be a fool!" Magdalene snapped. "I *served* in places like that!" Her lips twisted bitterly the next moment at the expression on his face, but her voice did not falter. "I am well aware of how to deal with such people. I offer money or advantage; I do not use threats.

And they know who is my patron. We are all in one basket, some at the bottom and some at the top, and unless I become a danger to them, no one will hurt me."

"And will anyone tell you any more than you would tell them?"

Magdalene smiled more easily. "We deal with different clients and offer different services. No, I would tell them nothing, but for a price, most of them will talk to me. They know I will use what they tell me but not in such a way that it would hurt *them*. As for hurting a buyer of their wares . . . most would not care; a few would be amused. In fact, Stav was delighted to tell me what I wanted to know."

Color flooded into Bell's face, dying his fair skin bright red. "Stav! Have you no sense at all? I am sure he has heard that Diot is with you. Did I not tell you that she kicked him in his privates and absconded with two farthings? He will—"

"He will do nothing. That was more than two weeks ago, and other outrages have overlaid the first fine fury. Besides, I soothed his loss and hurt with five shillings, so Diot need not look over her shoulder when she walks abroad. She will pay it back out of her earnings as she can—although I think Mainard will be glad to make up the sum and maybe gift her, too, because what I paid greased Stav's tongue so well that he told me where we can lay hands upon the man who collected the payments Bertrild demanded."

Bell's mouth had been open, perhaps to continue the argument. It snapped shut as she spoke the last words, and his eyes widened instead as he asked, "However did you learn that?"

"Never say God, or perhaps Merciful Mary, abhors a whore, for it is through being whores—and a series of coincidences so long that they must have been meant—that we learned," she began and told him about de Genlis's man Borc, Diot's remembering the name Bertrild because of her proud Saxon neighbor, and Borc confiding where his money came from to Stav.

"The direction will be worthless," Bell said, biting his lip in chagrin. "Those kind of people do not stay in one place. Of course, I will go tomorrow and see if anyone there knows where he is likely to have gone."

"No need. This is not that kind of direction. Stav knows Borc and his kind too well to hope he will sleep more than a few nights in any one place, but he learned that Borc always eats his dinner in one cookshop in the East Chepe. It seems that Bertrild could not afford, or did not wish, to pay Borc to serve her, but she did pay the cookshop a weekly sum to serve the man one meal a day. I suppose to keep him from starving because he had been her father's man, but it does seem out of character for her to have done so."

"It was not to keep him from starving," Bell said, grinning tightly. "It was so she could reach him to give him orders without ever allowing him to come to the Lime Street house. I am not quite certain whether that was because she did not wish her neighbors to see Borc or did not want Borc to know where she lived."

"Both, I suspect," Magdalene said, "considering what Diot said about how he looks and what I know about what he was, even in better times."

"I hope he has not yet heard of Bertrild's death," Bell said next. "I will have my men waiting for him at the cookshop tomorrow."

"Not your men. They are too obviously what they are, and I think it likely that Borc can smell a soldier from the end of the street. Let me send the watchman, Tom, who does odd jobs and runs messages for me. I suspect it is just the kind of cookshop in which Tom would eat, so he will not look out of place and Borc will not be warned. Diot can describe how Borc last looked to him. If Tom sees the man, he can signal your men when he leaves or, if Borc leaves first, Tom can follow him out.

"Good enough," Bell agreed. He hesitated, looking past her, pursing his lips. "Borc is a good lead, but not enough, even if we can lay hands on him. Besides, I doubt he knows more than from whom he collected. Bertrild would not have told him anything significant. I think I will go and see those five tomorrow morning."

Magdalene nodded agreement. "I think you should. You have reason enough in their being, with him, members of his Bridge Guild and having all come to visit him on Friday morning. Will you tell them about Codi's knife?"

"I am not sure. I may say a leatherworking knife was used to stab Bertrild and ask if any of them saw one of that description." He sighed and got to his feet. "I should be free in good time if my men take Borc. I will have a man watching from a candlemark before Sext until a candlemark before Nones. If Borc does not come in that time, Tom can try again on Wednesday."

Magdalene had also risen. "You will not stay and have the evening meal with us?"

Bell shook his head. It was far too dangerous to stay. With Sabina in the bed he usually occupied when he spent a night at the Old Priory Guesthouse, there would be no place for him but in Magdalene's bed if he stayed very late. And it always seemed to happen that he did stay late, talking and playing silly games with Magdalene and her women. He had the five pence for her charges—these days he always had five pence tucked into a recess in his belt—but he was not ready to yield; he was afraid he would be angry, hate her, if she made him accept her on those terms.

"Perhaps it is just as well," she went on with a sigh. "I doubt we could avoid talking of the murder, and Ella has been paying attention because she remembers Bertrild."

"Not she too?" Bell exclaimed, grinning. "Is there *no* person in England who did not want to kill that woman? I thought Ella, at least, would be exempt. Do you know where she was on Sunday between Nones and Vespers?"

Magdalene laughed heartily over the idea of Ella killing anyone, particularly with a knife, which she feared so much to handle that someone else had to cut up her food. Smiling, she walked with him to the door, lifting her face to the afternoon sunlight when they reached it. Although he knew he should not, Bell bent and kissed her lips. She permitted the caress, even encouraged it, allowing her mouth to open. Bell's tongue darted forward in response—but only once. He jerked back to pull away. Magdalene laughed again, leaned toward him before he could get any distance between them, and kissed him on the nose.

Ten

22 MAY
SOUTHWARK

Face flaming, Bell went down the path and slammed the gate behind him. He turned right in the direction that would take him to the bishop of Winchester's house, then shook his head, crossed the road, and headed down the street that went eventually to the priory of St. Saviour at Bermondsey. He was in no temper to go back to the bishop's residence where doubtless several clerks would each have thought of ten more questions to ask about the business he had completed after dinner that day.

"That woman!" he muttered to himself. "Between tormenting me and blithely going her own way without even asking me for an easier road, she'll drive me crazy."

Fury lent energy to his stride, and he soon reached his goal. Just far enough down the street to protect it from casual intrusion, but near enough for men-at-arms to get to the main focus of trouble near the docks, was the house of the sheriff of Southwark. Bell was received without question. As the sword arm of the bishop of Winchester, who was responsible for large properties in the area, Bell and the sheriff were well acquainted.

"Do you remember," he asked, after having explained that he was trying to get to the bottom of a murder that had nothing to do with either the bishop or Southwark, "that some four or five years ago there was a stew where they sold more forged parchments than women?"

"More than one, I fear," the sheriff replied, "but I suspect you

mean the really infamous one run by Goden. It was before my time,"
he added, and then raised a hand to stop Bell from moving. "But I
know about it because my predecessor was so furious at not being able
to lay Goden by the heels that he left me the records of the case and
begged me to go forward with it if I could."

"Likely that solves my problem," Bell said, "unless this Goden is
dead?"

"Only the good die young," the sheriff said wryly. "Goden thrives,
but I can assure you he no longer plies a trade in forgery. The women
went elsewhere, but he kept his bully boys and now rents them out
and is a beggarmaster." The sheriff's smile was a show of teeth without
humor. "I hope you do not need a forged document?"

Bell ignored that pleasantry. "I think that the woman Bertrild, who
I told you was murdered, was extorting money from one or more men.
Only five had the chance to take a particular knife that was used to
stab her. I want to know whether any of those five obtained false documents from that whoremaster."

"I will give you the direction of where he does business. He lives
elsewhere but shifts lodging so often it is not worthwhile to trace him
each time." The sheriff smiled grimly. "And you have my permission
to wring what you can out of him any way you want, but would it not
be a great coincidence that Goden should be the one to provide the
false documents? There are others who do such work, probably more
in London than in Southwark."

Bell grinned broadly. Idiot woman. She was always saying she
whored because she needed money, but she had wasted several pence,
he was sure, in trying to bribe Goden's direction out of the current
whoremistress of that house when he had obtained the information in
a few moments at no cost at all. He would rub her nose in *that*.

"No," he said. "Actually it is likely they chose that place because
four of the five were regularly in this neighborhood for other purposes
and for them—wealthy men and well known in London—such a stew
might be more private. It would be their word against Goden's if he
tried to betray them, and Goden would not even be able to identify
which document he was claiming was forged because he is, I assume,
illiterate."

"I do not think so. I think he is a defrocked priest, but we could never prove it." The sheriff shrugged.

He then gave Bell directions to where the man dealt with the beggars, and after a civil farewell, Bell set out to find Goden. As he progressed east and north through dark and narrow alleys, he loosened both sword and knife in their sheaths and glanced up, to be sure no one was about to leap down upon him from beams stretched from roof to roof, and from side to side at the fetid doorways more than he watched ahead. When he arrived, he almost regretted not being set upon, which might have diverted him from his goal.

Bell was not delicate. He had served as a man-at-arms for over fifteen years, some of that time aboard ships where the crew was packed tighter together than the animals they carried, and he had searched battlefields days after the battle was over for friends and enemies among the dead. However, the stench that surrounded the hovel of rotten boards and stinking mud stopped him in his tracks.

The house on one side had collapsed completely; on the other the building was in the process of falling in, leaning away from Goden's lair. Bell eyed the heaps that littered the area around the building and what had once been a small court in which a counter could be set. Most were a mixture of rags, decaying straw and leaves, rotting offal, mud, and from the smell, probably turds. A few, however, were men or women—under the debris that covered them it was hard to tell.

First, Bell drew his sword. Then, picking his way carefully through the filth, he prodded one of the heaps that held a body. The pile of dirty straw stirred, fell apart, and from it emerged a tall, skeletally thin creature, who shouted something at him.

"Go in and tell your master to come out," Bell said in English. "I want information, I will pay for it, but if he does not come out, I will have his house down around his ears."

As he spoke, he swung around, his sword cutting hard an arms' length behind him. Something screamed and fell, a clatter betraying a dropped weapon. Bright red made a shocking contrast with the brown-black filth encrusting what he had struck. Without examining what he had brought down, he swung back toward the thin creature he had bidden to fetch his master. He did not turn all the way, however; with his back now to the building, he slammed his boot heel into a cracked board. A satisfying sound of splintering wood followed. The tall creature turned and ran.

Bell occupied the delay that followed by pounding away at the weak spot in the wall. From the corner of his eye he noticed that whatever he had wounded had managed to crawl away. He grimaced, sorry the blow had not been fatal. Not that he was sorry he had struck it—whoever was creeping up behind him had not intended him any good—but death from the sword blow would have been merciful compared with the death from slow rotting the creature would now face.

His next kick was almost one too many, as his foot went through the wall. Had anyone noticed, he would have been at a dangerous disadvantage, but he was not deeply caught and managed to free his foot and be standing on both when two mismatched forms rounded the building. One was the tall, thin beggar; the other was wider than he was tall, but at least he was not encrusted with filth.

"Stop!" the fat man blustered. "Why are you damaging my house?"

"Because I wanted you out of it. I did not fancy going in after you." Bell laughed. "Tastes differ, of course, but the aroma was not to my liking, even outside. I did not think a stronger dose would agree with me."

"You are one man. I could set ten against you!"

Bell laughed again and gestured with his bloody sword. "I hope you will not. Twelve dead bodies will not improve the smell or appearance of this place, and yours would be the first, as you are closest. Now stop acting a fool, which I know you are not because you have warded off hanging for so long. I want information and I will pay for it."

"What information?" Goden's tone changed from bluster to whine. "You want to know who begs on what corner? That is the kind of information I have."

Suddenly Bell took three swift strides, thrust away the tall beggar with his sword, and pressed the knife he now held in his left hand into the fat man's belly. "You would not wish to die of a gut wound, I am sure," he said. "Let us walk to the end of the street, where I hope the air is cleaner, and—"

Goden jumped backward with surprising agility, but he was not quick enough. Bell thrust hard, heard the thin man cry out, and instantly drew the sword back, pressing outward. The edge caught Goden on the arm and ran across his chest. He screamed. Bell drew his arm back and set the point of the sword where his dagger had been.

"Walk!" he ordered. "Yes, backward. Your belly is a softer place to thrust than your back. If you try to run again or if any of your creatures tries to attack me, I will open your belly and let your guts run out. Walk!"

They did not progress very fast, but no one interfered. In that area, the few in the street melted quickly away when they saw the quality of Bell's clothes and the drawn sword. Eventually Bell and his captive came to a more open street where an old wall provided a place for Bell to put his back. Swiftly, he pulled the sword back and struck Goden on the head with the flat of the blade. The man folded to the street. Bell pulled a leather thong from his pouch and tied the old whoremaster's thumbs together. Then he sat down, took three pennies from his purse, and waited for Goden to recover his senses.

When he saw the faint quiver of Goden's eyelids, before he was conscious enough to close his eyes more firmly and pretend he was still unconscious, Bell rattled the coins in his hand. Goden's eyes opened.

"I know you were whoremaster in a house that sold forged documents. No, no, do not bother to deny it. I have no proof, no matter what you say to me here. There is no one else to hear you. I want you to sit here and name every single man or woman who did business with you—"

"Name them? How? Do you think they told me their names? And that was years ago! How would I remember?"

"Goden, do not annoy me. I have done you no harm so far, but you are not a man who would be a loss to the world, and I would not be averse to ridding it of you. I know that you were once a clerk or even a priest." Bell knew no such thing, but Goden's flinch proved the sheriff's guess right. "You can read and doubtless not only wrote down but kept in memory the names of those who bought false documents or had them made. Never mind how I know; not every man and woman who worked for you in the past loves you deeply."

"Who?" Goden muttered. "Tell me who and I will gladly tell you everything you want to know."

Bell shrugged. "I do not need to bargain," he said. "If I like what I hear, I will give you these three pennies and go my own way while you go yours."

Goden shook his head, frantically whining that he didn't know any names. Bell smiled and unsheathed his dagger. Goden gasped and began to name men, one after another.

Bell listened without stopping him or giving any sign that any name was familiar to him. He heard many that he knew, a few that confirmed his own suspicions so neatly that he nearly nodded, and one or two that really surprised him because he would have sworn they were men of probity. When Goden stopped speaking, Bell did not prod him for more names. If he was keeping back a few special tidbits, Bell did not care. He simply handed him the three pennies, hauled him to his feet, and shoved him back along the way they had come.

Among the names were three men from Mainard's Bridge Guild, three men who knew the Old Priory Guesthouse, three men of the five who had been in Mainard's workroom the day Codi's knife disappeared: John Herlyond, Lintun Mercer, and Perekin FitzRevery. He would still need proof; Goden's word was worthless, but those three would merit close scrutiny.

---

22 MAY
OLD PRIORY GUESTHOUSE

When Bell rushed out, Magdalene stood a moment looking at the gate and sighed. She had been more stirred than she liked by Bell's response to her innocent reaction to the spring warmth of the sun. If she had pulled him into her arms instead of confirming that she had been teasing him by kissing his nose, he would have turned back and satisfied the desire his kiss had wakened . . . and stayed for the evening meal and for the rest of the night.

Perhaps that was what she needed. Perhaps she had been celibate too long. The last time she had coupled had been with William, in

April, a few days after Baldassare had been killed. William . . . Magdalene shook her head. She did not want William; that was duty, although that last time a surprisingly pleasant duty. Bell would be different. He liked to play. She felt again the quick dart of his tongue, not a brutal thrusting invasion, but a tentative invitation.

Who would it harm if she yielded to him, took him as a man, not a client? Magdalene turned sharply and reentered the house, took her usual seat, and began, hardly seeing the pattern, to embroider. Who would it harm? Bell. As long as he did not accept that she *was* a whore, that there would be, must be, other men, and that she could and would only belong to him for the time he was with her, he would be jealous. Three men who had desired her were already dead.

The needle glinted as Magdalene drew it from the cloth, and she saw again the glint of light on her husband's well-honed blade as he waved it, threatening to cut off her nose and her ears to save her from becoming a whore. Magdalene laughed softly, bitterly. That was funny. It was that threat that had turned her into a whore.

She had given him no cause for jealousy; she dressed plainly, worked hard, kept her eyes down when any man spoke to her. She kept to herself as much as possible, but there were times when it was necessary to go to market to purchase what the manor lands would not supply, to sell her embroidery and buy more cloth and thread, and she was lonely; she needed sometimes to laugh and talk with other women. But once Brogan had seen that stupid mercer's journeyman following her, pleading with her, her husband had *looked* at her and noticed what she had grown into from the gangly child with too-big features that he had married. Nightmare followed.

Magdalene bit her lip. Her hand lay idle on her embroidery frame — and then a pair of shadows blocked the sunlight coming from the doorway and Haesel's high voice broke her thoughts. Magdalene called a welcome and Sabina came toward her, smiling, while Haesel ran off to the kitchen.

"A good party?" Magdalene asked. "Did the betrothed pair seem satisfied?"

"Well, Haesel said both were smiling nearly all the time. Both spoke to me and their voices were . . . light. So I think it is a good match. Master Chandler made nothing of there being a death in my 'family' and thanked me for coming to sing, but he did ask a hundred questions about Bertrild." Sabina shrugged. "I told him Mainard and I knew nothing because we had been at Master Newelyne's christening feast until nearly Compline, and Bertrild had died before Vespers. I said nothing about her being killed in the Lime Street house because I thought Bell might not want that known, and it does not matter. Mainard could not have killed her."

Magdalene swallowed a sigh. Poor Sabina. Surely the funeral guests were now gone and Mainard could have come or at least sent her a message. It was cruel of him to put her aside without even telling her — but she was only a whore and likely, to his mind, did not merit even common courtesy.

Still, Magdalene said nothing to Sabina. If it gave the poor girl comfort to deny to herself that her lover had dismissed her, let her have that comfort as long as she could. Only Magdalene silently renewed her vow that no man would ever be able to do that to her. It was not only for Bell's good that he must accept her as a whore, but for her own.

Meanwhile Sabina had been prattling happily about the fact that two more men had invited her to entertain at small functions and, she said, smiling broadly, a *woman* had offered an engagement to sing at her husband's birthday dinner. Of course, Sabina went on, she had taken the woman aside during one of her rest periods and told her that she had once been a whore, but the woman had not withdrawn the invitation. She said she assumed all female players were also whores and then asked whether Sabina had been the husband's whore. Fortunately, it transpired, when the woman brought the husband to where Sabina could touch and smell him, that she had never met him before. And, Sabina said, laughing, as she listened to the husband and wife she became sure the poor man had never dared to go with any whore.

Soon after, Ella joined them, her explosive and impatient client "Bam Bam" having left. Because she was eager to hear all about the party at which Sabina had entertained and Sabina, still excited by her success, was happy to go through the tale again, Magdalene was left to her own thoughts. Those, as she watched Sabina's lovely, happy face and thought how soon it would be marred by tears, became more and more sour until, at last, she resolved that she would visit Mainard the next morning and force him to tell Sabina to her face that he did not want her any more. Likely that would cost her a good client because he would not return to her house when his second marriage soured, but it would be worth it. Clients she had plenty. Women like Sabina were few and far between.

---

23 MAY

LIME STREET HOUSE

A restless night did not change Magdalene's decision that she must speak to Mainard; however, it did alter a trifle what she intended to say. She also wondered, as she set out across the bridge, whether free of his personal devil Mainard would even let her in the house. However, the servant who opened the door, although he was surprised to find a veiled woman on the doorstep, only said, "You are too early. You will have to wait, but I will tell the master that you are here."

Fortunately Magdalene was made speechless by a burst of fury, and the servant went away before she could speak. It seemed to her that Mainard had already arranged for women to come to his house so he could choose among them. In the moment the thought formed, Magdalene was already laughing at it. Many things changed, but not Mainard's face. And then she wondered whether her own bitterness was tainting the man rather than anything he had done.

"I am sorry I do not have the clothes sorted yet, Sister," Mainard said, coming down the stair. Then he saw who it was and said, "Magdalene! I thought you were the sister sent to collect whatever of Bertrild's clothing is not good enough to return to her uncle. Good God, I was just about to send one of the servants for you. Please, will you come abovestairs? There is something I must show you."

His expression was worried, but not guilty. Apparently no thought of Sabina or her fate troubled him. Torn between fury and a fear that her prejudices might drive her to a hasty and incorrect conclusion, she held her tongue and followed him back up the stair. The solar was large and surprisingly lavish, one end of the room holding a massive, carved bed, better fitted to a nobleman's bechamber, and the other two chairs—real chairs with backs and arms—set before the hearth. Just now the chamber was littered with more gowns, under-tunics, stockings, and every variety of female finery than Magdalene thought reasonable.

She was so bemused by the state in which Bertrild had apparently lived that she had not noticed what Mainard was doing until he thrust a cloth packet at her.

"Look!" His voice was strained. "Did Sir Bellamy tell you about the tally sticks I found yesterday?" Magdalene nodded, but Mainard hardly waited for her head to bend, thrusting the packet forward. "Look what I found today when I emptied the chest in the storeroom. Look!"

He unfolded the cloth, and Magdalene drew in her breath.

"They are not mine," Mainard cried. "I never gave her anything like that, not even for a betrothal gift. I make a good living, but not what would buy such jewels as these."

"Merciful Mother," Magdalene breathed, touching a row of wink-ing diamonds and rubies set in elaborately worked gold. Beneath the neck piece, fitted to go on a man's collar, was what appeared to be a matching bracelet, and a glint of blue suggested at least one more piece set with sapphires.

"Whatever could Bertrild have done to obtain these? What am I to do with them?" Mainard asked.

"Bring them to the justiciar?" Magdalene hazarded.

"I don't dare," Mainard said. "I don't even dare give them to Leon Basynges, my own goldsmith. If her uncle hears about them and claims they were Bertrild's as an inheritance from her father, he could de-mand that I return them to him or pay him their worth."

"I never thought of that," Magdalene admitted, knitting her brows.

"You take them," Mainard said, thrusting the packet at her.

"Me?" Magdalene gasped, backing away. Did the fool mean them for Sabina? "Do you have any idea what would happen to a whore caught with such valuables, valuables that she could not prove she had bought or had been given to her?"

Mainard laughed shakily. "Forgive me. I am so shaken I am not saying what I mean. I did not mean for you to keep the jewels. I know that among your clients are goldsmiths. I hoped that you could show them the pieces and ask if they knew who made them. The work is very distinctive, I think. Then, if we knew who made a piece, we could ask that goldsmith who had bought it and thus come back to who had given it to Bertrild."

"The plan has some merit," Magdalene admitted, "but I am afraid to take such valuable items into my house. Let me speak to Bell about this. You know he can hold his tongue. And speaking of Bell reminds me about the tally sticks. Have you retrieved their worth from Master Gerlund yet?"

"No! I cannot think *what* to do about that. I suppose it is wrong to leave the money with Master Gerlund, and I do not want Sir Druerie to hear about it. Nor do I want to touch the money myself, and I cannot imagine how to return it without frightening those who paid Bertrild — supposing I could discover who they are and what they paid."

Magdalene smiled at him. "There Bell and I may be able to help you. We hope to lay hands upon the man who collected the money for Bertrild. He should be able to tell us from whom he collected and perhaps how much each paid, so I think you would do well to get the money from Gerlund."

Mainard closed his eyes and put a hand to his head. "I cannot go just this moment. I still have all this to sort out — " he gestured at the clothing " — and chests I haven't opened. And now I am afraid to let anyone else look through her things. God alone knows what else is concealed."

Magdalene glanced out the window to judge the angle of the sun. She had time. "Let me sort the clothes," she said. "I know what is valuable enough to keep for Sir Druerie and doubt I will make any horrible discoveries among them. You go to Master Gerlund."

After some polite protests, Mainard agreed to Magdalene's suggestion and, snatching up the tally sticks, which were in the bottom of an empty chest, rushed out. Magdalene made much shorter work of the clothing than Mainard would have done, and when the lay sisters arrived from a charitable order that fed and clothed the poor, she had two substantial bundles ready for them. Two dark, sober gowns, unornamented but scarcely worn, she saved out for the cook and the maid, together with three chemises and three pairs of stockings for each. Whether they were to remain with Mainard or be sold, they should have something for their years of harsh service.

It was not until she had completed these tasks that Magdalene remembered neither she nor Mainard had said a word about Sabina. Having seen him and been reminded of his goodness and his transparent honesty, she found it harder and harder to believe he would thrust Sabina out without a single word to her. Magdalene revised her approach yet again, from accusation to a simple question about his intentions. She had no time to ask, however, because when Mainard returned, he was even more shaken.

"*Ten pounds*," he gasped as soon as he saw her. "Gerlund was holding *ten pounds* for Bertrild. He did not have all the money to hand. I will have to go again tomorrow or the next day. But he was also holding this." Mainard held out a parcel, wrapped in oiled leather, tied with several cords, and sealed on every fold and knot. He swallowed hard. "I cannot open it. I cannot." Tears stood in his beautiful eyes. "I cannot bear to know what evil I allowed that woman to do, all because I did not wish to contest with her. For my own ease, God knows what agony I allowed her to inflict on others."

"Do not be ridiculous, Master Mainard," Magdalene said. "There is no controlling that kind of person. If you blocked her one way, she would have found another." She shook her head. "But I *am* beginning to doubt whether it is just to seek and punish her murderer."

"If he had not taken Codi's knife . . . That was as cruel as anything Bertrild did." Mainard sighed. "I know you are trying to comfort me, but I have done wrong. I did not even try to discover and prevent her evildoing. And I am too much a coward to look at this, which must be more evidence of it. Do you think I can burden Sir Bellamy with this also?"

"Actually he is the very person. If it is more jewelry, it is barely possible that he might recognize a piece. As the bishop of Winchester's knight, he is often at Court and has business among the great men. And such pieces as you showed me are from a nobleman's strongbox. When I next see Bell, I will ask him to wait on you —"

"Oh, please, Magdalene, please take this away. It is all sealed. If you are questioned about it, I will stand witness that I took that box from Johannes Gerlund and gave it to you to hold for me, just as it is, and Gerlund will have to stand witness, too. Give it to Sir Bellamy and tell him that I pray I will never again need to see it or its contents, whatever they are."

He looked utterly distraught, his normal skin so pallid that the birthmark fairly flamed against it. Magdalene remembered how he had blamed himself for Bertrild's evil. This was not a man who lightly sloughed off responsibility; he truly was driven beyond endurance just now. She reached out and took the box.

"Thank you," Mainard breathed. "Thank you." Then he frowned slightly. "I am so sorry," he said. "I remember now that you came without my sending for you. I had meant to ask if you would, but you came—" His eyes widened. "Is something wrong? Sabina . . ."

"Yes, Sabina," Magdalene said. "I wished to speak to you about Sabina."

Just at that moment the bell at the door pealed. Mainard looked away, grabbed a purse from the top of a chest, and pushed it into Magdalene's hand. A horrible grimace twisted his lips. "Please, take this for her board and lodging. Please do not force her to ply her trade." Then the pallid natural skin flushed, and he bent his head in resignation, although he still would not look at her. "I am not trying to forbid Sabina any pleasure she desires. If she wishes to take other men, me being what I am, I will understand, but I want what she does to be her choice, not out of need."

"Master Mainard," Magdalene said indignantly. "I do not run a common stew. I do not force—"

Footsteps sounded on the stair, and Magdalene fell silent. There was no need to spread broadcast who and what she was. The still too-thin but no longer terrified servant stopped in the open doorway, grinned, and said, "Master Thomas FitzNeal and his lady are here to offer what comfort they can, Master Mainard." He did not look as if he believed any comfort was necessary.

Mainard's lips parted, but Magdalene put a hand on his arm. "It will do you no good to have me discovered in your bedchamber, Master Mainard," she said softly, drawing her veil over her face and pulling her cloak forward so that it covered the parcel and purse she was carrying. "I will leave as soon as it is safe for me to go."

The servant, who had been looking around the chamber, had lifted his head alertly when Magdalene said it would not be good for her to be found there. "I have shown Master FitzNeal into the common room, Master Mainard," Jean said, now speaking much more softly. "If you will go down to him, I will take this lady out the back way. No one will know she was here, except me, and I will never, never say what could hurt you."

"I am sure you would not, Jean," Mainard said, almost smiling. "Nor is there any wrong in what I have done, but to have another woman in the bedchamber the day after my wife's funeral would not look well, perhaps."

"And such a woman as me!" Magdalene said, laughing, as she turned to leave.

---

23 MAY
EAST CHEPE

Bell woke in a much better humor than Magdalene had. He was rather looking forward to his morning's work, but it was too early to begin so he lay abed a while — a rare indulgence — before he rose and broke his fast. While he lingered abed at his ease, he ran over in his mind the behavior of the five men at Bertrild's funeral. That all five had come was interesting; even more interesting was how they all clung together; most interesting of all was the air of nervous expectation that hung about them. Bell reconsidered that while he was eating. All had acted as if they were waiting for something to happen, but each reaction to the expectation seemed different.

Having finished his meal in a leisurely manner, Bell bade a servant see that his palfrey was saddled while he fetched his cloak and his purse. He had determined to begin his questioning with Jokel de Josne, who had seemed more thoughtful than worried at the funeral and had left the group to speak to others most frequently. Bell had not been able to overhear any of those conversations, but from the expressions on the faces of those Josne approached, they were not best pleased with what he said.

A reason for that occurred to Bell when he had entered Josne's shop. Although he called himself a mercer, Josne seemed to deal mostly in small foreign luxuries—sandalwood boxes, delicate bamboo fans, brass hinges and latches, and suchlike; however, his shelves were remarkably bare of goods. Items were well spread out but could not completely disguise the dearth of stock. It was possible that Josne had been explaining late deliveries or cancelling promised deliveries.

He still hoped to do business nonetheless, Bell thought, as Josne hurried into his shop in response to the ringing of a bell on the shop counter, but Josne's expression changed from a broad welcoming smile to a grimace when he recognized who his visitor was.

"What can I do for you, Sir Bellamy?" he asked sharply.

"I am looking into the death of Mistress Bertrild, the saddler's wife, at the behest of Master Octadenarius, the justiciar."

The man nodded, lips twisting wryly. "I cannot think why anyone should bother. She was such a woman as the world will rejoice without."

"You are not the only one to think so, but the law is the law, and a man who kills for a justifiable reason once may do so again for less reason or no reason if he finds killing easy."

Josne shrugged. "You do not need to look far to find one who had the best reason in the world to be rid of her. She was a shrew and expensive and took joy in hurting and belittling her husband. He is not a man prone to violence, but once he found a woman who professed love for him, likely he decided to be rid of his encumbrance."

"That is reasonable, only Master Mainard could not have murdered his wife. There are witnesses to say he was elsewhere at the time she was killed."

"The whore, no doubt." Josne shrugged again. "She will say anything that will profit her, I don't doubt."

"No, not the whore. A dozen or more men who knew him well. Thus, Master Octadenarius and I are constrained to look at any who had reason to wish to be rid of the woman. You had trouble with her, I know."

Josne snorted. "When the Bridge Guild to which I now belong was first proposed and members solicited, Bertrild's father, Gervase de Genlis, was proposed as a member—"

"By whom?" Bell asked.

"I do not remember," Josne said, thrusting forward his lower lip. "He was not accepted, but he did come to a few of the early meetings—one at the Old Priory Guesthouse. Somehow his daughter heard of that and when, not long afterward, Genlis was killed in an alehouse brawl, she blamed the other members of the guild who had attended that meeting." He laughed suddenly. "Bertrild said we had corrupted her father, who was so corrupt already that the whoremistress of a good house would not let her women serve him."

"I have heard Bertrild did more than blame you. She came to your shop and made a scene, and when you put her out, she stood in the street and cried aloud her charge of corruption. It might have been worth your while to silence her if you suspected she would create another such disturbance."

"Do not be ridiculous," Josne replied, without the smallest look of uneasiness. "If I did not murder her then, why would I do so now, several years later?"

"Because she had learned that your business was . . . ah . . . not as prosperous as it once was and she threatened to renew her accusations. What did not matter when all was going well might cause a disaster in less prosperous times."

"Who said I was less prosperous?" Josne snapped.

"My eyes and the expressions of those you spoke to at Bertrild's burying."

"Nonsense!" The man's eyes shifted. "It is true that a ship with my goods is a little delayed, but an accusation years old will not change that."

This time Bell shrugged. "Where were you on Saturday between Nones and Vespers?"

"Not killing Mistress Bertrild! I was here, I think, or out walking for a while. Anyway, I did not hold any grudges over her hysterics. I had my revenge for that long ago." Josne uttered a bark of a laugh. "Did you not know that it was we five, who had formed the Bridge Guild and whom she accused, who bought Master Mainard a night with Sabina? Perekin FitzRevery thought of it, and the five of us each contributed a penny. It seemed just. She had accused us of corrupting her father—who even Satan could not have spoiled, he was so rotten already—so we corrupted her 'innocent' husband."

"Did she know that?" Bell asked blandly.

Josne showed his teeth in what was not a smile. "I am sure she did not. Had she known, she would have told the whole world—and that might have hurt me, since it is often women who buy my wares, and women might not think it so fair and funny that we led her husband to use a whore. But I did not kill her and would not for such a cause."

"Perhaps not." Bell half raised a hand in farewell, and added over his shoulder, "But I would try to find someone who can speak to your whereabouts on Saturday—and preferably not one of your men or one easily bribed."

He stepped out while Josne was still fuming, but once he had mounted and turned his horse's head west, he permitted himself to smile. That had been interesting. He had known about Bertrild's attacks on the men leading the Bridge Guild, but he had not known how Mainard came to Sabina's bed. He had assumed that being dissatisfied with his wife he had gone to Magdalene's house and chosen Sabina because she was blind, but apparently FitzRevery had chosen Sabina for him. So that was why Mainard had said FitzRevery had done him as great a favor as a man could do.

Could he have done Mainard an even greater favor and removed the cross he was bearing? Bell almost passed Lintun Mercer's shop to go on to FitzRevery's, but decided to keep to his original plan of working the men from east to west and dismounted at what had been William Dockett's mercerie.

This time the journeyman at the counter recognized him and waved him past into the shop. The young man looked almost cheerful, and Bell remembered that he had never mentioned the possibility that the bolts of cloth he had come to inquire about might have been diverted between the shop and their destination. If that half-smile was an acknowledgment perhaps he should. . . . No. It was none of his business. It was as likely that the journeyman had just had a very good day or hated his new master and hoped a second visit from the bishop's knight would mean more trouble for Lintun Mercer.

An apprentice scurried up the stairs, and Master Mercer came down without delay. "I saw you at Bertrild's funeral yesterday," he said. "I did not know the bishop knew her or Mainard."

"He does not, as far as I know," Bell replied. "I attended as the eyes and ears of Master Octadenarius, the justiciar, who is interested in determining who killed her. He has on record a report of several disturbances caused by Mistress Bertrild and has asked me to determine the whereabouts of the men she accused of evildoing."

"That was years ago," Lintun Mercer said indifferently. "Master Dockett complained, and she was warned not to break the peace again. She did not."

"What had Master Dockett to do with Bertrild?"

Lintun Mercer laughed. "Master Dockett was the one who was interested in the Bridge Guild, but he had sent me to the meeting at the Old Priory Guesthouse in his stead. That was how I came to be Bertrild's target."

"And you have had nothing to do with Mistress Bertrild since then?"

Mercer shrugged. "She stepped into my shop once or twice on her way home from Mainard's place. I spoke to her as a courtesy to a fellow merchant's wife, but I do not believe she ever bought anything." He cocked his head in thought. "No. No. She never bought anything."

"Just to satisfy my curiosity. I am asking everyone she caused trouble. Where were you on Saturday between Nones and Vespers?"

"I was out in the morning for perhaps half a candlemark, but I had dinner here. Then I had to go Greenwich where there was a showing of Flemish cloth, so I rode out. I was still on the road at Vespers, and I was worried about reaching home before dark—and, of course, my beast cast a shoe. It is so whenever one is in a hurry, is it not?"

"You rode your own horse?"

"Yes . . . well, actually it was William's horse, but at need anyone in the household can use the beast."

Hamo had said the horse and saddle looked as if they were from a livery stable. Still, a tale of a cast shoe was easy to tell. "Did you have the shoe replaced?"

"Yes, of course. I did not wish to lame the horse, but it is useless to ask me who did it or where. It was some hole in the wall past Deptford. I did not even ask the smith's name."

"Oh well," Bell said blandly, "if it should become necessary, I am sure you will be able to retrace your steps. Did you perhaps buy any cloth at the showing?"

Mercer cast him an angry glance and said, "No, I did not. It was very fine cloth, but above the price my customers would like to pay."

"Ah, I am sorry you had a wasted trip. If you saw anyone there you knew—"

"I am sorry to say, I did not. The showing had been mentioned to me in passing as a private hint. Of course, I am sorry now I did not tell my friends, but I did not."

"Too bad. It is nice to have confirmation. If you remember anyone who might recall that you were there, let me know. You can leave a message for me any time at the bishop's house opposite the front gate of the priory."

Mercer nodded. "Perhaps there is a man . . . I did not get his name, but he lives there in Greenwich and I spoke to him. He might well remember me."

As he rode from Mercer's shop, Bell repeated to himself what the man had told him until he was sure he would have it word perfect for Master Octadenarius. If it seemed worthwhile to the justiciar, he could send men to inquire about whether there had been a showing of Flemish cloth in Greenwich on Saturday and to look along the road for a smith who had replaced a shoe on a horse on Saturday not long after Vespers.

It was very annoying that two out of the five men could not account for themselves on Saturday afternoon. It would be just his fate that no one had witnesses to clear him of suspicion. FitzRevery had said he was in the shop all day, but his journeyman had supported his statement with such an expression of surprise that Bell was almost tempted to arrest FitzRevery and try a little physical "persuasion" to wrest the truth from him. In the end, he left him with no more than a strong warning not to leave the city without first informing him or Master Octadenarius.

His interview with John Herlyond left him even less satisfied. The man grew pale when he entered the shop and introduced himself, upon which his two journeymen came forward with such aggressive expressions that Bell dropped his hand warningly to his sword hilt. Herlyond immediately called them sharply to order and sent them away, but Bell wondered if they would have offered him violence had Herlyond not done so. Nor were they too willing to go, and left with lagging steps, looking over their shoulders as if Bell were going to attack their master.

The behavior woke dark suspicions in Bell and at the same time testified to the total lack of any practice in hiding guilty secrets in Herlyond's household. "You have loyal servants," he said.

Herlyond looked at him with the sick fascination of a paralyzed bird eying a snake. "I hope I have been a good master to them," he said, and then as if the words were wrung out of him, added, "But I am sure you did not come here to talk about my household. I saw you at Mistress Bertrild's funeral, did I not?"

"Yes, and with Master Octadenarius's concurrence, I am investigating the cause of her death."

"I know nothing about her death! Nothing!" Herlyond exclaimed, growing even paler. "I was away all day on Saturday. My sister's husband died a month since, and I was helping her move from her house in Windsor to a new house I found for her in Lambeth. She will thus be closer to me, and I can be of more help to her."

"You went to Windsor Saturday morning?"

"No, of course not. I went on Friday after Sext. Windsor is all of thirty miles. We left there at first light on Saturday and came to Lambeth perhaps a candlemark or two before Nones. Then the place had to be swept and some walls painted. I do not know exactly when I left, but it was well before Vespers, after which I came home, and I did not go out again."

If he had left on Friday afternoon, would he have had time to find Saeger and give him the knife? Perhaps . . . barely. Also, it seemed he thought Bertrild had been killed near the time she was discovered in Mainard's yard—or he wanted Bell to believe that was what he thought. So Bell told him that Bertrild had been killed on Saturday, probably soon after Nones and in the common room of her own house in Lime Street. Herlyond wavered on his feet, clutching at a table edge for support.

"No. No. That is not possible," he whispered.

Bell's eyes were like balls of barely tinted ice. "The time is what Brother Samuel of St. Catherine's Hospital told me, and the place I found for myself, marked by bloodstains on the floor under the rushes. Why do you say it is not possible?"

"I . . . I do not know," Herlyond mumbled, staring at his own hand clutching the edge of the desk. "Somehow such violence is not fit for daylight in a well-furnished room. I thought. . . . I was sure that she had been set upon in the street, in the dark. . . ." He shook his head. "There is nothing more I can tell you. Nothing. I must attend to my business now."

That was another one who would bear careful sieving out, Bell thought as he left Herlyond's shop. His reactions bespoke guilt, but it was also almost certain that Herlyond did not know where and when Bertrild had been killed. He wondered, as he crossed the street toward Ulfmaer FitzIsabelle's establishment, whether he should have pressed Herlyond harder while he was still in shock or whether he was correct in believing he would get more out of the man if he gave him time to recover and make up some lies. Well, if worse came to worst, Octadenarius could wring the truth from him.

FitzIsabelle came out of a chamber behind a small showroom, which held some truly lovely pieces of silver—a set of candlesticks that easily rivaled the work of Master Jacob the Alderman, a set of brooches in gold that could have been made by the ancient Welsh masters.

"You are the bishop's man and were at Bertrild's funeral," he said. "What do you want with me? I owe nothing to the Church."

"The bishop of Winchester is no way concerned with this matter. It is with the concurrence of Master Octadenarius, the justiciar, that I am looking into the death of Mistress Bertrild. I have come to ask where you were on the Saturday she was killed."

"You are a busybody and likely serving the whore who lives with Mainard rather than Octadenarius. The one who had the best reasons to see Bertrild dead is Mainard. Where was *he* on Saturday?"

"At a christening party at a Master Newelyne's house in the West Chepe," Bell said, smiling. "And I have questioned a dozen men who also attended that christening party. There is no doubt that Mainard arrived just about Sext and did not leave until almost Compline." Bell felt a little guilty, but what he said was perfectly true, and FitzIsabelle annoyed him.

"I am sure the whore says he was with her at night."

"It does not matter where Mainard was at night. According to Brother Samuel at St. Catherine's Hospital, Mistress Bertrild died before Vespers. Mainard did not kill his wife. There are others, however, who had reason to wish her still and silent. You are one of those she caused trouble for."

"That was years ago, and she was silenced by order of the then sheriff. Why should I suddenly act against her now?"

"Because Mistress Bertrild seems to have found a more effective way to punish those she hated."

Bell did not smile with satisfaction at FitzIsabelle's reaction to his statement. He just waited. The man's face did not pale, but it was as if it had frozen.

"Whatever you think she found, it was nothing to me," he said, but his voice was strained. "Still, I had nothing to do with her death, and if it was near to Vespers, I can prove it. I was here in my chamber or my shop Saturday afternoon. My journeyman and apprentices will bear witness for me. You can ask them as you leave."

Eleven

Magdalene did not get to deliver Mainard's parcel to Bell until Wednesday morning and had little time to think about it until then. She came home to find four of William's captains and a clerk she did not know seated around the table and devouring bread, cheese, and cold pasty, washed down with William's wine. Letice, Ella, and Diot were cheerfully entertaining them. Sabina was nowhere to be seen.

"Just let me take off my cloak and I will welcome you properly, my lord," Magdalene said, hurrying toward her own room.

"Liar," Giles de Milland called after her. "You *never* welcome a man as a proper whore should do."

Magdalene laughed and flirted a dismissive hand at him as she entered her chamber and closed the door. She pulled off veil and cloak and threw them on the bed over the purse she had dropped there first, then took a heavy key from the pocket tied around her waist under her gown and opened a chest so heavily bound in metal that little wood showed. From that she lifted out her strongbox. She dropped Mainard's parcel in, put the strongbox atop it, and relocked the chest. Then she rushed out into the common room.

"To what do I owe this pleasure?" she asked the men as she lifted a flagon and refilled wine cups.

"To Oxford being packed like a barrel of herrings," Sir Niall de Arvagh snarled, lifting his head from Ella's shoulder where he had been nuzzling her neck. She froze at the tone, and he patted her and said gently, "Sorry, sweeting, I wasn't angry at you. You're good and lovely, not like the damned king."

"What has Stephen done now?" Magdalene asked lightly, laughter in her voice.

"Asked Lord William to send his men away because the city is like to be too crowded when the other barons and bishops arrive," a smooth voice, totally without passion, replied.

Magdalene shifted her attention from Sir Niall to the opposite side of the table and dropped a sketchy curtsey to the man she did not know. He was dressed in clerical robes, very rich clerical robes; he had dark hair, smoothly combed; dark eyes; and a neat moustache that joined a short well-trimmed beard, which surrounded his mouth and covered his chin but left most of his cheeks bare.

"Surely that is very foolish, my lord," she said. "If Oxford becomes crowded with many nobles' and churchmen's meinies, there is sure to be conflict. Who is to keep the peace if not William's men? They are accustomed to lodging in tents or even in the open and are mostly foreign mercenaries that could not care less about parties in England."

A corner of the dark man's mouth twitched. "Perhaps someone does not desire that the peace be kept."

"That is even more foolish. The king's peace must hold with safe conduct for all when the king calls a Great Council or the barons will not come."

"Unless the king has become so powerful that it is more dangerous to refuse to attend when summoned than to come without safe conduct."

Magdalene looked at him steadily for a moment and then shook her head. "My lord, I understand your words, but the true meaning of what you say is not clear to me."

He laughed. "I doubt that, Mistress Magdalene. I doubt that very much, indeed, but it is much clearer to me why Lord William is known to frequent this house so often. This is no common stew."

"No, indeed," Magdalene said, laughing in response and also to hide her uneasiness. "It is very *uncommon*, as you will discover if you allow Letice or Diot to show you what they can do to ease a man."

He shook his head but without any sign of being shocked. "My calling does not permit. I will ride on with Sir Giles to Rochester as I have messages for Sir Somer de Loo, but these other gentlemen will be staying in Lord William's house by the Tower, I believe. They will not need to hurry."

Magdalene made some light remark about never interfering with a gentleman's vows, and Sir Giles began loudly to bemoan his deprivation, saying he had certainly made no vow of celibacy. That was no more than a jest. He rose and left readily when the stranger finished the last sip of wine in his cup; William's men did not delay in carrying out his orders to pleasure themselves. It was just as well, because Magdalene had not been able to think how to accommodate him and still have her women ready for their regular clients.

Sir Niall de Arvagh left in good time to make room for Ella's first client. He had enjoyed her lively ministrations but had little taste for her childish chatter. Even so, Magdalene had to entertain two men, who fortunately did not know each other, with tidbits and wine until Diot and Letice were able to be rid of their company. That delay, of course, caused further delays. By the time Ella and Letice were bedded down with all-night visitors, Magdalene was exhausted. Diot told her to go to bed, and she was very happy to do so, very happy to know that if the bell rang Diot would answer it. She uttered a brief prayer that the woman would continue to prove as satisfactory as she was now and slept.

⚬

24 MAY
OLD PRIORY GUESTHOUSE

The next morning, Bell arrived in time to share their breakfast. Unfortunately, his men had not laid hands on Borc. Either Borc had not appeared at the cookshop, or Tom had not been able to pick him out from the description Diot had given. On the other hand, the justiciar had been most cooperative. His men had questioned the neighbors on Lime Street, and he had passed the information to Bell.

First, the likelihood that the messenger had killed Bertrild was considerably increased. She had not left the house after she returned

to it at about Nones and no one, except the messenger, had gone in —
at least at the front door. That left the possibility that someone had
sneaked down the alley and come in through the back, but it was not
great. The alley behind the house opened into the Chepe. There were
stalls on either side, and they were so close together that to pass into
the alley took great care not to knock the goods to the ground. Both
merchants remembered the servants leaving and returning, but they
swore that no one else had passed them all afternoon.

At the front, the messenger had been seen arriving and leaving by
a grocer's wife across from Mainard's house. She loathed Bertrild, who
had quarreled with her and insulted her, and she was hoping that so
unusual an event as a mounted visitor could be used to Bertrild's dis-
credit. She had watched carefully and confirmed the time Jean had
set for the messenger's arrival. He had left perhaps a candlemark later,
in a great hurry, heading west. Then she had gone next door to gossip
and found her neighbor had also watched, so she had that woman's
witness to what she said.

The information about movement after dark was less certain. Bertrild's slaves had seen and heard nothing. Their pallets and blankets
were spread under the table and wall shelves in the kitchen, and all
had been so exhausted by the terrors and excitements of the day, not
to mention the long walks to accomplish the errands on which Bertrild
had sent them, that they slept like bludgeoned oxen.

There was one report of violation of the curfew, however. A
woman who lived in the corner house, which also backed on the alley
that exited into the Chepe, had been up nursing a new babe and said
she had heard a horse's hooves passing some time before Matins. She
had not got up to look at who it was; she had been tired and, frankly,
did not *want* to know if one of her neighbors had business that took
him out in the dead of night.

"I think that, with what you saw in the wheelbarrow and the
fresh dung outside Mainard's back gate, it is reasonably certain that
Bertrild was—" Magdalene glanced at Ella and continued cautiously
"—ah . . . moved from the house on Lime Street to the yard of Mainard's shop."

"She will not come here, will she?" Ella asked, frowning. "The
last time she shrieked so that I was frightened to death."

"No, love," Magdalene soothed, wishing that certain random events did not fix themselves so firmly into Ella's usually faulty memory. "That was a long time ago, and Mistress Bertrild has gone away. She will never come back."

"Oh, good!" Ella said, and put a spoonful of preserves onto a round of bread with great satisfaction.

"Then it must have been the messenger," Sabina remarked. "And if it was, did he do it for himself or for her uncle?"

"She knew him personally," Bell reminded them. "She called him Saeger."

"That is not a name one hears very often," Diot said. "I wonder if it is local to where Bertrild's father lived and whether Borc also knew Saeger."

"Hmm, yes," Bell said. "I hope we will be able to catch him today. Is there anything more you can tell Tom that will help to identify the man, Diot?"

She shook her head slowly. "I would know him if I saw him, I am sure, but to paint what he is in words . . ."

She looked sidelong at Magdalene as she spoke, fearing that her whoremistress would think she was holding back deliberately. And then she looked down, studying intently the rich, white cheese and soft, fresh bread at her place. She would not lose what she had, she vowed, remembering how willingly Magdalene had trusted her to watch the house in her place last night.

Then Diot almost smiled. She might be able to kill two birds with one stone—show that she wished to be helpful and test Magdalene's assurance that Stav was not still hunting her. Magdalene had said she had paid Stav to forget his grievance, but Diot was not sure he would not have taken the money and then had his bullies set upon her anyway. That had made her shy of going out even with one of the other women. But if she went with Tom and Bell's men were also watching, she would be safe. If Stav's men came for her, they would be driven off, Magdalene would know Stav had violated his promise and set her powerful friends on him, and she would be free. If, on the other hand, no one troubled her, she would also know she was free.

"Is it really important that this Borc be taken?" she asked.

"Yes," Bell replied with some force. "More than ever now that I have questioned the five men who were in Mainard's shop on Friday. Several of them have no witness to where they were when Bertrild died; others have only the word of a too-devoted household. So, not only will Borc be able to tell us whether he extorted money from those five, but if he did know Saeger, he could tell us what Saeger looks like."

"Then if Magdalene can find some clothes fit for a whore who would eat in such a cookshop, I will become what I was not so long ago and go to the cookshop with Tom. I doubt Borc will know me, but even if he does, he will only recognize me as a whore from Stav's and not be suspicious."

"Why, thank you, Diot," Magdalene said. "That will be very helpful." Then she looked at Bell. "Unfortunately, knowing what Saeger looks like will not be much help if he has gone back to Bertrild's uncle."

"If he ever came from her uncle in the first place. Do not forget that one of Mainard's servants—I think it was Hamo, but I am not certain—told me that the messenger's boots were wrong. They were polished leather with thin soles, not the kind of shoe that a messenger from the country would wear."

"That is very interesting," Sabina said softly. "And there is something else to consider. I am not sure how many of Mainard's friends knew that Bertrild had an uncle who lived outside of London. She did once go to stay with Sir Druerie, but I doubt any of the men asked for her, and Mainard never mentioned her if he could avoid it. The only one I am almost certain knew was Master FitzRevery because he has lands in that area also."

"So he does," Bell said, eyes narrowing with interest.

"Yes, he keeps his shop as a mercer, but he is also a wool merchant and ships his fleeces down the Itchen. He has a farm. . . . I cannot remember the name, but Mainard would know."

Magdalene noted that Sabina said her lover's name easily with no hesitation and no vocal tremor. Her confidence in him seemed to have grown rather than diminished since the day she left her rooms above Mainard's shop, despite the fact that two full days had passed since Bertrild's death and he had not come or sent any message. It was significant, also, that she had retreated to her room and stayed there the entire time that William's men had been in the house and that clients had been with Magdalene. Clearly she had no intention of taking up her past role in the Old Priory Guesthouse.

As soon as she had a moment to be private with Sabina, Magdalene decided to discuss with her the purse Mainard had handed over. There had been more money in it than Magdalene expected, far too much for a few weeks' or even a few months' board and lodging while he sought a new wife. The amount had left Magdalene unwilling just to give Sabina Mainard's message, which implied that Mainard wished to take Sabina back into his keeping. Nearly a pound in silver was more in keeping with a farewell gift or a payment for silence—unless Mainard was in the habit of giving Sabina large sums of money, or in his hurry he had not remembered how much silver was in the purse. That thought was such a relief that Bell's voice penetrated Magdalene's concern with Sabina.

"Does a lot of business with lands across the narrow sea, does Master FitzRevery?" Bell was saying. "I wonder if he was ever involved with the rebels in Normandy? Could that be what Bertrild knew? If it was, and she threatened him, he would have had good cause to—" a glance at Ella "—ah . . . send Mistress Bertrild away. King Stephen is usually a most good-natured man, but that fiasco in Normandy cut deep, and I think he would not be too ready to forgive anyone who was mixed into that business."

Sabina shook her head. "Mainard would never tell even me a thing like that if he suspected it. He and Master FitzRevery are good friends and have been for many years."

Bell recalled the ambivalent things FitzRevery had said when he spoke to him and the doubts he had had that FitzRevery was truly pleased when he learned that Mainard probably had witnesses to his whereabouts when Bertrild was killed.

"I hope Master Mainard will not be disappointed in his friend. It appears that Master FitzRevery was one of the men for whom Letice lifted a seal."

Magdalene's lips parted, and he grinned at her with friendly malice. "You do not always know best about everything, even in your own trade," Bell continued. "I told you you should have left that matter in my hands. I found the old whoremaster without any trouble. The sheriff of Southwark was happy to tell me his name and current place of business—if it can be called that."

Magdalene giggled. "I never thought of going to the sheriff, not that he would have told me anything if I had thought of it. We each follow our own paths by habit, and this time yours *was* the easier way. But did you get the man to tell you anything?"

"Oh yes." Bell's smile turned grim, and he touched the hilt of his knife. "I can afford to use threats."

"Oh, Bell," Ella said, looking reproving, "that is not polite, and it could be dangerous. You are not usually so unkind."

After a minute pause and a quick swallow, Bell said, "I try not to be, sweeting, but sometimes one must use a little unkindness to make life easier for such good, innocent girls as yourself. This was not a nice man. Letice knew him and she will tell you."

Letice nodded vigorously and made a horrible face, then pretended to twist her own arm and strike herself. Ella looked horrified.

"Not to worry, love," Magdalene said. "You may trust Bell not to hurt the good and innocent."

Ella smiled and blew Bell a kiss, then examined the supplies on the table and chose another round of bread and a pot of honey. Magdalene nodded at Bell, who made an apologetic moue, promising wordlessly to be more careful.

"The whoremaster's name is Goden, and the sheriff is still trying to find enough evidence to . . . er . . . remove him. I . . . ah . . . convinced him to tell me the names of the people who had patronized that side of his business and among them were three who had been in Mainard's shop on Friday: John Herlyond, Lintun Mercer, and Perekin FitzRevery."

While he was speaking, Letice had slid off the bench and gone down the corridor. Now she returned slate in hand. "Cudl Ber woreed" she wrote, and proffered the slate to Magdalene.

Magdalene pursed her lips unhappily. "Yes, and Letice reminds me that she told me the client she calls 'Cuddle Bear,' who is one of those three, has been badly worried for a month or six weeks. Likely he is one Bertrild was draining."

"Oh fine!" Bell remarked sourly. "I have a wonderful case against the man. Goden's word, which is utterly worthless, and a whore's opinion, which is inadmissible. Has no one a piece of real evidence against anyone?"

Real evidence! The package Mainard had given her might well have something worthwhile in it. If Bertrild had sent it to a goldsmith for safekeeping, it must be valuable or dangerous. Not jewels, then, but documents—dangerous enough to cause Bertrild's death. Magdalene slid off the bench and rose, plucking at Bell's sleeve to bring him with her.

"Come to my chamber," she said. "I have something to show you."

There was nothing special in her face or voice. For one joyful instant, however, Bell thought that something he had said or done had sparked desire in Magdalene and she had decided to satisfy it before any of the day's duties fell upon her. When she closed the door behind them and pulled in the latch string, he started to reach for her, but she evaded his grasp without even seeming to be aware of it, fumbled in her pocket, and withdrew a key.

With that in hand, however, she proved she *had* been aware of his attempt to take her in his arms. She cast a single roguish glance over her shoulder at him and smiled mischievously. "Do not you dare try to grab me," she warned as she bent to unlock the metal-bound chest that sat beside her bed. "This is not an invitation," she added, moving the strongbox aside. "It is business only." Then, lifting out Mainard's packet, she handed it to Bell.

"What is this?" he asked, smiling to hide his chagrin as if he had been teasing her.

But she did not respond to the smile. "Something of Bertrild's, I believe," she said soberly, and went on to tell him about going to see Mainard at Lime Street to ask what he intended to do about Sabina, about the way he had greeted her, and about the jewels he had found hidden in one of Bertrild's chests.

"I will look at them," Bell agreed, "but I doubt I will know them. Mainard's idea of asking goldsmiths who made them seems more reasonable, but there is no sense confining the questioning to your clients. If Mainard will come with me to the justiciar and swear as to where he found the pieces and that he believes they are the fruits of a crime, they will be protected from seizure by Sir Druerie—although if it is the man I believe it to be, Mainard need have no worries about him. But that doesn't tell me what this so carefully sealed package is."

"Because I don't know what it is. That came from Johannes Gerlund, Bertrild's goldsmith, who told Mainard that in addition to the packet, she had ten pounds banked with him."

"Ten pounds!" Bell exclaimed. "If she was draining her marks to that extent, I am surprised she lasted as long as she did."

"Well, what do we do with that package?" Magdalene asked. "Should we open it?"

"What do you think is inside?" Bell held the package up near his ear and shook it. "Something is moving within," he reported, "but it does not clink like metal. Of course, if it is more jewelry, the pieces may be wrapped in cloth. Perhaps I should take it just as it is to Octadenarius."

"But what if it does not hold jewelry?" Magdalene said, following her earlier train of thought. "What if it is the evidence on which Bertrild was collecting the money? If Octadenarius opens this, he is an official and he *must* take notice of any illegalities. Surely some of these men have paid already for their crimes both in money and in agony of spirit. Would it not be well to temper justice with mercy for Bertrild's victims?"

"You want me to overlook murder?"

"No, I do not mean to excuse the murderer, although as Mainard said, if the man hadn't stolen Codi's knife and tried to put the blame on the poor journeyman and Mainard, I might be tempted to do so." She sighed. "And the purpose of beginning this was to clear Mainard's name. If he had been seen throughout the day at Newelyne's christening party so there was no chance at all that he had gone to Lime Street . . . But he *could* have done it."

Bell did not reply to that directly. He was still very angry with Mainard, not only for hurting Sabina but for making his own lot more difficult. How could he ever convince Magdalene that she would be better off in his keeping than running her own very profitable business—even if it was a whorehouse—when her woman had been thrown away like a dirty rag? Instead of answering, he turned the package over, examining it carefully and hefting it in his hand.

"I do not think this holds jewelry," he said. "Why should Bertrild make such a large, flat package?"

"Parchments? Records?"

"I think so, and though my conscience is pricking me, I am enough of your mind that I will open it to make sure some relatively innocent—"

"Wait," Magdalene said as he drew his knife. "Let Letice lift the seals if she can. Then we can decide whether we wish to destroy what is here or restore it and bring it to Octadenarius."

Bell looked at her uneasily. "You mean pretend we never looked inside this as you pretended you had never seen the papal messenger's pouch?"

"Yes," Magdalene replied, her eyes laughing although she managed to control her lips. "Just exactly as I treated the papal messenger's pouch. No harm at all was done by the delay of a few days in its delivery. And, Bell, did you ever stop to think what a disaster would have befallen the bishop of Winchester if that pouch had been given into his hands immediately after Baldassare died?"

"Never mind the bishop," Bell said, not as successful in controlling his incipient grin as she. "Consider what would have befallen you. He would have had to say he got it from you, and you would have been hung."

"Oh, I did consider it. I did. I did not mean to play the innocent. All I meant to say was that there are times when a small subterfuge provides benefit to all and harms none."

Bell sighed. "There are such things as the principle of honesty—"

The smile had left Magdalene's eyes. "To a whore there can be no consideration of principles at all, only first what is necessary for her, then, if possible, what is best for all."

"But you *have* principles, Magdalene. I have seen them at work—"

"Perhaps I have," she interrupted hastily, "but I am also a woman, and women—" the smile came back into her eyes and lifted the corners of her lips "—seldom allow a principle to interfere with good common sense."

At that Bell laughed aloud. "Somehow I do not believe that many men would agree that women have any common sense at all as well as not having any principles."

"Men," Magdalene said, "would not recognize common sense if it grew teeth and bit them."

Bell opened his eyes wide. "No. Certainly not in that case," he agreed too soberly.

Magdalene laughed, but shook her head. "No, but listen. Say there are documents in there from the past that would besmirch or even incriminate a man grown more cautious and honorable, a man who has been honest and upright in his dealings for many years. I do not say that the ill that man did should not be amended if it is possible. Such a thing could be addressed privately, by a priest or . . . or a bishop's clerk. All I say is that to show proof of such ill doing to the sheriff or justiciar, who would have no choice but to demand public punishment, would accomplish little except that man's ruin."

"I hear you." Bell's lips were turned down wryly. "Amended by a bishop's clerk, eh? You mean to make me drag Winchester into this? And what of those cases where real harm has been done — murder or rape or lands reft away?"

"That," Magdalene said, looking triumphant, "is why I desire that Letice lift the seals. For such cases, if there be any, we will return the documents to the packet and seal it all up again. Then it can be delivered to Master Octadenarius with the true story of its coming from Master Gerlund, who held it for Bertrild. Octadenarius can do with it what he wishes."

Bell groaned and shook his head. "I am not a very good liar," he said faintly.

"No, but I am," Magdalene responded, going to the door, lifting the latch, and pulling the latchstring into its usual position. "And I know Master Octadenarius well enough to explain how Mainard happened to give me the parcel but that you said it would be best if he had it. You need not even be there."

"Likely he will ask me about it the next time I see him and I will turn red. . . ."

Magdalene blinked and then opened her eyes in a stare of innocence. "Just say 'That Magdalene' or something like. You do look like a ripe radish when you lose your temper." Whereupon Bell promptly proved the truth of her statement by flushing. She laughed aloud, but only said, "I will get Letice now and ask if she can undo the seals."

At first, poor Letice simply stood and shook her head, making clear by sign that she had never done such a thing, but when Magdalene explained the purpose, she took the packet from Bell and examined it with minute care. Finally, she showed Magdalene that the leather on one side had been folded over all the other folds in a final closing, and because that was a short side, there was only one cord that passed over it. This had a thick wax seal over the place where it passed over another cord, but there was no knot there. If that seal and one farther up on the same cord could be loosened, the cord could be slid side-ways over the end of the packet. Perhaps then Letice could raise the seals on the edge of the closure and that one end of the leather wrapping could be unfolded. From that opening, with luck, the contents could be extracted.

Bell and Magdalene discussed it for only a couple of moments before they urged Letice to try. Letice bit her lip and looked worried. Bell patted her shoulder.

"Do not let it trouble you if you cannot open it without any sign," he said, looking relieved. "If worse comes to worst, I will simply discard the wrapping and tell Master Octadenarius that Mainard, having no idea what was within but wanting no part of anything of his wife's, asked me to look at the contents. I did, and when I saw evidence of crimes, I brought it to him."

"Good enough," Magdalene agreed and began to clear off the table where she did her accounts.

Letice went to the kitchen to find a broad-bladed knife, and Dulcie followed her back, carrying a small brazier on which to heat it. Although the task had looked far more formidable than lifting the flat seal on a document, it turned out to be easier than expected. The seals were thick blobs of wax without any delicate impression that must not be distorted. Then, instead of being attached all across a broad, flat surface, the wax only adhered to the leather in a few spots. Letice was able to slide the hot knife under the wax without even distorting the shape the seal had taken on when applied, which meant they had only to slip the cord under it and press it down again when they wished to reseal the packet. As to any marks on the leather that showed the seal had been moved, the thick blob could be spread just a little to conceal such marks without showing signs of tampering.

In a surprisingly short time, the leather wrapping was unfolded. Fortunately, it was not very tight and it was easy enough to slide the box out. All three stared at it for a long moment. Then Letice put her hands over her eyes, then over her ears, and shook her head. She did not want to know. Bell patted her again, and Magdalene gave her a brief hug. She and Dulcie removed the evidence of their crime and closed the door behind them as they left. Bell opened the box.

Twelve

24 MAY

OLD PRIORY GUESTHOUSE

The bell at the gate pealed, and Magdalene folded her lips together over an obscenity. This was one day on which she really did not want any extra clients. Ella and Letice were already occupied with men, Diot had not yet returned, and Sabina was in her own chamber giving Haesel a lesson in French. Still, she rose and went out to deal with whoever was waiting, resolved to send the man away despite the loss.

She and Bell had spent all morning poring over the contents of Bertrild's box with mingled horror and disgust. At first they thought they had nothing more than a set of accounts, for the pages of the first collection of parchments, neatly holed and tied together with silk ribbons, were filled with names and dates, followed by a second number, and amounts of money. Neither Bell nor Magdalene could think of why a set of accounts should be wrapped with such care and stored with a goldsmith, but then Magdalene recalled what Sabina had told her about Bertrild's obsession with her father's lands and mentioned it to Bell.

Both agreed if the wrapping and deposit in the care of a goldsmith was merely a mark of obsession, the parchment could be sold to a scribe to be scraped clean and the contents of the box forgotten. They almost set the sheets aside at that point, but Bell, idly leafing through them, noted that the names were almost never repeated. That would be impossible for estate accounts. The same people paid rent in kind—

usually a share of their crops—or performed a service for their landlord season after season and year after year.

That was strange enough to make Bell open the second bound-together package of parchment sheets. Here he found the reason for the care and secrecy with which the packet had been treated. The sheets did not record estate accounts but the means by which Gervase de Genlis, Bertrild's father, had lived after he had ruined his estates.

Apparently, Gervase sold his name and seal to any man who wanted a noble witness to a transaction, legitimate or not. He was paid for this service, and the first collection of records listed who paid him and the date on which he affixed his seal as witness. The odd number beside the date, Magdalene discovered, referred to the second collection of sheets, which, beginning with the number, gave a surprisingly full description of what Gervase had witnessed but did not indicate for whom nor the date.

Bell and Magdalene soon became so fascinated by what they read that they ate their dinner in Magdalene's room. Not all the records referred to cases of false witness. One whole sheet explained the jeweled necklet and why neither Gervase nor Bertrild had dared sell it. Gervase had taken it as a bribe to transmit letters from several known rebels to Robert of Gloucester, most powerful of Henry I's bastards and a key to many English barons' acceptance of Stephen as king. To encourage Robert of Gloucester to cry defiance against King Stephen—and letters from such notorious rebels as Geoffrey Talbot, Ralph Lovel, and William FitzJohn could have no other purpose—was treason. But Gervase was dead and had never left England while he was in London. Someone else had carried those letters.

The number at the end of the page sent them hurriedly to the first set of sheets they had examined. When they found it, they nodded at each other. This was the man who was a wool merchant as well as a mercer and made frequent trips to Normandy. Both reached for the second set of sheets at the same time. Magdalene was a hair quicker and ran her fingers along the lines on each sheet until she found the number.

When she named a place, Bell said, "The farm. The farm that must serve as his collection and storage place for the fleeces. The place is less than a league from the river." He took the sheet from her, read the item, and nodded. "Gervase swore that the farm was freehold and had been in the possession of FitzRevery all his life. There must have been some doubt cast on the title of the property."

"To keep her from disclosing this — his delivery of the letters and how he was forced to carry them — is reason enough for murder," Magdalene said slowly, "but can this man be Saeger also? Surely it was the man Bertrild called Saeger who killed her. Yet she must have seen FitzRevery often because she came to Mainard's shop every week to collect money. Why did she never call him Saeger?"

"Do we know she did not? I never asked Mainard. I will check on that and see if I can use the name in FitzRevery's hearing, too. When I questioned him, he said he was at the shop all day, but his journeyman looked so surprised when he agreed to FitzRevery's claim that I have my doubts it was true."

Magdalene nodded. "Nonetheless," she said, "I do not think we should forget about the rest of these documents. Others may turn out to have as good a reason as Master FitzRevery for murdering Bertrild. I wonder what these small rolls are?" She pulled them from the box and unrolled one. "Oh, here are the numbers again."

Examination disclosed that the parchment rolls recorded further dates and sums of money. Checking back soon made clear that the extra sums had been paid by those involved in rebel activity or whose documents revealed the worst dishonesty. Apparently, Gervase had collected more than his pay for false witness or silence from those men.

"God, the man was as clever as he was evil." Magdalene sighed. "Each set of sheets alone means very little. I suppose they were kept apart during Gervase's lifetime. After he died, Bertrild must have collected all the documents into one place. Do you suppose that was when she learned what her father was doing, or did she always know?" She frowned. "But if she learned right after Gervase's death or always knew, why did she only begin to ask for money about a month ago?"

"I have no idea, except that from what I have seen, most of the money came from those in Hampshire who had agreed to welcome an invasion force under Robert of Gloucester. Yet Gervase must have been part of the group. I wonder how he planned to protect himself?"

"*I* wonder if Bertrild tried to touch those outside of London and found they no longer cared?" Magdalene remarked, "And only after that began to squeeze the men in London."

"No longer cared?" Bell echoed. "Why should they—" Then he struck himself a sharp blow on the forehead. "What a fool I am. If they were on the very border of open revolt, of course they would no longer care, but that implies that Gloucester is actually . . ."

The bell at the gate pealed, and Magdalene lifted her head.

"If you want to go and attend to your women, I can go on with this myself—" Bell urged.

"No," she said, grinning at him and shaking her head; once he realized there might be political implications, he was not so willing for her to examine the contents of the packet. "If there is any trouble, Ella and Letice know where to find me. For the regular clients, they can manage by themselves."

Bell grunted irritably and they returned to an examination of the documents. The bell at the gate rang once more, but Magdalene kept her eyes on the neatly written entries. She was doing her best to commit to memory the names of the men in Hampshire from whom Gervase had extorted money so she could send a message to William.

She did not know whether the information had any value, but knowing it could do no harm—at least not to William—and three of his captains were at the house near the Tower and could send a messenger with the news. If only she could get rid of Bell for a while, Magdalene thought, she could write down the important names and copy any details that William should know from Gervase's sheets. She did not dare do it in Bell's presence as he might object, and if he objected, he could take everything away.

Her disappointment on that score was kept in check by finding an entry for another of the men who had been in Mainard's shop that Friday with which she hoped to divert Bell's mind from politics. Bell had told her that Ulfmaer FitzIsabelle claimed to have been in his place of business all Saturday and that his staff supported him—and not for love, but Gervase recorded against him a dishonesty that was serious.

FitzIsabelle had not been named by Letice's old whoremaster as someone who had genuine seals affixed to a false document because the document Gervase had witnessed for FitzIsabelle was genuine enough; it simply recorded a date and facts that were not true. What it said was that a considerable sum of money had been drawn from Gunther Granger's account in Ulfmaer's bank and delivered to that person. Since the man was dead on the date the document was actually witnessed and noted by Gervase, delivery would have been difficult. The date on the document itself was a week earlier.

"Look here," she said, holding out the sheet to Bell. And then the bell at the gate pealed once more.

For a moment she stood undecided, then folded her lips over words no lady should know, and went to answer the summons. With her mind still on whether Ulfmaer's crime was serious enough to drive him to murder, she opened the gate. She was about to slam it shut again because the man who was ringing the bell was unknown to her and dressed in the boiled-leather armor of a common man-at-arms, when he caught at it and said, "Sir Bellamy? Is the captain here? He said to send a message here if we caught the man Borc."

Magdalene pulled the gate wide again. "You have him?"

"Yes, madam."

"Oh, good."

While Magdalene had been exchanging inanities with Bell's man, she had been thanking God and Mary for their mercies. Now Bell would have to go to question Borc. All she had to do was induce him to leave the packet with her. As that problem came into her mind, another joined it. She did not think Bell would be pleased to have his man find him in her bedchamber. Another piece of good fortune. Likely she could get him out of her room in such a hurry that he would leave everything behind.

"I do not know whether Sir Bellamy brought his horse," she said to the man-at-arms. "Would you take a look in the stable and bring the animal out if it is there? If not, just come in. The door is open."

She then hurried into the house and virtually pulled Bell out of her room, saying, "Hurry into the common room. I sent your man to the stable to look for the horse that isn't there. They've caught Borc."

"Everything always happens at once," he complained, but jumped to his feet when he heard the door slam shut and hurried out without stopping to collect any of Bertrild's parchments.

Magdalene stood for a moment looking at the documents on her table, but not seeing them. Bell's haste confirmed her guess that he did not want to be found in her bedchamber. She suppressed a sigh, wondering whether she should give up any hope of teaching him acceptance. How could they even lie together if he was ashamed of it? But before the question really made sense to her, it was pushed aside by the memory of the slam of the door. The man-at-arms would not have slammed the door that way! She hurried out on Bell's heels to confront any client who had intruded in so crude a manner.

It was Diot who had rushed in, however, tousled and dirty-looking. She said nothing, merely waved and hurried toward her own room to wash and change her clothes. The door of the room beyond opened a crack and Haesel peered out, Sabina's keen ears having caught the noise. Doors seldom slammed in the Old Priory Guesthouse. When one did, it might mean danger of some sort. Magdalene smiled to relieve any anxiety and gestured for Haesel to come out; Sabina came, too, clutching her staff just in case the smile was false.

Magdalene went to open the door again, just in time as the man-at-arms was coming along the path. When he entered, Bell was talking to Sabina, who was standing with Haesel near the hearth; they provided a very innocent-looking group. Bell raised a hand to his man and started to turn away, but he hesitated, and Magdalene, fearing he guessed that she wanted to glean information for William, promptly offered to put the materials from Bertrild's box away and not look at them until he returned, if that was what Bell would prefer.

He shook his head at her, his eyes thoughtful. Then, as if he had read her mind, instead of responding to her words, he said, "About the reason for her having the necklet, I had thought I would speak to the bishop first, but now I think that is something of which he would rather stay ignorant." He turned toward the man-at-arms, saying, "Go ahead, I will be with you at once," and then looked back at Magdalene. "As for our guess about why she was raising money here in London rather than in Hampshire, I will warn Winchester but perhaps it is important for Lord William to know also."

Magdalene nodded at him, smiling warmly. Perhaps she should not despair so easily about teaching him acceptance. Usually he tried to pretend that William didn't exist. Was his remark only because he knew William would be involved in pushing back and defeating any invasion, or was it a sign that he recognized he must share her attention and loyalty with her patron? And, as for being ashamed of being caught in her bedchamber—she swallowed a giggle—she had noticed that Bell was a little shy of any mention of the union between man and woman. A Church schooling, perhaps? Mayhap he would be just as eager to avoid being caught in his own wife's bedchamber.

"No, do not put the parchments away," he continued, the faint frown of thought still wrinkling his forehead. "Find out whatever you can, especially about the five who could have taken Codi's knife. With what Borc can tell us, we might have evidence enough for an arrest."

"God willing," Magdalene said with virtuous solemnity, grateful that he had not read her last thoughts.

<hr />

24 MAY

SOUTHWARK, TOM WATCHMAN'S LODGING

Bell instinctively turned left toward the bridge to London when he came out of the gate of the Old Priory Guesthouse, but his man caught his arm and directed him to the right.

"That whore," he said, "she saved us a lot 'v trouble. Tom said she went right up t' that Borc and said she knew him. She begged part 'v his meal from him, as if she was hungry, and then asked if he'd like a little private treatment—any special kind he liked. Whispered in his ear, Tom said, so he couldn't hear what she said, but it must 'v been good, 'cause Borc stopped eatin' for a minute. When he was finished, she whispered again, and he got up 'n went with her. We was wondering how to grab him without starting a riot, but she must 'v told him she had a place, 'cause he went with her easy as easy."

"So where did she take him?"

"Tom Watchman's lodging." The man-at-arms laughed. "She's one clever bitch, that one. Must 'v asked Tom where he lived or got him to show it to her before they came. Never did a thing to start Borc worrying—no looking around like she wasn't sure. And it's just the kind of place a good whore might keep."

It was, indeed, just the kind of place that a whore who did a brisk business away from the stews might keep. Down a dark, slimy, but not unbreathably fetid alley, they came to a door still sound enough to retain a latch and open on its hinges but already showing signs of rot. The rail was gone from the stair, if there ever had been one, and the stairs groaned and creaked but did not tremble. The odor inside the building was only faintly redolent of urine; mostly it smelled of turnips and cabbage.

Bell's man led the way up that flight of stairs to a landing that gave evidence in the sounds coming from behind a thin door that at least one whore did find the place convenient. Another flight—more ladder than stair this time—rose to a second landing, lit dimly by openings under the eaves of the roof. Two doors at right angles opened off the small platform. The man-at-arms, leaning past Bell, opened the door to the right.

The room was so small it was overcrowded by the three men, one sitting groggily on a stool, the other two standing over him, but it was not unpleasant. On the top floor, it rose above the adjoining building, and the small window looked out over other grimy roofs to the sky. The bed was right under the window, which provided a pleasant breeze in the spring weather, and being no more than a pallet on a wooden frame with leather straps, it could be easily moved to a warmer corner in winter or if it rained. The room would have smelled better than the rest of the building too, if not for the stench that wafted from Borc.

His face was so ingrained with dirt that the wrinkles which showed around his sparse but unkempt beard were like black lines on lighter gray earth. The beard hair was clotted with dried spittle and bits of God-alone-knew-what. His hair, a greasy mat, plastered to his head, had a few tangled cords hanging by his ears and down his back. His tunic was so clotted with old spilled food and less identifiable layers of filth that its original color was unrecognizable. Nonetheless, the tunic was no rag; it was of good, sound cloth as were the equally filthy chausses that showed beneath it.

Bell eyed a splotch, which was a familiar dull-rust brown, on one side of the tunic near the only tear in the garment. That was old blood.

He wondered whether Borc had killed the man who originally wore the tunic, but the slack face and limp posture raised doubts as to whether Borc was capable. It was something Bell needed to find out.

Having examined the unappetizing specimen, Bell raised his eyes to the two men guarding him. "I wanted him able to speak," he said. "Why did you hit him so hard?"

"Didn' 'it 'im atall," Tom said indignantly. "Didn' need 't. Diot brought 'im up smooth as silk. We ony came in later to keep 'im from grabbin' 'er."

"True, Sir Bellamy," the man-at-arms said. "He was like this when he came into the cookshop." Then he grinned. "He can talk, though. Been complaining about the whore getting away and telling us we'll be in deep trouble when his mistress hears that we're holding him."

Bell nodded. "Borc," he said fairly loudly, and stepped forward and slapped the man's face—not hard, just enough to get his attention. "Your mistress is dead. There is no one to protect you, so you had better answer my questions or I will have you hung for extorting money from respectable tradesmen."

"Dead?" Borc lifted his head, his bleary eyes clearing a little. "Don' believe you. Cookshop fed me. She must've paid."

"Likely she paid on Saturday when she took her money from Master Mainard. Likely the cookshop owner doesn't yet know. I am Sir Bellamy of Itchen, the bishop of Winchester's knight, and I am looking into Mistress Bertrild's murder—"

"Murder!" Borc exclaimed, and burst out laughing. "So the saddler finally had enough of her. I warned her when he took the whore into his house that her time was short."

"I am sorry to disappoint you," Bell said, not sounding at all sorry, "but Master Mainard did not kill his wife. We have substantial witnesses to prove that he was at a christening party in the West Chepe."

Borc laughed again. "Witnesses," he repeated scornfully. "All liars. They all hated her. They all liked him. They'd have said he was in France, even if they'd stood right by him while he bashed in her head."

"Perhaps." Bell smiled unpleasantly. "But they are all honest tradesmen, known and respected in the city, which I doubt can be said for you. If they stand and say that Master Mainard could not have committed the crime, they will be believed. Will you? Why, if that tunic you are wearing could speak, I am quite sure that it would testify against you and say you were no stranger to murder."

"No!" Borc shrieked, half rising from the stool. "You can't hang me to save him! I didn't do it! I didn't!"

He was forced back down onto the stool, but he shook his head violently, struggling against the hands that held him. Now fear showed in the sudden tightening of the slack muscles of his face, and he began to weep, the tears making lighter tracks in the dirt. He was well aware of how often a common man, specially an outcast of society like him, was punished for a crime committed by a man or woman with higher status.

"I didn't kill her," he wailed, beginning to shake. "I didn't. Why would I? She paid for my food. She gave me money for carrying messages. Why would I kill her?"

"If you didn't wish to kill Mistress Bertrild, you are probably the only person who knew her in England who did not," Bell said sourly. "Where were you on Saturday between Nones and Vespers? Who can stand witness that what you say is true?"

The questions were a challenge meant to impress upon Borc how helpless he was. Bell expected no answer, but Borc suddenly went still.

"Saturday . . . Saturday . . ." The man's eyes shifted from side to side and then widened. "Saturday!" he exclaimed and then laughed weakly. "Yes, I can tell you where I was on Saturday. That was the day the men were supposed to bring whatever Bertrild demanded from them to the cookshop. See, I carried a message from her on Thursday—"

"To whom?" Bell interrupted.

Borc shook his head, refusing to meet Bell's gaze, and his lips curved in a sly, secretive half-smile. "Don't matter to who I carried the messages. Ain't them who'll stand witness for me. See, I was in the cookshop. I was in the cookshop all day on Saturday from maybe a candlemark after Prime until just after Nones. And the cook'll remember because he kept trying to get rid of me. So I do have a witness—a good, honest tradesman—who'll stand witness that I was in the cookshop in the Chepe nearly all day Saturday."

Since Bell had never suspected Borc of killing Bertrild, he was not in the least disappointed over the man having a witness of his whereabouts. He was, however, seriously annoyed by Borc's resistance to telling him the names of the men Bertrild was blackmailing. Those names, provided by even so unreliable a witness as Borc, would be the first actual piece of evidence that someone beside Mainard had a reason to kill Bertrild. The fact that she might have known of evildoing by a person, that she kept the evidence carefully, was no proof that she had ever used the information or that anyone mentioned on the parchments ever paid her or even knew she had the information. The documents were her father's, not hers, nor was there any mark on them in a different hand.

"The cook is not enough," Bell said. "You need two witnesses."

"The pie seller was there near Sext, and he'll remember because I nearly knocked over one of his trays when the cook grabbed me to throw me out. And—"

"And nothing. I want the names of the men to whom you carried messages on Thursday. I want to know how many of them and which ones came to the cookshop on Saturday."

Bell's frustration grew as he realized that if Bertrild had been killed by someone who could not or would not permit more extortion, that man would not have bothered to go to the cookshop to make a payment Saturday morning.

"Don't remember," Borc muttered. "Mistress Bertrild told me where to go and I went. She didn't tell me any names. Show me the men, and I'll say if I remember their faces."

Borc smiled when he said that, and Bell barely refrained from gritting his teeth and exposing how important the information was. Bell knew Borc understood it was safe enough to offer to identify the men if Bell brought them before him. Obviously, if he didn't know who the men were, he couldn't bring them for Borc to examine.

Instead of expressing his rage, however, Bell sighed ostentatiously and pointed out that if Borc thought he could continue the extortion, he was mistaken. No one would believe him against the word of rich merchants and, besides, the men were dangerous.

"If you didn't kill Bertrild, don't you realize it must have been one of them? Yes, you're a witness with important information. I'll stick you in protective custody until the sheriff's men can beat a sworn statement out of you."

He gestured to his man-at-arms, who jerked Borc to his feet. Tom Watchman stepped back, and the man-at-arms who had come to fetch Bell and had followed him up the stairs stepped around him and grasped Borc's other arm.

"Wait," the man whined. "Wait. Don't be so stinkin' mean. Let me go around one more time. They can all afford a few pennies more. Then I'll tell you, I swear I will."

"Hmmm," Bell said, as if he was considering what Borc said. "Show me some good faith. Tell me something else. You came to London with Bertrild's father, Gervase de Genlis, didn't you? So you knew most of Gervase's friends and tenants?"

"Well, most of the tenants. Can't say I knew his friends. I may have seen them, but—" he snickered "—Lord Gervase wouldn't want them to know how close we were."

"Did you know a man called Saeger?"

Bell was looking Borc straight in the face when he said the name, but then let his glance wander so Borc should not attach too much importance to the question. Before he looked away, he saw a frown of thought and honest puzzlement; there was no sly shifting of the eyes or twisting of the lips. Bell judged that Borc was willing to please by answering questions about life in Hampshire in the hope that his cooperation would mitigate his treatment at the hands of whoever would imprison him.

"Saeger," he repeated. "You know, it does sound like I heard that name somewhere, but it just don't come to mind. But I'll tell you this. If I get knocked around, it's sure to get rattled right out of my skull."

"That depends on how hard they hit you," Bell said. "If it's hard enough, I think the name might get hammered right in so you don't forget again. How about Perekin FitzRevery?"

"Him I do know," Borc answered, promptly and easily, his gaze suddenly steady.

Bell almost laughed at Borc's expression. That in itself was a banner waving in warning. In addition, Bell detected a flicker of the eye-

lids, a tightening of the corners of the mouth that betrayed the
intention of keeping some secret.

Still Bell asked with interest, "What do you know about Fitz-
Revery?"

"Had a farm on the west side of the Itchen. Ah . . . let me think. . . .
Hamble, that's what it's called. Nice farm. In the family for years."
Suddenly Borc's mouth twitched, as if he realized Bell was not convinced of his truthfulness. He looked down, and tears began to leak
from his eyes again. "Good years when we were out there," he muttered. "Good years. But I was hot to come to London when Lord
Gervase decided to leave Moorgreen. I thought I would find wonders
in London. Wonders. Look at me now."

"No, thank you!" Bell said. "It is no pleasure." And then to the
men-at-arms. "Put a rope around his neck before you take him down
the stairs. If he wants to jump and hang himself, that can be as he
wills, but don't let him get away. I will meet you at the justiciar's house
on Gracechurch Street just south of the Cornhill road. Take him inside the gate, but not into the house. I do not believe that Master
Octadenarius wants his house fumigated."

Bell thought of going back to the bishop's house to get his palfrey,
but decided the time he would save on the less-crowded streets would
be offset by the time lost getting across the bridge and through the
Chepe on horseback. He went down the stairs, ignoring Borc's cries
that he was now prepared to tell him anything if he would let him go
afterward. Bell was sure Borc had managed to think up a half dozen
names, possibly even names Bertrild had mentioned, but not those
from whom he had collected money. He would talk just as freely or
more freely after a few days in prison.

As ever, when he reached the bridge, Bell's gaze passed down the
street to where he could just make out the wall of the Old Priory
Guesthouse. His lips twitched as he recalled Magdalene's hurry to get
him out of her bedchamber. He had been grateful at the time for her
thoughtful protection of his reputation. Second thought had exposed
her clever device and associated that rush with the documents he had
left strewn on her table.

His lips twisted again but with understanding, not amusement.

Her eagerness to keep the documents was not for her own sake or even
Sabina's. Magdalene was a good friend. No "out of sight, out of mind"
for her. Despite the fact that William of Ypres would never have known
of Gervase de Genlis's records, she would glean whatever might be
useful to Ypres from them—just as she had made sure Ypres would
know when and where the papal messenger's pouch would be discovered. She was fiercely loyal, yet she was not Lord William's woman.
She could and sometimes did take other men into her bed.

She said the one thing had nothing to do with the other, that her
body was like a roll of cloth that she cut a length from and sold. The
severed length had no effect on the quality of the remainder of the
cloth on the roll, and until the roll was all used up or her body worn
out, each piece of cloth that she sold was as good as any other and as
worth the price. Her loyalty was an entirely different matter.

Bell turned his back on the Old Priory Guesthouse and started
across the bridge. Lord William, he knew, had done Magdalene many
favors and always supported her against any attack from the Church
or the Law. He remembered how Master Octadenarius had said he
did not press Magdalene for information she did not wish to give lest
he receive a visit from William of Ypres. And yet—Bell almost bumped
into a counter thrust a little too far into the walkway; he stopped and
remonstrated with the merchant and the counter was withdrawn a few
inches. And yet—his thought continued exactly where it had left off—
she had offered to put the parchments away and not look at them if
that was what he wanted. A warm glow suffused him. She had put his
desires ahead of William of Ypres's interests.

The glow lasted just long enough for him to enjoy it; then common sense removed it. Magdalene had put his desire ahead of Ypres's
interests for a few insignificant hours. As soon as they looked at the
records again, she would have learned everything anyway and would
send the information off to Ypres. Bell was surprised at how little an-
imosity he felt about that thought, but he grinned as he lengthened
his stride. Putting jealousy aside, passing such information to Ypres
was a practical necessity, and he himself would have seen that word
got to Lord William if Magdalene had not.

Robert of Gloucester had abjured his oath of fealty to King Stephen the previous autumn. If the fact that the men in Hampshire

would not pay for Bertrild's silence did mean that Robert of Gloucester was planning to invade, William of Ypres would certainly be involved in the defense of the country. The sooner he knew of the possibility of Gloucester coming to England, the better his defense could be.

As he executed a neat twist to avoid a man with a tray of ribbons and a woman with pails of oysters hanging from a yoke over her shoulders and got off the bridge, Bell's brow furrowed. Perhaps it would have been better if the news about the possibility of Gloucester's imminent arrival came through his own master, the bishop of Winchester? He and Ypres had had their differences from time to time, but now they were drawing together, both worried about the influence of Waleran de Meulan on the king.

The frown cleared. No, it was better this way. He and Magdalene could do it by both roads. He would send a messenger to Winchester tomorrow. The bishop, although he still had not forgiven his brother for denying him the position of archbishop of Canterbury, would still send the warning on to King Stephen. From there, it might or might not actually get to William of Ypres, depending on Stephen's mood and Meulan's advice, but since Ypres would already have had Magdalene's warning, he would doubtless inform the king himself. Perhaps the double alarm might stir Stephen to action.

When Bell looked around, he was coming out into the western end of the market and the sun was casting long shadows to warn of oncoming evening. He looked from John Herlyond's place of business to that of Ulfmaer FitzIsabelle. The goldsmith had stolen a dead man's money, Bell mused as he walked along. Octadenarius would have to know about that in case there were heirs who had been defrauded. What Herlyond had done, he did not yet know. He could guess that FitzRevery's crime had to do with the farm at Hamble. Borc's quick, smooth comment that it had been in FitzRevery's family for years — by the reverse logic that must be applied to anything Borc said — implied that a problem lay there.

Recalling Borc made Bell quicken his pace as he came onto Gracechurch Street again. There were still shops, but the press of people was less, and in a short time he was pulling the bell at Octadenarius's door. He was shown in immediately, directly into the justiciar's private closet this time.

"You are early today," the justiciar said, putting aside a roll of parchment he had been examining.

"We have laid hands upon the man Borc, who collected the money Bertrild extorted."

"I hope the sheriff is not going to complain to me about a riot in the market."

"No, my lord Justiciar." Bell smiled. "As ever the whores of the Old Priory Guesthouse have been most helpful. One of them, a woman called Diot, knew Borc—as I told you yesterday—from a stew where she worked in the past. She induced him to give her part of his meal and offered to pay for it in the usual way. Then she led him to the lodging of Tom Watchman, and my men seized him quietly. They are bringing him along and should be here soon."

"Bringing him here? Do you suspect him of being this Saeger and murdering his mistress—perhaps for the money he had taken and did not want to share with her?" Octadenarius sounded hopeful.

Bell knew it would be convenient if the murder could be fixed onto so worthless a character. He shook his head regretfully. "Unfortunately you know he could not have got into the house by either the front or back doors. The grocer's wife was watching the front and could never have missed such a creature as Borc entering, and the merchants with booths at the mouth of the alley would never have let him pass. Beyond that, he can prove where he was all day on Saturday. In fact, he was in the cookshop where Bertrild's victims delivered their sacrifice, watching to make sure they came. Some of them may have noticed him too."

Octadenarius snorted with displeasure. "Then why bring him here where I will have to take note of his capture? Could you not squeeze the information you wanted out of him wherever you were?"

"Oh, I am sure lots of things would have poured out if I squeezed him, but little or nothing of it would have been true, and I really have no way to prove or disprove his accusations. If we play him right, however, his actions should tell us what we need to know."

"If we play him right." Octadenarius sighed, but under his heavy brows, his eyes twinkled, belying the mournful expression. "Why can I foresee my role in this will be busy and costly? If you had more strength of character and had resisted the importunities of Mistress

Magdalene, I would have accused and hung the journeyman and not had all this trouble."

"You would have been sorry for hanging Codi," Bell responded, laughing. "He is really a most estimable young man and will be a fine saddlemaker some day. Would you really wish to exchange him for a man who not only knifed a woman but plotted to lay the blame on an innocent?"

Octadenarius sighed again. "I suppose not, although such a woman as Mistress Bertrild . . . well?"

"I would like you to put Borc in the Tun for a night or two and let them squeeze him there—but not too hard. I want him reasonably lively when you let him go. When he believes he has convinced them that he has told them everything, he may be released—with several of your men on his tail. They are to watch him close. Sooner or later he will go into a number of respectable shops, shops where he could not possibly afford to buy and that would not employ so ragged and disgusting a person. Let your men make note of whose shops he tries and, if they can come close enough without being marked, what he said and whether he was given anything."

This time Octadenarius's face showed approval. "Very good. Bringing the creature as a witness might not convince a jury of a decent man's peers, but the testimony of my men as to what they saw will be more effective. Did you learn anything about the messenger, this Saeger?"

"That was a question I think Borc answered honestly. He said he did not know, but admitted the name was familiar to him. That is possible, if Saeger was a servant of Bertrild's uncle, Sir Druerie, rather than of Gervase de Genlis, whom Borc served, or was Genlis's tenant or friend. But we should soon have an answer to whether the messenger was truly from Sir Druerie or not. Master Mainard sent a letter to Sir Druerie with a man of Perekin FitzRevery's. FitzRevery has a farm at Hamble, west of the Itchen River, not far from Swythling."

"Yes, I suppose the uncle had to be appraised of Mistress Bertrild's death."

"And it gave Mainard the opportunity to say to Sir Druerie that he had not been at home when his messenger came, and Bertrild had been killed before he saw her again. Thus, he had no idea whether

Sir Druerie's message required some action or information from him. Even if Sir Druerie only answers that the message was irrelevant to Mainard, which he might do if the messenger was a paid assassin — but I cannot believe that. I knew Sir Druerie when I lived at Itchen and he had the reputation of a good man. Well, whatever he answers will tell us whether he actually sent the messenger."

Master Octadenarius rubbed his chin reflectively. "And if he did?"

"Then I will ride out to Swythling and take Saeger for questioning. I suppose you can give me a letter for the sheriff. We have evidence enough for that."

The justiciar nodded. "When will you need this letter?"

"Likely on Saturday or Sunday. FitzRevery's messenger left on Monday and would deliver the letter to Sir Druerie first because Swythling is on his way to Hamble. That means Sir Druerie would probably have the letter on Wednesday. I will be busy with the bishop's affairs all day on Thursday, but we will likely not hear from Sir Druerie until Friday or Saturday. I can leave as soon as I know his answer."

"You will have to remind me as soon as Sir Druerie replies. Depending on what he says, I will know better what to write to the sheriff." Octadenarius lifted a bell from the end of his table and rang it lustily. The door opened at once, as if the servant had been waiting right outside it. "Have Sir Bellamy's men arrived with their prisoner yet?" the justiciar asked.

"Yes, my lord."

"Call out four men from the guardhouse and bid them take the prisoner to the Tun, and send in my clerk."

As the servant closed the door, Bell remembered something he had not told the justiciar. "Mistress Bertrild was getting a round sum from her victims," he said. "I told you that Master Mainard found a bundle of tally sticks hidden in her clothes chest. When Mainard brought them to Johannes Gerlund, the goldsmith who had issued them, he discovered that Bertrild had ten pounds in keeping with Gerlund."

"Ten pounds!" Octadenarius exclaimed. "No wonder — " He broke off as the clerk came in. "There is a prisoner being taken to the Tun," he said to the man. "Write an order for the Warder there. The prisoner's name is Borc. He is to be questioned about men from whom he extorted money on the orders of a Mistress Bertrild, wife of Master Mainard the saddler. She was stabbed to death on last Saturday. Note that Borc himself is not suspected of the murder and should not be damaged too severely. We believe one of the men from whom the money was extorted killed the woman, and we need their names."

The clerk sat down at the end of the table, pulled a sheet of parchment and an inkpot and quill toward him, and began to write. Doubtless orders to the Warder of the Tun were familiar to him.

"So she had collected ten pounds," Octadenarius said, going back to the subject the clerk had interrupted. "That is a round sum. Do you know for what she wanted the money?"

"I am not sure, of course, but she tried to get Master Mainard to buy back the mortgages on her father's property of Moorgreen. He would not do it. He said he had not enough money and, more important, that he had never held land and would not know how to restore the property."

"Wise man."

"I suspect Bertrild cared nothing for restoring the land. She wanted to be the lady of the manor and expected Mainard to remain in London so that the proceeds of the saddlery would support the house and servants in Moorgreen." Bell shook his head. He was a landowner's son and knew the costs of keeping up such a property.

The clerk finished his writing, sanded the parchment, and passed it to Master Octadenarius, who perused it briefly and handed it back. "Send it." The clerk went out and he looked back at Bell. "Is there anything else?"

"Only that I questioned the five members of Master Mainard's Bridge Guild—those that his wife had harrassed two years ago—mostly because they came to Bertrild's funeral but looked most uneasy. None has any witnesses, except the members of his own household, as to where he was on Saturday between Nones and Vespers."

The justiciar shrugged. "That is not surprising. For now, let it go. If Borc marks any of them as having paid extortion to Bertrild, I will look into their whereabouts more carefully. As for Borc, I will see that he is released just before Nones on Friday, my men having had a good look at him from hiding while he is being questioned. I will send one of the men to let you know where he went and what he did at about Vespers, or later if he is still abroad."

"Thank you, my lord Justiciar. Send the man to the bishop of Winchester's house by the front gate of the priory of St. Mary Overy."

"Not to the Old Priory Guesthouse?" Octadenarius asked, laughing.

Bell laughed too. "It might be too tempting for him," he said. "And their prices, which I cannot afford, would surely put your man in debt."

Thirteen

Bell had been amused rather than infuriated when Master Octadenarius teased him *because* he was going to the Old Priory Guesthouse as soon as he left the justiciar. Had he known that he would have to fight temptation as he passed Magdalene's gate, he would not have found Octadenarius's jest quite so amusing. When this fact made itself clear to him as he walked down Gracechurch Street toward the bridge, his amusement faded somewhat. After he completed the bishop's commands and seen Bertrild's killer taken, he had better go back to Winchester and remain there, away from temptation.

He forgot the resolution as soon as Magdalene came to open the gate for him, her face alive with delight. "Oh, I am glad you are come. Never have clients been so tedious. All I wanted was to see them in the proper beds and get back to those records, but for some reason or another every one of them had something he *must* tell me." She stepped back and gestured him in. "You look tired and dusty. Do come in. At least now all our guests are safely away, the evening meal is on the table, and we can talk in peace."

"Look, it is Bell," Ella cried as they entered, sliding out from the bench on which she was sitting. "This is the second time you have been here today. Surely not for business again. I have no one for tonight. I could—"

"Thank you, Ella," Bell said, turning her around and giving her a little push back toward her seat. "I thank you for your offer, but I am a poor man. I could not afford your price, my pet."

"But surely—" She began to turn toward him.

"No, Ella," Magdalene said. "You know you must not offer to reduce the price or to go with a man you fancy or pity for nothing. If you did that, all the guests would soon want the same, and we would not have money to pay the rent on this house or to put food on the table."

"But he is *such* a pretty man," Ella said, pouting as she sat down again. "And I am sure—" her glance slid down from Bell's face to his crotch, all but exposed by his thigh-length tunic, "—that he is more than sufficiently endowed below to make me very happy."

Magdalene was choking on laughter at the appalled astonishment on Bell's face and the brilliant color his ears had turned, and it was Diot who interrupted Ella, by saying, "Love, it is not very polite to discuss a man's parts right in front of his face."

"Oh, yes, I forgot. But it is very confusing because Bell isn't a friend and yet he is here so often and mostly Magdalene talks to him as if he were one of us but she once said he was not family. If he is not family and not a friend, then . . . then I am not sure what rules apply to him."

"Well, he is a man, love—" Magdalene began.

"I can see *that*," Ella said, giggling faintly and glancing again at the hem of Bell's tunic.

"I think you had better sit down, Bell," Magdalene said in a strangled voice. Then she cleared her throat and went on, "Here on the corner near me. I have a good deal to say to you. Sabina, love, move down a little. And what I meant, Ella, was that men are more sensitive and delicate than women, so you must not talk about—" she coughed and cleared her throat again "—about their privates or how hairy they are or any such thing, even if they are not friends. We do not want to hurt *anyone's* feelings you know."

Ella sighed heavily. "Very well, Magdalene, I will try to remember, but it does seem silly. I don't mind if anyone talks about my privates or my breasts or . . . or anything."

"I know, love, I know. You are so sweet-natured that you never take offense, but not everyone is like you."

Fortunately Haesel had peeped out of the kitchen when she heard a man's voice because she knew Sabina would want to withdraw to avoid solicitation. When she saw Bell and heard Magdalene tell him to sit down, she got across to Dulcie that someone else needed a trencher and a cup, and Dulcie brought out a large round of stale bread, a bowl of pottage, and a cup large enough for ale. Her arrival distracted Ella, who went to the shelves that lined the walls at the back of the room and brought a spoon, which she laid next to the bowl Dulcie had deposited in front of Bell. Letice reached for the flagon of ale, leaned across the table, and filled his cup.

"I am very sorry," Ella said meekly as she laid down the spoon. "I did not mean to offend you. I only meant that you are pleasing to me, desirable. . . ."

"That's all right, love," Bell said, patting her hand.

She understood no more than a child of five, if she understood that much, but he hastily plunged the spoon she had brought into the soup and took a mouthful. Comforting Ella had its dangers; she was very likely to forget why she had needed comfort and begin all over again.

"I am behind in my eating and must catch up," he mumbled around the food, and Ella nodded and went back to her seat to pick bite-sized pieces of cheese and cold meat off her trencher.

The moment she was busy, Bell said to Magdalene, much more clearly, "Well? Were any others than Ulfmaer mentioned?"

"All of them!" Magdalene replied in an exasperated voice. "All five. But I do not think that Jokel de Josne or John Herlyond would have 'removed' her to prevent disclosure of their secrets. As Letice told me, Josne deals in stolen goods. Genlis 'witnessed' half a dozen bills of sale for him, but from the kind of goods, I think they must have been stolen from foreign merchants, who likely are long gone from London. And Josne's reputation is not lily white anyway, so I do not see how her evidence could have done him much harm. I am not even sure why Josne paid her, unless she asked very little—or unless there was something more serious that might have been uncovered even though Bertrild did not know it."

"That should go to Octadenarius," Bell said, taking a swallow of ale to wash down bites of meat and cheese. "Goden mentioned Josne. He may, indeed, have more to hide."

Magdalene nodded agreement and then said, "Herlyond is just the opposite. He is a typical case of what we were talking about, a man who I believe has redeemed himself. He was a runaway journeyman from Southampton. Way back in 1125 Gervase 'witnessed' for Herlyond a letter of release and a recommendation from a Master Mercer who was actually recently dead. That mercer was not Herlyond's master. His own master had refused to propose him for mastership in the guild and would not release him to find someone who would."

"So he came to London, found a master, made good, and has been working here for nearly twenty years. Yet it was he who admitted he rode a horse out of London on Saturday and almost fainted when I told him Bertrild had died between Nones and Vespers."

Magdalene shrugged. "He has some guilty knowledge, that is sure; however, there is nothing more about him, and I suppose that Genlis would have squeezed him or added to the record. . . . Well, he would have if he recognized him. Genlis was such a sot that he might not have remembered his own mother's face."

"I will ask around among the mercers and speak to the guildmaster. If Herlyond has a good reputation, I would agree with you that he should not be exposed—except for one thing." Bell paused to break off a piece of his trencher and soak it in the pottage, scooping out some vegetables with it. "He comes from the same area." He popped the bread in his mouth and added, rather indistinctly, "If he were Saeger—"

"No, he is not," Magdalene assured him. "In fact, I know a great deal about Saeger. He came from a tiny village near Swythling, not from Southampton. There are two wills in which Saeger is mentioned, one obviously false, and a indictment in absentia against him for poisoning his wife and possibly her father, too."

Bell swallowed hard to down another piece of bread and then let out a long, low whistle. "That's worth killing over, since exposure would mean hanging in any case."

"I will show you those documents. I have put aside for you to look over at once everything relating to the five who could have got Codi's knife. Perhaps you can find something in them that will hint at which man was Saeger, or knew Saeger and could have given him the knife."

"Given him the knife," Bell echoed and then scowled. "Good God, I never thought of that. There is nothing to say where the man who arrived at the Lime Street house actually came from. In fact, I think Hamo told me the horse did not look as if it had traveled far. What if Saeger went first to one of the five and was given Codi's knife—" he nodded "—that might have been why he ... ah ..." he glanced at Ella across the table "sent Bertrild away with his belt knife instead of Codi's. It would not have been so important to him."

"There is another possibility," Magdalene said hesitantly, "that ... oh, you will not like this at all." She sighed. "It came to me that *Bertrild* could have taken Codi's knife."

Bell stared at her, his mouth open, his spoon halfway from his bowl. He put the spoon back in the bowl. "But then any man in England could have been the one who ... did it. No, no one mentioned her as being in the workroom on Friday."

"No one would think to do so. She was in there often, and certainly would not take the knife to ... to hurt herself, and that's what we were both asking about. Who could have taken the knife to ... ah ... hurt her."

"Knives are dangerous," Ella said. "I will never touch one. My mother taught me that."

Sabina and Diot, who had been following the conversation between Bell and Magdalene with great interest, both took deep breaths to answer Ella when the bell at the gate pealed. Letice rose, nodding to those around the table and pointing to the back door to indicate she would bring her client in that way. Haesel came to lead Sabina to the back room, but she shook her head.

"I will sit by the fire and sing to Ella," she said. "Diot's guest is one of Lord William's men and was never my client, so he will not care if he sees me."

"Thank you, Sabina," Magdalene said with heartfelt gratitude and smiled as Ella jumped to her feet and went to her stool near the hearth. She loved Sabina's singing.

Stepping so carefully around the words "kill" and "murder" lest they spark anxiety in Ella was a nuisance. Beside that, Magdalene felt it would be better to stay in the common room with Bell. She could use the excuse that the table was larger and better for spreading out the documents, but the truth was that she found her eyes and thoughts straying too often to the bed when she was in her room with him.

"Finish your meal," she said, keeping her voice low as Sabina tuned her lute. "I will bring the documents in here. Both Letice's man and Diot's will be staying all night, so they will not trouble us." She lowered her voice even further. "But it cannot be *any* man in England who killed Bertrild. We know who did that. It was the man called Saeger."

She rose from the bench and went to her room, coming back with a box, which now held the two tied sets of parchments, the small parchment rolls, and the two flat-folded sheets of parchment. Having set down the box, she pushed aside the remains of her meal, removed the flat-folded sheets, and opened and spread them at her place, angled so Bell could see them and continue eating.

In the background Sabina's voice could be heard softly singing a happy, lilting melody. After a little while, the bell rang at the gate, and Diot rose to answer it. Magdalene also got up when Diot and Sir Giles came in and walked down the corridor with them, talking softly to Sir Giles and then making a brief detour into her room to get the letter she had written to William. Bell glanced up; his lips tightened, but he went on eating steadily and, aside from that single look, kept his attention on the documents he was reading.

When Magdalene seated herself at the table again, he made no comment on what she had done but said, "You are right. The information about Saeger could hang him. But I find it hard to believe Saeger could be the messenger sent by Sir Druerie." He shook his head. "Sir Druerie was not at all like his brother and would never consider harboring a murderer—unless he believed the charges to be false. . . ."

Bell had cleaned his bowl and finished the cheese and meat he had taken. He shoved the remains away, and reached for the other documents. Magdalene pointed out the relevant places, and Bell read them.

"Lintun Mercer. Yes. And I even know about the case. Mainard's friend Newelyne told me about it. So, the agreement that gave Dockett's whole business to Mercer *was* a false document, witnessed by Genlis, and with a seal lifted from the real agreement, which divided the business just as the son claimed. Genlis said Mercer destroyed Dockett's will also. That would have cost Mercer a heavy fine and much good will from Dockett's customers. I can see why he would have been willing to pay for Bertrild's silence, but what he did was not a hanging matter."

"I did not think it reason enough to kill her," Magdalene agreed.

"Ah," he said with satisfaction when he had found Perekin Fitz-Revery's name. "I knew there was something rotten about that farm at Hamble. Borc was so sure and easy about the FitzReverys owning it for years. So the local priest claimed that FitzRevery's father had made over the farm to him on his deathbed. FitzRevery swore that his father would never have done such a thing, refused to yield the farm, and carried the case to the sheriff. Eventually, FitzRevery claimed to have found the deed and produced it—but that must have been the one that Letice transferred a seal to. And Genlis knew about that and did get FitzRevery to carry letters to Normandy for him. He does not say here from whom, but I would not be surprised if we combed through these rolls of parchment that we would find the letters were from Talbot, Lovel, and FitzJohn."

Reminded by Borc's name where Bell had rushed off to earlier that afternoon, Magdalene was about to ask what else he had learned from the man, but she was distracted by a more urgent idea. "If the letters were from those men, carrying them was treason, and exposure would mean drawing and quartering. That is no pleasant way to die. And FitzRevery could have known Saeger, coming from the same area." Magdalene shrugged. "He would even have the additional temptation of relieving his good friend and neighbor of a personal devil. Moreover, if Bertrild stole the knife, FitzRevery may be excused from trying to get his friend in trouble."

Bell snorted gently. "Not from dropping—or helping Saeger drop—the body in Mainard's yard. But that would have been stupid, bringing the body closer to him. . . . No, what if Saeger brought it because he knew he had been seen with Bertrild in the Lime Street house and wanted the death to seem to have taken place elsewhere? In desperation, FitzRevery could have dumped the body next door.

He would be very familiar with the alley and probably with Mainard's habit of not locking his back gate. Yes. FitzRevery is a definite possibility. As you said, he could not *be* Saeger—not if his father owned Hamble before him, but he could have employed Saeger."

"To commit murder? Is that not jumping from the cooking pot onto the coals?"

"Maybe not." Bell pursed his lips thoughtfully. "If FitzRevery knew of Saeger's indictment, he would know Saeger could not afford to present a complaint against him. Their evils would cancel each other, I think. And FitzRevery's journeyman looked very surprised when FitzRevery said he had been at the shop all day Saturday."

"So what do we have? FitzRevery, but I cannot for the life of me see how we could prove anything, even that he hired Saeger."

"We must lay hands on Saeger first. Borc said he did not remember him—and I think that was true—but a little jostling and perhaps a mention of the wife-poisoning might jolt Borc's memory. What a shame I cannot attend to that tomorrow, but I have the bishop's business to do."

"Borc? I forgot all about him again. So he told you that Fitz-Revery's family owned that farm. What else did you learn?"

"Nothing. He would not name the men from whom he collected money, and to tell the truth I did not press him. If we added torture to what the man already is, no one would believe a word he said. What I did was leave him in the Tun. He will be released on Friday afternoon, and Octadenarius's men, whom he does not know, will follow him. Do you wish to lay odds against me that he will go directly to those who paid Bertrild and try to collect something for himself?"

Magdalene chuckled. "You must know I am too clever to wager against a sure thing. Yes, you will then know who he squeezed for Bertrild." She was silent for a moment, then sighed. "I am certain FitzRevery will be among them, but I wish it were not so. He is a nice person. It is almost impossible for me to believe that he would order or pay another man to kill. Letice has always called him 'Cuddle Bear', and you know, Bell, it is not easy to fool a whore who serves you time after time."

"Fear is an urgent prod," Bell said. "Did you not tell me that the man has been very uneasy for about six weeks?"

Magdalene sighed again. "Yes."

She looked downcast. Bell was stung with jealousy that she should care and, because he knew how senseless that was, he said, "FitzRevery is the most likely, but it could be possible that Jokel de Josne was driven to kill, not for what Bertrild was squeezing him but for some more important secret he wanted to keep hidden. Ulfmaer FitzIsabelle is also barely possible, if he could have slipped out without his people noticing. Although the worst the law would have done was to make him repay Gunther Granger's heirs and fine him, had Bertrild exposed his stealing of Granger's funds, who would have ever trusted him to bank money? Without clients who would give him money, he could not lend at interest. Possibly more than half his income would be lost."

"True." Magdalene looked a little more cheerful. "I had not thought of the moneylending aspect of what exposure would mean to FitzIsabelle." Her eyes narrowed. "I think I will go see Mainard, to-morrow. I am a little annoyed with Mainard. He still has sent no word to Sabina. I do not know whether that purse he gave me was a farewell gift or not, so I do not know what to say to her. Also, Mainard has done virtually nothing to help himself while you and I have been running about asking questions and thinking about this murder until we are exhausted. Mainard knows those men. I will discover what he knows, and whether any of the others could have known Saeger."

Bell laughed and stood up. "Poor Mainard. Do not skin him alive. He may have a good reason for his silence. And remember that Sabina has lost nothing—"

Magdalene stood up also. Her gaze met his. "Except her faith in a man she trusted . . . loved. Yes, loved. Whores, like all mortals, can be fools and love."

"That was not what I meant," Bell snapped. "You did not let me finish. I was about to say 'has lost nothing yet' and warn you against being so fierce in defense of your woman that you do more harm than good and drive the poor man away. And you can cease jumping down my throat and pulling out meanings I never intended."

They stood for a moment, glaring at each other. Bell, struggling against his desire for her, had a violent impulse to pull Magdalene into his arms and kiss her into submission. Magdalene could feel her breasts swell against the confinement of her shift and gown, could feel a warmth in her loins and moisture between her nether lips. She backed up a step and shook her head.

"It is true. I am blaming you for Sabina's pain, and I have no right to do that. Forgive me."

She did not hold out her hand to him, however, and Bell did not reach to touch her. He had the feeling that sparks would fly between them, as when one had been stroking silk and then touched the fur of the trimming.

"I will not come tomorrow," he said. "As I told you, I will be busy on the bishop's affairs and must go up to Saint Stephens, where some miller who rents a mill that was willed to the diocese has gone mad and damaged the church. It is close to Saint Albans, so I will probably stay the night at the abbey."

Magdalene giggled. "To purify yourself?"

Bell rolled his eyes. "Unfortunately, I have no reason to need purification. Are you ready to give me one?" He paused significantly.

"Oh!" Magdalene exclaimed, stamping her foot. "You must always have the last word!"

He smiled slowly, suggestively, but made no direct reply. "If there is any urgent news," he said, "you can leave a message for me with Philip, who acts as the bishop's secretary here when the bishop is in Winchester. He is more reliable than Guiscard de Tournai was, and will let me know as soon as I return."

Fourteen

2 5   M A Y

M A I N A R D ' S   S H O P

Magdalene arrived at Mainard's shop soon after Prime. Henry was already at the front counter, clumsily arranging tooled leather reins. Two pairs had been pushed off by themselves to the very end of the table and then a pile of others, tied two by two. The ones at the end were more crudely done, the design less finished and showing a miscut place here and there. A man in the rough garments of a farmer visiting the city was examining one pair of the cruder work.

"They are sound and solid, even if they are not cut *perfectly* straight," Henry said, "and very pretty despite the two or three little mistakes. Take them in your hands and pull them—you can see, I cannot do that. You are stronger anyway. Yes, look at the place the knife missed and be sure that the leather is sound. And think, you said these are for your woman when she rides into town. She has not your strength and when riding will not be hauling at the mouth of a cart horse."

The young man pulled at the rein with the cut as he had been told and then laid both down. "I do not know. Two pence. That is a lot of money."

"Those reins will last for twenty years," Henry said. "And every time your wife rides anywhere in that whole twenty years, she will be reminded that you denied yourself the pleasures of London, just to bring her a fine gift. And each time one of the other women in the village sees those reins, she will burn with envy for how good a husband your wife has . . . and your wife will know it. Oh, yes, she will know."

The young man picked up the reins again and stroked the polished leather. There might be a fault or two in the tooling, but the suppleness and polish of the leather was very fine—as it should be since that was the first process the apprentices learned and the one most often practiced.

Behind her veil Magdalene grinned. Henry certainly could sell. He had flattered the customer by praising his strength and his generosity; he had pointed out the flaws in the goods, which the customer could not fail to see anyway, thus giving an impression of honesty— and Magdalene was certain there were no other flaws or Mainard would never have offered the reins for sale at all; and he had dangled the wife's pleasure and likely gratitude, hinting at her willingness to repay her husband's sacrifice over many years.

The sale was soon concluded, and Henry turned to her. "Why did you not go through, Mistress Magdalene?" he asked switching to French. "Or do you want to buy something?"

"No." She kept to English. "I wanted to ask you if you remembered that Friday before Mistress Bertrild was killed. We talked about the customers who came to the shop and went into the workroom. By any chance, was Mistress Bertrild also here that day? Or if you do not actually remember her being here, could she have slipped past you and got into the workroom without your knowing?"

"Was she here that Friday?" Henry repeated slowly, also in English, obviously thinking hard, but after a moment he shook his head. "I don't know. I know she was here on Saturday because she had a big fight with Codi. She wanted him to make her a belt of the blue leather that Lord Baltom brought on Friday for his wife's new saddle."

"Oh," Magdalene said. "Then she probably was here on Friday. How else would she have known about the blue leather Lord Baltom brought? Very good. Thank you, Henry. Is Master Mainard within?"

"Yes, he is." Henry made an odd sound. "He's a strange one, that Mainard. Glum as a cold winter's day. You'd think he'd be ready to float with that burden lifted from him, but he's sad, and as short tempered as I've ever seen him. You'd think that he lost something precious in that accursed wife. I wish you had some good news to cheer him up."

"I wish I did, too," she sighed as she edged around the end of the counter and went into the shop, dropping her veil.

Codi straightened from tapping something with an odd-shaped hammer when Magdalene came into his line of sight and came to the door. "Oh, Mistress Magdalene," he said with a broad grin. "Will you come into the workroom, or shall I send Master Mainard out?"

"I think it would be quieter if he came out here," Magdalene replied, "but before you ask him, will you try to think back to the Friday that you lost your knife? Was Mistress Bertrild here that day? You remember, that was the day Lord Baltom and his lady came."

Codi blinked and frowned. "She did not come every day," he said. "Why did you think she had been here that Friday?"

"Because she knew about Lord Baltom's blue leather. She asked you to make a belt from it for her the next day, the day that she was killed."

Codi blinked again. "So she did, and she asked for the belt while she was still in the shop. Yes, I remember. She never went into the workroom at all that Saturday. I gave her the money from the box that Master Mainard had left for her, and she demanded more. I said there was no more and showed her the open box, which was empty. Master Mainard always left exactly the right amount and no more. Then she demanded the belt from the blue leather. I told her the leather was not ours. We argued about the belt. Mistress Sabina heard us. When I kept refusing, she said I would be sorry and stormed out of the shop. But I don't remember seeing her in the workroom on Friday."

"Thank you. Would you ask the boys if they remember her being there?"

"Yes, I will. And I'll send Master Mainard out to you."

But it was Stoc, the younger of the apprentices that came out. "Master Mainard is putting away his tools," he said. "He will be here anon. But I saw Mistress Bertrild. She *was* there on Friday, but I don't remember whether it was morning or afternoon. It was after Lord and Lady Baltom came. I know that because I had to stop working to be out of their way, and I was just standing and looking around."

"You're sure?" Magdalene asked.

Stoc nodded. "I always watched her when she came in. Once she came up behind me, real quiet, and pushed me when I was using a knife. I got cut." He held up a hand, showing a long scar. "Usually she came in like a bad storm and tramped over to Master Mainard's table to yell at him, and she'd knock things off the worktables. But if Master Mainard wasn't in the shop, sometimes she kind of sneaked in, soft and quiet like, looking for something to take. Once she took a buckle off Codi's table. Codi's a little bewildered sometimes. He would of thought he lost it and then paid for it, but I told Master Mainard who took it."

"Go back to work, Stoc," Mainard said from the doorway. "What can I do for you, Mistress Magdalene?"

The last sentence was in French, and Magdalene thought it was to make understanding more difficult for Codi and the boys. They all spoke some French; it was necessary to deal with the nobility, who were the largest customers for saddles and for whom it was a first language, but they had to think about anything said in French. English was their native language.

"You can give me some help in trying to discover who murdered your wife," Magdalene said, her tone tart. "You may think you are safe from accusation—and that may be true as far as the law goes—but your neighbors will always wonder unless someone is proven guilty. So far, Bell and I have done all we could. Now it is your turn to help catch the killer."

He looked aside, by habit turning the birthmark away from her, and passed a hand over his face. "I do not know what to do," he said. "She tortured them."

"That does not excuse taking Codi's knife to implicate him and bringing the body here to implicate you," Magdalene snapped. "Jean said she called the man Saeger. I assume Bell told you that she sent the servants away, and no one else entered the house until the servants returned. That means that this Saeger killed her."

"But Saeger was a messenger from her uncle."

"He *said* he was a messenger from her uncle, but we know Saeger came from the area and could easily have known Sir Druerie as well as Gervase, so he could use that excuse to get to see Bertrild even if it was not true. And the man who killed Bertrild did have Codi's knife. Either he took it himself or—if he was a messenger from Druerie—he was given the knife by one of the men who was here on Friday and told to use it." Magdalene was not going to mention her idea about Bertrild taking the knife and perhaps furnish Mainard with a path to escape helping identify the murderer. "You have been in business here in London for more than twenty years. Who, among those five men, could have lived near Moorgreen from 1131 to 1136?"

Mainard gestured Magdalene toward one of the tall stools in front of the counter, waited until she seated herself, and also sat down. "Perekin cannot be Saeger," he said. "It is true that he lived at Hamble most of the time until 1136, but he could not have been a wool merchant at Hamble and a farmer near Moorgreen at the same time. And he was here in London most winters."

"But he could have known Saeger, could he not?"

"I do not know," Mainard said. He had put his elbow on the counter and was resting his head on his hand, his voice redolent with misery. "If Saeger had sheep, it is possible. If he was a farmer, it is less likely."

Magdalene could not help but feel sorry for him—he was truly a good-hearted man—but she also felt impatient. He should be a little less tenderhearted to his male friends and be more aware of the misery he was causing his loving and patient whore.

"How about Ulfmaer FitzIsabelle?"

"No. Aside from a few weeks now and again, Ulfmaer has never been much out of London. He inherited the business from his mother, Mistress Isabelle in 1131. I do not see how he could have known Saeger either."

"Herlyond will be fine-combed by Master Octadenarius so you can forget about him. What of Lintun Mercer?"

"He came to London in 1136 from near Lincoln where he was born. He was a mercer there also, but his partner had several sons and bought Lintun out so the boys could share the business."

"How did he meet Dockett?"

"I have no idea. William did not say. At one time he had offered to combine his business with Perekin's, that was after William's daughter married the goldsmith and his son was already a journeyman apothecary, but by then Perekin was thinking of being rid of the mercery and dealing only with wool and fleeces. Anyway, William came to tell Perekin that Lintun Mercer was interested in buying a half share of his business and to ask if Perekin had changed his mind. I happened to be there, which is how I was included in the discussion and came to stand witness for the son and daughter. I suppose William felt he owed it to Perekin to give him a final chance. It was a good business."

"Could Master Dockett have been uneasy about Mercer? We learned from the packet you gave me that the agreement Mercer presented giving him the whole business after Dockett died *was* false— and Gervase de Genlis believed that Mercer had destroyed Dockett's will, too."

Mainard shook his head. "I do not know. William and I mostly talked about business when we met—whether he had suitable cloth for padding saddles or for decorative bits. . . . He never complained about his partner."

"And do you like Mercer?"

"Well enough," Mainard said, looking up. "He has been late on delivery a time or two, but nothing I could really fault him for, and a handsome apology if I had to remind him, which was only once."

"Jokel de Josne. He used false sales receipts."

Mainard sighed heavily, but his lips firmed, and he looked severe. "Josne never said from where he came—he does not speak much of his past—but he knows Norwich. He arrived in London in 1136 and made a big splash. He came with a large stock of French goods, some of it very good, some . . . I am sorry to say it . . . shoddy. I do not deal with him. I am not sure how he became a member of our Bridge Guild, I suppose through Ulfmaer, who is his good friend."

There was a little silence while Magdalene tried to think of something else to ask. Then Mainard said, "Magdalene, cannot those records of my late father-by-marriage be destroyed?"

"Good God," Magdalene breathed, "I had forgotten that Gervase de Genlis was your father-by-marriage. I can see why you want to let the whole mess sink in silence, but the chances are no public disclosure of the information will be made. And what of those who were defrauded, like William Dockett's son and daughter and the kin of the dead man Ulfmaer robbed? I can promise you that if Perekin Fitz-Revery and John Herlyond are not guilty of murder—but to my mind if either one gave Saeger the knife and the order to kill, then he *is* guilty—we will certainly forget about the sins of their youth."

"Whichever way one turns, there is evil."

"So there is," Magdalene said briskly, stepping down from her stool, "and many say I and my women are purveyors thereof. Nonetheless, we are human and have our hopes and dreams, and we hurt when those are damaged. Why have you not come to see Sabina? She misses you."

Suddenly there were tears in Mainard's beautiful eyes, and he turned his head fully away. "I cannot bear it," he whispered. "I have always told her that if she needed relief from me and took other men, I would look aside, but now I do not think I could look at her sweet face, and know . . ." His voice broke on a heavy sob.

"What a fool you are," Magdalene said. "If you do not understand what Sabina is, you should not have taken her as your woman. Sabina has not touched another man, has not even spoken to any of her old clients. She retreats to the chamber for which you paid whenever clients come. She is waiting for *you* to take her 'home,' which is what she calls her rooms above your shop."

He was staring at her now, the natural skin pallid, even the purple birthmark paler than usual. "Can I believe you?" he whispered.

"Me?" Magdalene said. "No. I do not ask you to believe me. What you need to believe is what you know Sabina is. Do not load on her *your* feeling of ugliness and lack of worth. Remember that to her blind eyes, you are beautiful. You are kind and generous to her. You are a good lover. Why should she seek another man? You must decide whether you believe that because she became a whore to save herself from starving, she is a whore at heart and will spread her legs for any man for no reason at all, or that at heart she is a decent woman who will cleave only to the one man to whom she has sworn herself."

He swallowed hard. "Sabina is a good woman, but how can she not know. . . ." He paused to take a deep breath. "She thinks me beautiful?" The words were less than a whisper. "I . . . I will come . . . soon."

Magdalene shrugged, lifted her veil to cover her face, and went out. She could not fight Mainard's battle for him. He was not jealous in the ordinary sense, only so uncertain of himself that he might destroy Sabina out of fear. But telling him that she loved him could only do so much; he needed to be with her, when her constant reassurance could have an effect.

Because she could do no more on that score, Magdalene dismissed Sabina's fate from her mind and turned toward Gracechurch Street to walk south to the bridge. Her eyes unseeing as she considered what Mainard had said, she passed the counter set before the next shop only to be stopped by hearing her name called aloud.

"That is my name," she said, turning toward the voice, "but I am sorry I do not know who calls me."

As she spoke, she looked blankly at Perekin FitzRevery, who was standing behind a counter laden with small bolts of cloth and richly dyed hanks of yarn, as if she had never seen him before in her life. That was how she and her women treated every client. The men paid not only for the services of clean, sweet-smelling, and willing companions but also for security; thus, no client was ever recognized outside of the walls of the Old Priory Guesthouse.

"Come within," Perekin said, gesturing to her. "I have some beautiful ribbons to show you. I think they are almost worthy of your embroidery."

"Thank you," Magdalene said, walking around the counter. "It is kind of you to have thought of me."

Inside the shop, Perekin sent his journeyman out to watch the counter and then laughed. "You are thoughtful also, more careful of my reputation than I am myself—but then, there is no one who can be hurt by my sins but myself. My wife, bless her, is dead these five years, and I still remember her too fondly to take another woman into my home in her place. My daughter is well married and away in her own home, and if my son does not understand what I do, he is not the man I believe him to be."

Magdalene smiled and lowered her veil. "All very well," she said, although she thought cynically that he had quickly enough taken up the chance of an excuse she had given him by talking of her embroidery, "but it must be the client's choice to acknowledge us. Our business at the Old Priory Guesthouse is not to impinge on our clients' lives in any way outside of their visits to us. Now, how may I serve you?"

"By making a place for me today. I find myself in a mood for celebration and now have a few extra pence to indulge myself."

Magdalene raised her eyes to the ceiling and bit her lips as if she were thinking over her women's appointments, but she was trying to be sure that FitzRevery could not make out her expression. Celebrate what? Surely Bertrild's death. And the extra pence were no doubt what he would have had to pay her.

"This evening, if that is satisfactory," she said, bringing her gaze down to meet his. "Letice will be free from after Vespers. You can stay the night if you like, and you know we will gladly feed you."

"Excellent!" he almost caroled the word in his good humor. "And, oh wait. Here are the ribbons." He walked around the inside counter and from a shelf below it took a wrapped package. "I had intended to bring them the next time I came, but when I saw you, I decided I deserved a little rejoicing at once."

"Thank you again, Master FitzRevery," Magdalene said, taking the packet and raising her veil.

"Until tonight," he said softly, seeing her out the door.

Oddly enough, FitzRevery's frank avowal of pleasure in his release made Magdalene less sure of his involvement in Bertrild's death. She could not put her finger on how she felt a murderer in fact if not in deed should act, but it was not with bouncy good humor. Mainard's gloom seemed less innocent, but then Magdalene reminded herself that the gloom was not over Bertrild's death but over concern for men he had known for years.

She was just in time for dinner with her women, and opening the packet of ribbon kept them all occupied after the meal had been removed until the bell pealed to announce the first client. Sabina rose at once, and started toward her chamber.

"Go take a bath, Diot," Magdalene said. "And stay there until I call for you. I will tell the Mayor" he was, in fact, no such thing but had a sufficiently pompous manner to fit him for the title "—that you had been shopping and come back dirty and sweaty and wished to be sweet and clean for him. I need to talk to him about his years in Norwich."

Diot ran off with a grin. She bathed often anyway, as if she could not rid herself of the filth of her time in the stews, and would have spent even more time in the tub if she had not feared she would be reprimanded for taking advantage. An invitation to take another bath was only too welcome.

Magdalene went out to answer the bell. It was not the "Mayor" but Ella's client. She, having seen him enter, came dancing out to greet him, bubbling with the beauty of the ribbons that Magdalene had brought and what she was going to embroider on them. Magdalene was prepared to intervene if he seemed bored, but that was not at all the case. In fact, he came to the table and looked through the different colors. Then, choosing one, he looked from it to Ella and smiled most oddly.

"Could you embroider that for me, my pet?" he asked.

"I could. I could. Magdalene draws the designs for me and—" she went to get her basket and produced her current piece of work "—you can see I embroider well."

"Indeed you do, little one." He looked at Magdalene and grinned broadly. "I would like white dogs running though some kind of fruit trees or marrow vines, and the fruit or marrows must show. How much would that cost?"

Magdalene's heart sank. She had the feeling that the man was going to play a bad joke on his wife, giving her his whore's work to wear, or perhaps wearing it himself, sewn onto a neckband. His relationship with his wife was no business of Magdalene's, but if the woman liked the work and wanted more or suspected and tried to find out from where the piece came, it could make trouble for the Old Priory Guesthouse. Usually she sold her work and her women's through a mercer in the East Chepe who did not know who she was and, from her speach and demeanor, assumed she was a lady of good birth fallen on hard times and selling her work to live. Still, she could only smile and nod, and smile more broadly when the bell rang again and she hurried out to answer.

This time the bell did announce "Mayor." Magdalene welcomed

him and produced her apology. "Would you like to sit with me in the common room, or would you prefer to sit in the garden behind the house? It is very pleasant there now."

He chose, as Magdalene had expected, the garden where he was less likely to see, or be seen by, anyone he knew. She fetched him a cup of wine and a small plate of cakes, and when she had put it down on the table, snapped her fingers.

"Aha, you are just the man I wanted to see, and I am delighted to be able to talk to you for a few moments. I could use your advice. Did you not tell me, oh, I cannot remember when but it must be a year since, that you were a master mercer in Norwich?"

"You have a long memory, Magdalene." He did not sound pleased about it.

She laughed lightly. "Not really. I only remembered because a mercer, not a client of this house" (that was not true, Josne was a client if not a frequent one, but Magdalene did not mind prevaricating in a good cause and the lie actually protected Josne after all) "—approached me to sell me some particularly fine yarn from Norwich. I liked the yarn very well, and the dyes were rich, but I did not like the man. The name he gave was Jokel de Josne—"

The "Mayor's" brow wrinkled. "Éoqule de Éosné? From Norwich? My advice is that you should not buy from him lest you have the sheriff at your door seeking for stolen goods. Has he had the impudence to go back to Norwich? I did not think there would be a man in the city who would do business with him."

"You mean he is not from Norwich or has been away from there?"

"Gone from the town for years. He was never actually convicted of any crime, but that was because he fled before evidence could be found. Rumor and complaint followed him and grew until the sheriff was about to examine his premises for stolen goods. He disappeared only the night before the sheriff came. It was said that one of the sheriff's men was in his pay."

"Oh, when was that?"

"Hmmm. I left the city myself—except for visits—for I married very well in London in the spring of 1130. It was not long after that, perhaps the summer or autumn, that my father wrote to me that Éosné had cleaned out his warehouse and salesroom and disappeared—and taken with him all the goods he had 'bought' but not yet paid for and all those he had 'sold' and not yet delivered. It was quite a scandal, which is why I remember his name, also because it was French, and we of Norfolk are mostly named in the Danish mode. My father's letters were full of it for weeks."

"Ah, well." Magdalene shrugged. "It was very fine yarn, and as you know, we do embroidery in this house, but the last thing I desire is to draw the sheriff's attention. I will not deal with the man. Thank you for telling me."

"You are a wise woman to seek advice when you are not sure," the "Mayor" said.

Magdalene smiled sweetly and did not call him a pompous fool. In fact, she sought his advice on several other small matters, until he had finished his wine and cakes. Then she said Diot had surely had time enough to scrub herself clean and went to fetch her woman, who came from the back door of the house looking fresh and very beautiful and holding out her hand with seeming pleasure.

Watching discreetly from the kitchen window, Magdalene nodded with satisfaction. Diot seemed even more reliable and eager to please now that she had been told she would not be put out even if Sabina was forced to return to whoring. Of course Diot knew that any infraction of the rules—stealing, deliberately offending a client, speaking about clients to anyone except her "sister" whores—would still result in her expulsion from the Old Priory Guesthouse; however, except for that, Magdalene had told her, her position was assured. She had sat, frozen-faced, and then burst into tears, sobbing that it was as if she had died and had come awake in heaven. Magdalene had been somewhat startled. Whoring, even in so good an atmosphere as the Old Priory Guesthouse, was not her idea of heaven.

When Diot's door had closed, Magdalene walked down the corridor toward the common room, pausing as a squeal came from behind Ella's door. Then she heard the girl laughing and protesting that "that tickles," and she sighed, recalling that Ella's client not only had a warped sense of humor but was the lunatic who insisted on eating various foods—most of them sticky, like ripe fruit or puddings—off

Ella's body and out of various orifices. Ella enjoyed it, but it did make a mess of her and the bedclothes.

Letice's client must also have come, Magdalene thought, because Sabina was sitting near the hearth, softly strumming her lute, playing a false note now and again as she worked over a new song. Magdalene gathered up the ribbons strewn over the table, stopping to consider one of clear blue and another of green. Both, she thought, laying them aside, would suit Bell's fair coloring and embroidered would make a good name-day gift for him; the green could be embroidered with his coat of arms, the blue with a hunting scene. The idea of hunting brought to mind the white dogs the client wanted, and she sighed again.

Well, if it made trouble, she would cross the stream as best she could. No sense worrying now. She refolded the other ribbons into their packet and put them on one of the shelves on the back wall, coming by her stool to pick up her workbasket. Sabina, hearing her footsteps, looked up. Magdalene thought she was paler than she had been, and her lips did not curve gently into their usual almost-smile. Restraining her impulse to sigh again, for Sabina would hear that and want to know why, Magdalene took her sewing basket to the table.

From it she extracted a thin piece of charcoal with which she marked the smooth boards of the table with a long rectangle, the length and width of the ribbon Ella's client had chosen. Within this, she sketched eight lean greyhound figures; around them, more carefully, she drew squat, fantastic trees with drooping branches, among which she marked out pear shapes. Her lips twisted. Pears were a favorite of the client when they were in season, probably because they crushed easily into a sweet, wet, mess.

The sketch had to be corrected several times before she was satisfied, but when she felt she had a graceful, flowing design, she went to the back shelf and brought out a bottle of pale ink. Having pinned the ribbon to the table just below her sketch, she sharpened the quill that had lain beside the bottle and began to copy the picture onto the ribbon. She left the ribbon pinned to the table to dry and fetched Dulcie from the kitchen to scrub the table clean.

"You went to see Mainard," Sabina said softly, when Magdalene had seated herself on her own stool and begun to work on an elegant gown facing that the East Chepe mercer had ordered.

"However did you know?" Magdalene asked.

"I smelled the shop on you when you came in." Sabina smiled faintly. "I am very fond of the odor of leather." She paused, and then went on, even more softly. "I hope you did not . . ."

"I told him you missed him. He needed to know that, my love. When you are with him, he does not doubt you, but when he is alone, he thinks of how ugly he is and that you must hate to lie with him and crave other, whole men."

"No!" Sabina cried. "I know his face is not like other men's, but his body . . . oh, that is perfect, beautiful and strong, so strong. He is like a great wall or a great tree, able to shelter those who need him." She was silent for a while, her fingers picking minor chords from the lute. "I suppose he is inquiring about another wife. . . ."

"He said nothing to me about that, but I do not think he will seek a wife so soon. The woman, terrible as she was, is not dead a week, and the manner of her death, being what it was, might raise suspicions. No, I do not think Master Mainard is thinking about a second marriage."

Two tears oozed out from under Sabina's sealed lids. "That means I will have to wait longer. I do not think he would make proposals to a woman while he had his whore living above his shop." She bit her lip. "I wish he would find someone and be done. If he does not want me, I . . . I need to know."

"He will always want you," Magdalene said. "It is only you with whom he can be at ease, but if he wants sons of his blood to inherit his business . . . I am sorry, my love, very sorry, but a whore's child . . ."

"I know that." Sabina's voice trembled. "I would not dare to bear children anyway. What if they were born like me, without eyes?"

Magdalene sighed. It seemed to her that she was doing a lot of sighing this day. "He said he would come soon. When he does, you must convince him—although how, I have no idea—that you do find him beautiful and desirable. He is afraid, because he promised you that he would look aside if you took other men, and now he finds he cannot endure that."

"But I haven't! You know I haven't. I want only my Mainard. I *love* his funny face."

"Tell him, my love. Tell him over and over. Somehow you must make him believe you—no easy task when everyone, even those who love him, look away."

Sabina bit her lips, but her face looked more intent now than sad and after a while she began to sing again. Magdalene embroidered steadily, not thinking about how Sabina could convince Mainard she found him beautiful but wondering how a whore could convince any man she would be faithful. She thought of the terrible instruments of torture, the iron chastity belts some men who went on crusade had inflicted on their wives . . . and still were not convinced of their purity.

Magdalene chuckled softly. They had doubted with good reason. Any woman who did not find a way to remove such a shackle was mad. One could not even relieve one's bladder and bowels without smearing the belt and oneself with filth. In an attempt to be sure the spaces provided for such relief did not permit other usage, they were far too small. Her husband had shown her such a device, one his grandmother had worn, and spoken of the peace of mind a woman's patience could bring her man.

Even if he had not expected her to welcome the idea, he had been shocked at her response. Perhaps he had thought she would weep and plead with him not to force her to wear such a thing, promising to be faithful. Perhaps he had even thought she might accept it. Certainly he had not expected her to laugh and say she imagined there were locksmiths enough to make a duplicate key, perhaps many duplicate keys to assuage the insult of having her honor questioned. Brogan had hit her, but he had not mentioned chastity belts again.

As she opened her embroidery frame to move the work up some inches, Magdalene frowned. Why in the world was she thinking about chastity belts and a man dead many years? She felt a slight warmth in her cheeks as she rethreaded her needle with cherry-red silk and took the tiny double stitch that would fix the thread. Bell. Thinking about Mainard had brought Bell to her mind. And Bell's jealousy had made her remember Brogan.

Although her eyes were fixed on the pattern she was embroidering, she was hardly conscious of the needle setting the stitches to outline a rose. Never. Never would any man again have the right to demand she be faithful! But she could not hold back a little silent giggle when she remembered Bell's swift riposte to her suggestion that he was going to stay at Saint Albans to be purified. She shook her head. The greatest danger she faced in dealing with Bell was not his beautiful body or his handsome face but that he was so much fun.

Fifteen

W hen will soon be?" Sabina asked pathetically, interrupting Magdalene's thoughts.

"I do not know, love," Magdalene soothed. "Remember that it is not only because he is afraid you will have changed toward him that Master Mainard does not come but because Bertrild's death has caused him to be all behind in his work. Monday they did no work at all and Tuesday, although he sent Codi and the boys back to the shop, I fear they did nothing or did nothing well enough to be called work. Likely he spent most of Wednesday undoing the disasters they had created. And even today, I suspect little was accomplished."

"Perhaps tomorrow? Oh, no! Tomorrow I have an appointment to sing at a birthday dinner. Oh, what shall I do? If he should come and I not be here . . . what will he believe?"

"That you were singing at a birthday dinner," Magdalene said dryly. "How could you be so stupid as to lie about a matter so easily proven? Sabina, if he will not believe what you say—and what Haesel says—you must not go back to him."

"Oh, I must! I must! I care so much for him." She wiped away a few more tears and then smiled tremulously. "But I did not mean that he would be angry, only that he might think I was avoiding him. Perhaps I had better send a message to Mistress Saylor that I am ill and cannot come."

"Do not be so silly. This is a new client, and you must not disappoint her. Mainard will not come at dinnertime anyway. That would break up his day too much."

"But he often came at dinnertime. We mostly ate our meals together."

"Sabina! Your brains are rattled loose. It is one thing for him to walk up a flight of stairs and eat a meal that Haesel fetched and then walk down again. It is quite another to walk almost a mile from his shop, across the bridge, and then here and have to walk back again."

Sabina drooped. "Yes. I suppose I am being silly. And he might not come tomorrow. . . . But if he should come tomorrow or any other day and I not be here, I could not tell him how much I care for him. He might go away and . . . and fear to come back."

Ordinarily Magdalene would have scoffed, but recalling Mainard's pain she thought Sabina might be right. "You have a point, love. He is so unsure and suffers so much. . . . Yes. I will tell you what we can do. You can make a list of all of your singing appointments for the next week and the places you will be, and Tom Watchman or Ella and Diot can bring him the note. Oh, and I will write that you beg him to come any other time or to tell you if he wishes you to cancel any of the appointments because you are very eager to be with him."

"Yes, yes. That would be wonderful. Now, let me see. Tomorrow I must go to—"

"Wait, love. Let me fetch a pen and ink."

The list was made easily enough, although the directions for each place took some time. Sabina insisted on giving those in case Mainard wanted to be sure where she was. The letter explaining why she sent him the list and urging him to come to her took a great deal longer. Sabina was afraid to press too hard, lest Mainard think her bold or that she wished to impose her will on him, but she wanted to press hard enough for him to feel the sincerity of her longing.

She was just about satisfied with what Magdalene had written for her when Diot showed "Mayor" out the way he had come in. Sabina took her letter and her lute and retired to her chamber because the next set of clients would be coming soon. Letice, clinging and stroking, led her man out into the common room rather than down the back corridor a few moments later. He stopped beside Magdalene to admire her embroidery and to make a special appointment with Letice for Tuesday morning the next week. Magdalene did not often accept morning appointments, but he explained he would be sailing for France on the afternoon tide that day and wished to take a pleasant memory along.

The bell had pealed to announce Diot's second client before Ella and her messy eater staggered to the bathroom, giggling all the way. Magdalene shook her head. It was a harmless lunacy compared with some of the things men thought whores should be willing to do, but she could understand why his wife would not permit it—if he had ever mentioned it to her. Dulcie came from the kitchen to strip the bed and replace all the linens. Of course, they charged the client two farthings extra for the washing, but it was a nuisance.

Letice's second man came, a pale, frail clerk who slunk in from the back gate, having entered through the priory. Magdalene knew he made Letice anxious, but he would have no other woman. Magdalene could not decide whether, like the new sacristan of the priory, he had chosen Letice because she was not Christian or because of her exotic looks. But he had an almost abnormal desire for her. In fact, what made Letice anxious was that she was terrified he would die in his violent convulsions of mingled ecstasy and guilt. Magdalene heard him begin to whimper even before the door closed.

The bell pealed again, and Magdalene hissed between her teeth as she put her embroidery aside and got up to answer. That would be Ella's second client, and she and her fruit squasher were not yet out of the bath. She ran down the corridor and quietly tapped on the door of the bathing room. That would be a reminder to Ella not to encourage another passage at arms in the tub, which she would likely do if the man had the strength. Then she went out and opened the gate.

Her breath almost caught in her throat when she saw who was there. She had forgotten it was his day. He had canceled his regular appointments on Monday and Tuesday but kept the one on Thursday. How fortunate that Ella was busy! She would be able to talk to him, perhaps in the guise of urging him to come more frequently to test his reaction to Bertrild's death.

"Come in, do," she said in English, remembering that Lintun Mercer was not really fluent in French.

She stepped back from the gate and gestured him toward the house. "I am very sorry that Ella is not here to greet you herself," she continued as they walked toward the door. "She will be ready in just a few moments, but we had an accident with some dessert from dinner, which she took into her room. Dulcie had to change all the sheets, and Ella had to take a bath. She is sometimes silly—"

"Sometimes!" Mercer said, laughing as they entered. "The girl's an idiot! What did she do, take the pudding into bed and fall asleep on it?"

Although Magdalene bristled internally at the contempt with which Mercer spoke of Ella, who was childlike but within that not stupid, she only smiled and said, "Something very like. You know how timid she is. She was eating and a loud noise startled her. She dropped the pudding and in her attempts to clean it up, it got smeared all over. Sit down at the table, and I will fetch you some wine and cakes."

Since Mercer knew the Old Priory Guesthouse's wine and cakes from guild meetings that were held there, he was very willing and took a seat at the long table while Magdalene went to the kitchen, passing the bathing room on her way to and fro. Through the closed door, she faintly heard splashing and voices. Good, it would be some time before Ella was ready.

"Ella missed you Monday and Tuesday this week," Magdalene said as she set the refreshments before him.

"Does Ella know me from any other man?" he asked, raising a brow in doubt while reaching for a cake and lifting the cup of wine.

"Oh, yes. To be sure she does." Magdalene laughed, swallowing her irritation with the man's attitude. "Of course, she does not know your name, but if asked to describe you, she would give a very vivid picture."

He put down the wine cup without sipping from it. "I am not sure I wish to have Ella's other clients recognize me."

"Of course not!" Magdalene snapped. "My women never mention one client to another. You should know that." Then she reminded herself that, no matter how irritating, this *was* a client, a good one, worth, until Bertrild started squeezing him, nine pence a week, and that her purpose, now that Bertrild was dead, was to induce him to be worth that much again. "Anyhow—" she continued quickly, allowing her lips to curve in simulated amusement "—unless you have a wife or another leman, I doubt the description would mean much. Ella 'knows' you from the waist down." She laughed lightly. "I hope you are not overmodest, but she does tend to recognize men by their privates."

He relaxed, grinned, and lifted the wine cup again. "Since you say she missed me on Monday and Tuesday, I can take that as a compliment."

Still annoyed and thinking she would like to make those privates too sore for Ella to use, Magdalene murmured, "Oh, yes. Ella is very enthusiastic and proud of her skill."

"Skill?" Mercer's brow wrinkled.

"Ah," Magdalene said, clenching a hand nervously under the table and barely preventing herself from biting her lip in chagrin, "I meant craft. My mother was from the north, and I still use a word or two from that country, although I was born and bred in Oxford."

"Oxford is a good place for whoring, what with all the clerks and students from the schools there."

Mercer took another cake and Magdalene, lowering her angry gaze to the plate, reached for one also, so furious she was unable for the moment to control her voice. To call her mother a whore just because she was! Then she swallowed her spleen with the bite of cake she had taken. It was better for him to think that she had been born a whore from a whore than that he remember her slip into the speech of the north. It was better and safer if no one connected her with the north, where a drunken knight had been killed by a knife in his heart and his wife disappeared.

"Yes, it was," she said, her voice easy although her blood still pounded in her throat. "In fact, business grew so good that I found I needed larger quarters and so came to London. I hope business is mending for you, too, and that you will soon be able to come more often. As I said, Ella misses you. You are a favorite swain."

"What? She calls me a 'swine'? Favorite or not, that cannot be a compliment!"

"No, no." This time Magdalene did bite her lip. "Once I am reminded of my mother, I use her speech. The word was 'swain,' which in the north means lover. Do forgive me!"

"Hmmm." Mercer's eyes were cold. "I wonder what you women do call us when you are private? You should be careful, though, lest your slips of the tongue betray you. I—"

"I am so sorry, so sorry!" Ella cried, running in from the corridor with only a drying cloth around her; she was glowing pink from pleasure and her bath. "There was fruit and pudding all over me and my bed, and—"

"Yes, love, I already told your friend that a dessert of fruit and pudding was spilled in your bed. Do not bore him by telling the tale all over."

Ella laughed in a trilling crescendo. "I hardly ever talk to this friend. Talk is not for what he comes, and I am very glad of that, for he is strong and can futter me many times."

"Ella!" Magdalene reproved.

Mercer was laughing, however, obviously flattered and excited by what Ella said. He rose and put his arm around her, bending his head to kiss part of her breast, which was exposed by his pull on the towel. They went off together, leaving Magdalene staring down at the two cakes left on the plate. Had he been threatening her when he said she should be careful lest her slips of the tongue betray her? Mainard said Mercer was from Lincoln. Could he have heard of Brogan's death? that Brogan's very beautiful wife had disappeared, and somehow made the connection between the beautiful Arabel de St. Foi and the beautiful whoremistress Magdalene la Bâtarde?

Why? Why had she lapsed into the speech of her early life? She had not done so for years, having carefully extirpated any signs of her northern origin for fear she would be identified. Many years had passed, and Magdalene was reasonably sure that her husband's death, as she had planned, had been accounted the work of thieves, who had then abducted her. She rose from the table and went to her stool by the hearth, where she picked up her embroidery. So why had she slipped so stupidly? Mercer was not a man she would like to trust with any knowledge about her.

As she embroidered, she went over and over the conversation she had had with him, trying to remember all his gestures and expressions. By the third or fourth review, she was even more annoyed with herself. If she had not told him, he would never have known the words were northern; she could have told him they were Welsh or Cornish. . . .

Magdalene froze, the small embroidery frame dropping to her lap. But Mainard had told her that Mercer had been born and bred in Lincoln. Born and bred in Lincoln? No, that was impossible. She was sure Lintun Mercer had never heard the words 'skill' and 'swain' before. But that was the common speech of the area around Lincoln. Was it possible that in the city . . . No, merchants from Lincoln had come to the smaller town near her husband's estate, and they had spoken the same way she had. So Mercer was *not* from Lincoln.

Magdalene frowned, then snorted softly with disgust. Unfortunately that meant nothing more significant than that Mercer was dishonest, which they knew already, and had probably fled wherever he did come from because he was about to be exposed, like Jokel de Josne. Good God, was no one in that Bridge Guild honest except Mainard? She blinked. Was that why Mainard had been invited, no, pressed, by Perekin FitzRevery to join that Bridge Guild? Because his respectability and transparent honesty would lend credibility to all the others? Mainard was the only leather worker; the others were all mercers or goldsmiths.

She went over the five chief members of the Bridge Guild in her mind: John Herlyond, who had violated his journeyman's bond; Perekin FitzRevery, who had falsified a deed to his farm; Ulfmaer FitzIsabelle, who had stolen from a dead man; Lintun Mercer, who had stolen half the business from his partner's heirs; and Jokel de Josne, who had fled his home city before being arrested. It was interesting that he had left in 1130 before Saeger had married in 1131 and only appeared in London in 1136, after Saeger's wife was dead.

Then she sighed and picked up her embroidery again. That they were all dishonest was interesting, but it proved nothing. None except FitzRevery and possibly FitzIsabelle had done anything worth killing to hide. She clicked her tongue irritably against her teeth. But telling another to kill, another who would not dare expose those orders, was much easier than doing the killing oneself, and might seem worthwhile to be rid of the drain of money that Bertrild was extorting. Might . . . Possibly . . . She made another sound of irritation. Perhaps when Bell came and they pooled the information they had gathered, a finger might point in one direction.

By the time Letice had supported her exhausted, trembling, and weeping client to the back door and gone with him across the garden to the gate to the priory, Lintun Mercer and Diot's man were also gone. Magdalene had managed to dismiss Bertrild's murder from her mind in favor of concentrating on the day-to-day needs of the whorehouse. This was a subject in which all the women were interested, and a lively discussion ensued during the evening meal.

It was decided that Diot and Ella would go to the market the next morning. They would be able to buy soap, which would be in short supply if, as Magdalene expected, William's men, covered with mud and sweat from hard riding, visited on their way to and from Oxford and Rochester. Ella said apologetically that she had put her foot through one of her sheets and would need a new one again; the double washing and extra boiling to free them of food stains wore hers out quickly. And Sabina asked if they would pass anywhere near Mainard's shop so they could drop off her letter to him.

Ella was eager to see the saddlery, and Diot agreed with good humor that it could not be far out of their way. The remainder of the meal was then consumed hastily because all three women had all-night clients that day. And when the men had come and been closed in safely with their companions, Magdalene leaned wearily on the table, half asleep. Dulcie, coming in to clear the leftover food, told her mistress sharply to go to bed.

"No need fer you to sit listenin'. All th' men'r old friends. All this chasin' 'v murderers 's wearin' y'out."

"Right," Magdalene said, nodding so Dulcie could see she agreed without needing to raise her voice. But as she put away her embroidery and went to her room, she admitted to herself that it was not finding Bertrild's murderer that was wearying her, but Sabina's sadness and her own doubts about Bell. One part of her constantly nagged that for his good and hers she should drive him away, but the rest of her could not bear to do it.

———◆———

26 MAY
OLD PRIORY GUESTHOUSE

Not, Magdalene conceded, that it would have been possible to dismiss Bell when he arrived the next morning, yawning and red-eyed, too tired to be hungry but desperately in need of food and comfort. There was nothing in his voice or manner that could have been used as an excuse to tell him he was unwelcome in her house. He was distressed and seeking help, not from whores, not even from women, but from friends.

After Magdalene had got him to drink some unwatered wine and eat a thin slice of meat pasty, he had told them that he had gone to settle a minor quarrel between the priest and a parishoner and ended up killing an innocent man. While the others stared in consternation at that flat statement, Ella, who would ordinarily have shrunk from such a remark, got up and patted him consolingly.

"You could not help it," she said. "You did not want to do it."

He rested his cheek on her hand for a moment, his blue eyes dull and sad. Then Ella kissed him gently on the cheek, patted him again, and said she and Diot had to go out to the market.

"Tell it all to Magdalene," she advised him earnestly. "Even the parts you are ashamed of or afraid to admit. You will see. She will make it all better."

He smiled a little at Ella's innocent conviction that Magdalene could cure all ills, but he picked up a second slice of pasty that had been set before him, and when the last reminders about what to buy had been communicated and Diot and Ella had taken their cloaks and left, he drank his wine and told those still at the table that the miller had truly been mad.

"The thing was, he did not look mad at all. He was not dirty and unkempt. In fact, I was so astonished when he came into the church wheeling a dung cart and began to fork the dung into the aisle that I just stood there with my mouth open. But the priest knew. He must have known. Yet all he did was shriek, 'What are you doing?' and before the miller could answer, said he would make him pay for his blasphemy."

"If he attacked you, Bell, you had a right to defend yourself, even if he was mad," Sabina said.

"God! Do you think I would have drawn a weapon against a mad-man? It was not me he attacked. He flew at the priest and jabbed at his groin with the fork, screaming that the priest was evil and must not be fertile. I wrested the fork from him and turned to throw it out the door so he could not seize it again. In that moment, he had grabbed the priest by the throat."

"And you could not loose his hands." Magdalene sighed.

"I am a strong man," Bell said, eyes staring at nothing. "I am long practiced in arms. I know how to stop a fight, to control a ber-serker. I went behind him and seized each of his wrists and pulled, expecting to wrench his arms back and bind them. Not a hairs-breadth could I move him. Then I tried to pry his fingers loose one by one. They were sunk so deep into the priest's flesh that I would have had to tear out his throat to get my hand under the miller's. And the priest was dying! His eyes were bulging. His tongue was coming out of his mouth."

He stopped. Magdalene refilled his cup with wine and put it in his hand. He lifted it and drained the cup.

"Perhaps I should have let the miller kill the priest. That man is so stupid. . . ." He sighed heavily, then smiled ruefully at Magda-lene. "Ella said even the parts that I am ashamed of. I cut the poor miller's throat. God knows, I have killed many times. Still, I cannot get him out of my mind—the way I did it, pulling his head back by the hair and running my knife across his neck. It was as if he were not human, as if I were slaughtering a pig or a sheep. The blood gushed out over my hands and I thought . . . I thought . . . that was a waste. There should have been a bowl to catch it for blood pudding." He closed his eyes and swallowed. "Such a thought. I cannot seem to . . ."

Magdalene again covered Bell's hand with hers. "I am very sorry it was by your hand, Bell, but have you stopped to think that perhaps the man was no longer really human and that you did a mercy? Can you imagine what that poor creature's life would have been like if he had lived? He would have been chained like a beast or locked into a chamber. . . ."

"Oh yes," he said. "I went to beg pardon of his wife, and she wept but admitted she was glad. He had as yet done no harm in his family, but he had urged his son and daughter to couple together and grew quite angry when they said it was wrong and refused. She was afraid he would soon have become violent."

Magdalene smiled faintly. "It was for the best, but you wish it was not you who had the doing."

"Exactly." But his eyes were brighter and suddenly he laughed. "Ella was quite right. Tell Magdalene and feel better."

He looked around the table then and drew a haunch of cold lamb to him. Letice got up, dropped a kiss on the top of his head, and went off to her chamber. Sabina reached forward and felt for his hand. He gave it to her, and she squeezed it sympathetically. He returned the pressure and then let go to pull from its sheath the knife with which he had killed the miller. With a faint half smile, he carved off a slice of lamb, and having taken a hearty bite, he asked around the food if there was ale instead of wine.

When Magdalene poured it for him, he washed down the lamb and, in a voice that implied the subject of the miller was permanently closed, asked what, if anything, Magdalene had discovered about Bertrild's death. She told him that Bertrild had been in Mainard's shop on Friday and could have taken the knife, that she had stolen other things from the shop to make trouble for the journeyman and apprentices. Then she mentioned Josne's sudden departure from Norwich and Mercer's lack of familiarity with the speech of the north.

She was a little anxious when she told Bell that. Although he did not ask or pry, she was sure that he was more interested in her past than left her comfortable; however, he did not pick up on her state-ment and was eating with such concentration—probably he had skipped dinner and his evening meal because of the miller's death—that she could not read his expression.

"That does it," he said when she was finished. "There are too many possibilities for me to make an accusation. We must find Saeger and wring the truth out of him. Well, today I need to finish the busi-ness I began last Tuesday. I must be present when the justice gives his decision whether to uphold the bishop about those rents he claims for the diocese of London and Hugh le Poer claims belong to Montfichet."

Magdalene giggled. "I do not envy the poor justice who must make that decision."

Bell grinned back. "Nor I. Poor man, it hardly matters what he decides. He will be caught between the upper and nether mill—" His voice checked and his grin disappeared. Then he said, as if he had not spoken the previous sentence, "Probably I will also know this eve-ning from which men Borc extorted money."

"Oh yes," Magdalene said quickly. "You told me that Master Oc-tadenarius will loose him with men to follow."

"Then we will pick him up again, and I will see if I can shake loose his memories of Saeger. I hope he will be able to point to one of the men in London. If he does not or tells me nothing, I will stop at Swythling on my way to Winchester and speak to Sir Druerie." He shrugged. "Since I must report the results of the hearing and the death of the miller to the bishop, I can leave a day or two sooner than I intended and perhaps I will actually be able to lay my hands on Saeger."

"Would Saeger dare stay so close to where he was indicted for murder?"

"If he found a protector, perhaps." Bell pursed his lips as he thought and added, "I will take with me the two wills and the tale of the indictment."

"Shall I get them now?" Magdalene asked.

Bell looked at her. Restored nearly to normal, he was amused by her ready compliance. It was unlikely that William of Ypres would be interested in Saeger's false will or even the fact that he probably poisoned his wife. She might have been less willing if he wanted to remove evidence of FitzRevery's carrying letters to Normandy.

"No. I do not wish to carry them around with me, and I am not going directly back to the bishop's house." He cocked his head. "Don't you want to know why I want the documents?"

Magdalene raised her brows. "Because you will have to convince Sir Druerie of Saeger's guilt. You told me that you do not believe Sir Druerie the kind to shield a murderer unless he believed him to be wrongly accused."

He laughed. "Do you ever forget anything you hear?"

And she laughed in response. "How can you say that? I have the worst memory in the world. I cannot remember my clients' names or faces or when they come or anything that is said by them in my presence." She watched him push away the remains of the food, not that much remained, and drain the last of the ale from his cup. "When will you want those documents? I have put them safely away where I do not think they will be found without a real search, so I would like to get them out when no one is here to see."

"I will come by tomorrow morning before I leave, if I decide to go to Winchester," he replied, pushing back the bench and getting to his feet. "Ay, me, another day listening to idiots state the obvious— and I do not except from that the justice and myself."

Magdalene laughed again, and he went away. After that, the day was calm and ordinary, although Magdalene did from time to time find the death of the miller and the bowl for blood pudding intruding into her thoughts. She could not restrain a faint shudder each time, but it was for Bell's horror more than for the death of the man. It was odd that a soldier who had seen so much death should be troubled. No, it was not the death. Bell had not been at all moved by killing Guiscard de Tornai. Then Magdalene nodded, satisfied because she understood: Guiscard had been guilty of murder. The miller had only been mad.

Despite the calm, Magdalene grew more and more uneasy throughout the day, and she was much relieved when the gate closed behind the last of the clients just as the sun was setting. At least whatever ill portended would not affect them. But she had barely reached the house when the gate bell pealed. No clients were expected this night, and Magdalene did not want any. She gave the bell a malevolent glare as she returned to answer the summons, but it did not care and derisively bonged again.

"I am afraid—" she began as she opened the gate, and then swung it wide, her face wreathed in a broad smile. Suddenly she knew why she had been so uneasy; she had been waiting for this to happen and had been afraid it would not. "Master Mainard!" she exclaimed. "I am so glad to see you. Come in. Come in."

He hesitated, and Magdalene took him by the arm and pulled him through the gate, shutting it behind him. "Yes," he mumbled uncertainly, "but will she . . . Will Sabina . . ."

The door of the house had been open. Magdalene's voice had been loud with surprise and relief. Sabina's keen ears had caught at least her lover's name. She appeared in the doorway, without Haesel or her staff, hands outstretched.

"Stop!" Mainard cried. "There is a step." And he bounded past Magdalene to prevent Sabina from falling.

Magdalene knew Sabina was well aware of the step, but she called no assurance to Master Mainard. His running to offer support was a good sign. Uncertain about whether her presence would be helpful or intrusive—Mainard was staring at Sabina without saying a word, and she was clinging to his hands, equally silent—Magdalene hesitated near the gate.

A moment passed and then another. Magdalene began to grin. Whatever Mainard's intentions when he came, he was now as fascinated as a bird by a snake. She stood a while longer, watching the tableau, but she had just about decided that she must break it—after all, she could not let them stand there all night and get drenched in dew—when the bell rang again, right in her ear.

She started violently, then reached up to catch the clapper as she saw the bell tilt to ring again. If she could have done so without disturbing the two statues at her door, she would have shouted to whoever was outside to go away. Since that was impossible, she opened the gate just enough to peer out, opened her mouth to send the person away, and then opened the gate a bit wider.

The man outside was certainly no client. He was dressed like a decent servant, and his face was so twisted with anxiety that Magdalene had some difficulty remembering that this was, or rather had been, Bertrild's slave Jean.

"Is this the Old Priory Guesthouse?" Jean asked in a breathless voice. "Is Master Mainard here? I have just come from his shop, and Codi told me he was coming here."

"Yes, he is here," Magdalene said cautiously. "Can you give me a message so that he does not need to be disturbed?"

"I—I don't know," Jean faltered. "His uncle-by-marriage, Sir Druerie, is come from Swythling and is asking for him."

"Sir Druerie!" Magdalene echoed, and opened the gate wider. "Come in, Jean. You had better tell your master this yourself."

Sixteen

27 MAY
OLD PRIORY GUESTHOUSE

Magdalene woke in a foul mood on Saturday morning. That was not very surprising because she had gone to bed in a foul mood the night before and had not slept well enough to wipe away her anger and frustration. She had been furious with Mainard and even more furious with Sabina because she had not tried to hold him or make him promise to return. A quarter candlemark, Magdalene was sure, could have made no difference to Sir Druerie's business, whereas a promise of some kind would have been of great importance to Sabina.

However, when Mainard had heard Jean out and said, "Sir Druerie? What can have brought him all the way to London?" Sabina had only leaned forward, kissed him lightly, and said, "Go, love. You had better find out."

He had started away at once, then stopped and looked back. "You stay here, Sabina. Do not go back to the shop. I do not want you there while Sir Druerie is in London."

That could have meant anything at all. Sabina plainly took it to mean that when Sir Druerie was gone, Mainard would want her back. Perhaps there had been some silent communication between the two of which she had been unaware, but Magdalene was afraid that once Mainard was away from Sabina, he would fall prey to even stronger doubts. Then, remembering what had happened as soon as he saw her, he might resolve not to see her again because it was too dangerous. Poor Sabina would be hurt so much the worse for her period of hope.

The morning did not improve. There were two early clients—
Saturday was a very busy day—one for Diot, a man who came in
complaining bitterly because it was raining (as if Magdalene should
have arranged better weather for him), and one for Ella, this one dissatisfied because Magdalene could find no better time to accommodate him. Those had barely been tucked away with their companions
when Bell arrived, soaking wet, in a violent rage. Borc had escaped
Octadenarius's men!

"How?" Magdalene asked, taking his dripping cloak to hang
near the fire and coming hurriedly back to the table with a fresh
cup for ale.

"Herlyond," Bell said succinctly. "Borc went into Herlyond's shop
and never came out again. After waiting for him about a quarter candlemark, our man went in also, but the journeyman swore that Herlyond was not there and had not been all day. Of course, he equally
swore that no such man as Borc had entered the place."

"Good God," Magdalene breathed. "Herlyond must be Saeger,
but—but that is physically impossible! You mean Borc left the prison
and went straight to Herlyond's shop and disappeared?"

"No, no," Bell said. "Actually Herlyond's was the last place he
visited."

Magdalene shook her head. "Why did he go to Herlyond's last if . . .
No, I am only confusing myself. Tell me what happened from the beginning, please."

"Octadenarius was as good as his word," Bell growled. "There were
four men following Borc when he left the Tun. They had all had
plenty of chance to watch him, were sure they knew him, and Borc
gave not the slightest sign of suspicion that he was being followed."

"Are you sure he is not shrewd enough to hide that?"

"Perhaps he is, but he would not have been shrewd enough when
he left the Tun. Octadenarius had a brilliant idea. One of the gaolers
carried in two skins of bad wine, pretending he had mistaken Borc's
cell for another, one floor up or down. As you can imagine, Borc
wasted no time in drinking as much of the wine as he could pour
down his throat before the gaoler recognized his mistake. He was all
but falling-down drunk when he was released."

Magdalene raised her brows. "That *was* a good idea."

"It seems to have worked. Borc went straight south—well, as straight as a man that drunk could walk—to Jokel de Josne's shop. One of the men, realizing where he was going, beat him to the counter, but the journeyman there did not give Borc a chance to say anything. He came around the counter, struck Borc a violent blow, saying 'I warned you!' and drove him away with kicks and curses."

"That does not sound much like Josne fears exposure by Borc, yet he *could* be Saeger. His whereabouts are unknown over the right years."

"Borc may never have seen Saeger, you know. He seemed to know the name—he did not lie about that—but he may have heard his master talking about Saeger rather than having dealt with him."

She shook her head. "Where else did he go?"

Bell gave a disgusted snort. "To every man who was in Mainard's shop on that Friday—including Mainard himself. And none of the others was rid of him so summarily as Josne. He worked his way down the Chepe from Josne's shop. There was only an apprentice at the counter at Lintun Mercer's and Borc slipped inside, but he came out again before Octadenarius's man could follow. He may have got money there; the man said Borc looked smug and self-satisfied when he came out."

"Then?"

"He went on to Perekin FitzRevery's place. The man thinks he was handed a coin or two there also because he was smiling and just tucking away his purse in the doorway, and he certainly got money from Mainard."

"Mainard? You cannot mean that Bertrild was extorting money from Mainard. He's not in Gervase's notes at all."

"No, but Mainard confirmed that he had given Borc money. One of Octadenarius's men stopped him when he was leaving his shop to come here and asked what Borc wanted. Mainard said he had complained that he had been employed by Bertrild and that she had not paid him his week's wages. Mainard said he doubted the truth of Borc's complaint but gave him two pence anyway and told him he would give him no more."

Magdalene sighed. "Sometimes Mainard makes it hard to believe in his innocence. Would you give Borc money because he said your dead wife owed it to him? And two pence? Maybe two farthings for pity and to be rid of him without any noise, but two pence?"

"He got more from Ulfmaer FitzIsabelle. Our man was lucky—or clever. I think Octadenarius told his men about the five who could have got the knife and when they saw that Borc had already visited three of them, the man got into Ulfmaer's shop before Borc did. He was looking at some silver brooches when Borc arrived. Borc was pushed out of the shop, not into the street but into a back room where a shouting match soon began, during which our man heard something about five pence."

"Five pence," Magdalene repeated.

Bell nodded. "Our man did not hide the fact that he was listening. He pretended to be surprised by the loud voices and asked what was going on. The journeyman said it was a distant, ruined relative. Not long after, Borc came out looking very satisfied. He then walked across the road to Herlyond's place. That was as much as that man saw. Another took up the chase and said that at Herlyond's the journeyman actually invited Borc in—"

Bell stopped and sighed. "I suppose the man should have been suspicious at such a show of cordiality, but he was alone by then, the other three needing to keep out of the way because Borc may have noticed them at his other stops. He could not send anyone around to watch the back alley. . . ."

"But if he did not go out through one of the gates he must still be in the city. I am sure Master Octadenarius sent someone to question the gate guards, and Borc is fairly noticeable."

"Unfortunately he is not as noticeable as one would think, but it's true that the gate guards do stop the extra ragged to make sure they are not carrying out of the city valuables they could not possibly own. No, he did not pass the gates."

"Then he *is* in the city." Now Magdalene sighed. "There are bolt holes enough, but who would give him . . . Oh, of course, the man had at least seven pence and possibly more, depending on what he got from FitzRevery. He could easily buy a hiding place. Well, I will ask around—"

"Oh no, you will not—" Bell began.

The gate bell pealed, short and sharp. "No!" Magdalene wailed.

"Not now!" But she pushed back the bench and rose, shaking her head to forestall the comment Bell was about to make. "Saturday is always busy, but Letice is free, and I charge an extra penny for those who do not make an appointment ahead of time. I have rent to pay and need the silver."

She took her cloak from a peg near the door, threw it over her shoulders, and pulled the hood over her head. The bell pealed again. The door, which Magdalene had opened, was not pulled closed, and she cocked her head to listen. Then suddenly she ran out, leaving the door open. Bell jumped up and followed her, realizing that she had heard something unusual.

He heard it too, the moment he was out of the door, a child's voice wailing "Mistress Magdalene! Mistress Magdalene! Oh, please come. Please come."

She had the gate open by the time Bell reached her and Stoc, Mainard's youngest apprentice, stumbled in, shivering, weeping, and drenched to the skin. Instinctively, Magdalene threw part of her cape over him—although it was doubtful he could get any wetter.

"What is it, child?" she asked. "Is something wrong with Master Mainard?"

"Dead. He's dead. I saw him." The boy's eyes were staring wide.

"Oh, my God," Magdalene breathed, slipping to her knees in the wet grass. "Bell, did you hear?"

He took the child by the shoulder and shook him. "Stoc, where is your master lying?"

"Here," the boy answered. "Codi sent me to fetch him. He told me beyond the bridge, along the wall until I saw a gate and to ring the bell. I had to jump. The bell rope is too high. Master Mainard must come at once."

Magdalene drew a gasping breath. "Then who is dead?"

"I don't know," Stoc wailed. "He was some dirty, stinking beggar who came in the shop yesterday, pushed right past Henry. He hurt Henry's hand! There were horses out back yesterday, and when Codi saw it was raining, he sent me out to pick up the manure so it shouldn't get all over the path. He was outside the gate and his face . . ."

The boy turned his head into Magdalene's shoulder and began to tremble so hard she thought he would fall.

"Borc!" Bell said, then pulled Magdalene upright and pushed her and the boy toward the door. "Come inside before we all drown." And when they had closed the door behind them, he said, "You'd better wake Mainard and tell him there's another corpse outside his shop."

"He's not here!" Magdalene exclaimed. "That's why I nearly fainted when the boy said he was dead. His wife's uncle, Sir Druerie, arrived yesterday. The servant, Jean, came from the Lime Street house. Codi must have forgotten that he sent Jean here to tell Mainard that Sir Druerie had come. When the boy said he was dead, I thought Sir Druerie had killed Mainard in revenge for his niece's death."

"You mean without even asking Mainard whether he had done it?" Bell asked, starting to laugh, and then stopping abruptly to slam the fist of one hand into the palm of the other while using such language that Magdalene put her hands over Stoc's ears. When he was out of obscenities, he said, "If the dead man is Borc, we've lost him even more thoroughly than if he were hidden in London. And if he's dead, then that means he *did* know who Saeger is."

"And it means that Saeger must be here in the city." Magdalene's eyes widened. "Could he have come with Sir Druerie?"

"I'll find—"

"Please," Stoc said, hiccuping on tears, "where is my master? He must come to the shop and tell us what to do."

"He is at Lime Street, child. Do you not remember that Jean came to ask for him, and Codi sent Jean here?"

The boy cried harder for a moment, then sniffed and wiped his nose on the back of his hand. "I did forget, and Codi did, too, I guess. Now I'll have to go to Lime Street to get him. Gisel went for the justiciar, and Codi is with the body, so I'll have to—"

"No, I'll go," Bell said. "You stay here and dry off and warm up. Then you can go back to the shop."

"Right, Stoc. You go off to the kitchen now and tell Dulcie—she's deaf, so you have to yell a little and show her what you need—to dry your clothes and give you something to eat. Bell will bring Master Mainard to the shop." The boy went off willingly, and Magdalene smiled at Bell. "Thank you," she said. "I don't know if that child could have gone much farther."

"I was going there anyway to talk to Sir Druerie," Bell said. "It is possible that he brought Saeger with him, although how Saeger found Borc or Borc found him, I have no idea. But I think I'd like those wills and the report of the indictment. I want Sir Druerie to understand how dangerous the man is. To use him as a messenger and as a guard for a long ride implies a good deal of trust."

Magdalene nodded and went to her chamber. In a moment, she was back with a small parcel wrapped in oiled leather.

"I thought you said you had hidden the documents," Bell remarked, taking the parcel.

"So I did, but I took those out last night and wrapped them ready for a journey. You said you might go to Swythling today." She put a hand on his arm as he was about to turn away. "You be careful, Bell."

He looked down at her, a slow smile relieving the grimness of his mouth. "I live in hope," he murmured. "And I have no intention of dying until that hope is fulfilled."

———•◦•———

27 MAY

LIME STREET HOUSE AND MAINARD'S SHOP

Bell was welcomed to Mainard's house with exclamations of consternation at how wet he was. Hamo ran out to take the horse to the shed behind the house, and Mainard offered Bell dry clothing, grinning with the characteristic turn of his head that partially hid the distortion of his face as he said there were few to whom he could make such an offer because of his size. Since he was shivering and did not wish to take a chill, Bell accepted, and Mainard gestured him toward the stairs to the solar, but when Bell had climbed them, he stopped dead at the open door.

"What has happened here?" he asked, looking around at the obvious signs of a ruthless search.

Some effort had been made to restore order, but the cushions that had softened and decorated the chairs were slashed, every chest was open and its contents strewn on the floor around it, and the elaborate bed was a wreck.

"It was much worse when I arrived," a short, broad, gray-haired man said from a righted chair, and as Bell entered the room, "Bell? Bell of Itchen? Is it you?"

"Yes, Sir Druerie."

"Well, what are you doing here in London? The last I heard of you was that you had gone as a mercenary—and after your father and mother had paid well to have you educated for the Church."

"The Church did not suit my temperament, Sir Druerie, but the cost of my education was not wasted. I am now one of the bishop of Winchester's knights, and my ability to read and write and even my knowledge of Latin has made me valuable to his lordship—as has my skill in arms."

"Here." Mainard, who had paid little attention to the exchange, handed Bell a pile of clothing he had picked out from the mess on the floor.

"Change. Change," Sir Druerie said. "You are shivering. I would not like to have to admit to your parents that I was the cause of your death after all the dangers you have survived." He lifted a cup of wine from a table by the chair.

Bell laughed, sneezed, and began to strip off his garments. When he was naked, Mainard handed him a cloth to dry himself, and Bell put on the saddler's clothing. Big as he was, he found that everything was loose—and much more soberly colored than he was accustomed to. Moreover, he could not wear the shoes at all. For the moment, he contented himself with a pair of woolen stockings, but he had been staring around as he dressed, and he asked again when he was finished who had searched Mainard's house.

"I have no idea," Sir Druerie said. "When I arrived, the door was open, and the house looked like this. The common room was even worse. All the rushes had been piled in a corner of the room, the contents of the garderobe were on the floor, and the garderobe was pulled away from the wall. Every chair and table was overturned, every cushion slashed open and feathers all over. I went to the kitchen to look for the servants, heard cries and thumping, and I found them locked into the shed. If FitzRevery's man had not been with me and assured me it was the right house, I would have left."

"FitzRevery's man?" Bell asked.

"Yes, he who brought the letter from Mainard telling me that

Bertrild had been murdered. As soon as I saw that news, I decided to come, and I told the man to stop at Swythling on his way back so I could accompany him. I was afraid that Mainard had killed her, you see, and I wanted to testify for him and see if I could get him free on self-defense or justifiable homicide."

"I would not!" Mainard exclaimed. "She was not a good or kind person, but—"

"She was a devil—a devil to each person with whom she dealt. She turned my wife and daughter, a most loving pair always, into two cats, hissing and spitting at each other. She changed my daughter-by-marriage, a most cheerful girl by nature, into a watering pot. And clever with her evil! It took me months to realize what had caused the misery in my home. I was sorry to send her back to you, Mainard, but we could endure her no longer."

"I should not have allowed her to go," Mainard said, "but I believed she would be happier and thus more agreeable in your house. I thought it was only me she hated because she had married a monster for nothing."

"You are not a monster," Sir Druerie said. "I have seen worse in the small villages. And refusing to buy back the mortgages on Moorgreen was the wisest thing you ever did. She never intended to restore the land. She intended to make the house into a great manor and be the Lady of Moorgreen while the money from your saddlery supported her. You would have been ruined in no time at all."

Bell frowned. "Clearly you and your niece were not on the most loving terms, Sir Druerie. Why did you take the trouble to send a messenger—"

"I never sent any messenger!" Sir Druerie exclaimed. "That was the other thing in Mainard's letter that disturbed me. I could not help but wonder whether the man, whoever he was, was trying to involve me in Bertrild's death."

"I never thought of that," Bell said slowly, as Mainard appeared by his side and offered a mug of steaming wine, redolent of herbs. He nodded his thanks, but continued speaking to Sir Druerie between cautious sips. "We are sure that the man who said he was your messenger killed Mistress Bertild, but whether he made the claim just to get into the house or because he wished to do you harm, I do not know."

"But who in London could wish to do me harm? I am no great lord. I live quietly on my land, I have been to London twice, no, thrice, in my life before this."

"Saeger?" Bell said, carefully watching Sir Druerie's face through the slight screen of the steam from his cup.

"Saeger?" Sir Druerie repeated, looking first totally blank and then, after a breath or two, puzzled. "Wait. Wait. I have heard the name, I am sure."

"Will this help you remember?" Bell asked, reaching down to the pile of wet clothing on the floor and extracting the pouch in which he had carried the documents, which he handed to Sir Druerie.

Sir Druerie unwrapped the documents, looked at them, and shook his head. "These look to be wills," he began, his eyes still on the parchments, "but the names on both are the same. Two wills?" He looked at Bell and then back down at the documents. "On the same date? And this? A record of a case in which an indictment was obtained against . . . Saeger! For poisoning his wife . . . Good God! Of course, I remember now. My brother was supposed to hear the case because Saeger's farm was tenant to Moorgreen, but Gervase had already left, and it was presented before me. The man was guilty. No doubt about it, but we never caught him."

So either Sir Druerie had sent Saeger to kill Bertrild because he knew he was guilty all along and kept him for such work as most men would refuse to do, or, as he claimed, he had never sent a messenger and was not involved in Bertrild's death. From past knowledge Bell hoped the latter was true.

"Did you know this man Saeger?" he asked eagerly.

"Know him?" Sir Druerie echoed. "Of course not. He was the son-by-marriage of a man who held a farm on Moorgreen land. How would I know a farmer's son-by-marriage?"

"Sorry, Sir Druerie, I meant would you know him to look at. If you saw him again, would you recognize him?"

"I suppose so, unless he has changed out of all semblance. I was actually with him close to for several candlemarks. He was selling off some horses, and I had him bring them to Swythling for me to look at, since I knew Gervase could not afford to buy. They were good horses, well broken to the plough. I was surprised he was selling them."

"What did he look like?"

"Look like?" Again Sir Druerie seemed astonished and then he nodded. "Of course. You believe the man committed murder, and you want to catch him. Hmmm. What did he look like?" He frowned, wrinkled his nose, then sighed. "He was very ordinary. Medium height, brown hair. I don't remember the color of his eyes. He wore a brown smock, like most farmers. . . ." He hesitated. "Not much help, eh? But I think I would recognize him if I saw him."

"Perhaps we can arrange—" Bell looked around for Mainard, intending to ask him to think of a reason to collect the five men who could have taken Codi's knife when he suddenly remembered why he was in Mainard's house at all. "Good God!" he exclaimed. "Mainard, I was so shocked by this robbery—"

"But nothing was taken, so far as I can tell," the saddler said.

"Nothing was taken? But why. . . . No! I will not be diverted again. I came to tell you that there's another corpse out behind your house."

"What?" The saddler who had been sitting on a stool, just out of Bell's and Sir Druerie's line of sight, jumped to his feet. "Who?"

"I am not certain, but from what Stoc said, I believe it to be Borc."

"Borc? He was at my shop yesterday, after Nones, begging for money. He said he worked for Bertrild, and she had not paid him before she was killed. I cannot say I believed him, but he had been Gervase's servant—"

"Yes, he had. A most unsavory sort," Sir Druerie said, shrugging. "He is no loss, whoever killed him."

"I had hoped he knew Saeger and could point him out to us," Bell pointed out. "And, I suspect from his timely death, that he *did* know Saeger and tried to make him pay for silence." He stood up. "You are wanted at your shop, Mainard. I came to fetch you, but seeing the disorder here put my errand out of my mind."

"Yes, of course," Mainard said, looking distractedly around the room. "Codi will be out of his mind, poor boy. But how can I leave Sir Druerie—unless . . . would you be interested in coming with us, Sir Druerie, since the man was your brother's servant?"

Sir Druerie laughed and tilted his head toward the window where the storm drummed against the closed shutters. "Go out in that rain to inquire about the death of a common servant—and a bad one at that? No, I thank you. Go, if you feel obliged to do so, Mainard. I think your servants will have put the common room into order by now. I will have them carry down the chests holding Bertrild's things and look through them to see if there is anything my wife or daughters might find of use. The servants can give me dinner, I hope?"

"Of course. I will tell Jean. He will get Hamo to help carry anything you wish downstairs. I am sorry to leave you, but my poor journeyman and apprentices will be very frightened. Finding Bertrild was a terrible shock, and this atop it . . ."

While Mainard and Druerie were speaking, Bell had bundled up his wet clothing and picked up the wills and Genlis's report of the indictment from the table by Sir Druerie's chair. He pulled his pouch, into which he slipped the documents, over his shoulder and picked up his sodden cape."

"You can leave that here," Mainard said. "I'll have the women dry it out. I can lend you another."

While Bell struggled into his wet boots, Sir Druerie rose from his chair with a hint of reluctance, putting a hand on his hip and grimacing as he did. Bell, who had been a little annoyed by the man's seeming indolence and arrogance realized he was prey to rheumatics, intensified by the wet weather. His guess was confirmed by the care and difficulty with which Sir Druerie navigated the stair. Bell would have offered his shoulder as a support, but the stair was too steep and narrow and he suspected, too, that the older man's pride would have been hurt.

Since there was no place in which to leave his horse in shelter at Mainard's shop and the distance was no more than a street and a half, Bell did not have Hamo bring his palfrey from the shed but set out to walk the distance at Mainard's side. They turned the corner into the Chepe itself, and Bell recognized Lintun Mercer's shop (recalling and dismissing the memory that the bolts of cloth had arrived when promised) a few doors down. As they passed it—it looked strangely naked without its counter as did the whole market with only a few open stalls sheltered—Bell could see FitzRevery's shop and Mainard's, too. Lacking the crowds, even Herlyond's and FitzIsabelle's places of business. . . . Bell drew in a breath.

"What is it?" Mainard asked, looking anxious.

"Sir Druerie can recognize Saeger! He said so. That is our answer. You must arrange for the five men to come face-to-face with Sir Druerie."

"I? You are asking me to be a Judas goat!" Mainard exclaimed.

"I am asking you to lay an ambush for a man who not only killed your wife—who I admit might have deserved killing—but also, for her property, another woman in Hampshire, of whom I know no ill at all."

"But what if he did not kill Bertrild? What if someone came in at the north end of the alley from Fenchurch Street? If a man wished to conceal his movements, he would have chosen to go farther rather than pass the stalls nearer my house. It is not impossible that someone else—"

"Then if we lay hands on Saeger, he will have a chance to clear himself, at least of murdering *your* wife, and we will bring him to deserved justice for murdering *his*." Bell's voice was sharp, without sympathy.

Mainard wrung his hands under his cloak. "I suppose I must," he said faintly, "but what am I to say? I am no liar, and I do not do business with any among them except FitzRevery. I will choke on the words if I must ask them to gather to talk of the bridge. Truthfully, I have not given it a thought or a moment's time since Bertrild died. They will all know it is not the truth. . . ."

"Then tell the truth," Bell said. "Tell them that you collected ten pounds in silver from Bertrild's goldsmith and that you wish to return it to those from whom she extorted it. That is the truth. You do wish to return the money, do you not?"

"Yes. But then they will know that I know from whom she took the money and . . . and why."

"Hmmm." Bell thought that over, then said slowly. "I think they, or at least one of them, knows already. Do I not remember that you said nothing was taken when your house was turned inside out?"

"Nothing of real value. I have not counted up every shirt or pair of socks."

"Then do you not think it possible that whoever did it was searching for the evidence. . . ." Bell hesitated, sighed, stopped, and grasped Mainard's arm. "At the funeral, you told someone about Bertrild's tally sticks, didn't you?"

"Yes, I did. Was that wrong? I only told Pers, that is Master Newelyne. He has nothing to do with this, and he certainly could not have killed Bertrild or be Saeger."

Bell sighed again. "But you did not tell Master Newelyne to keep the matter in confidence, did you? And he had no idea how Bertrild had got that money, or how much it was, or that it was from extortion. Is it not possible that he spoke of the matter to others?"

"Of course he didn't know it was from extortion! Neither did I, until I learned the amount. Pers thought she had saved it from what I gave her and from starving the slaves. He always said I allowed her far too much. He was pleased because he thought I would be getting my own back again." Now Mainard sighed. "I suppose he did tell others."

"Which of the men was at the funeral?" Bell asked, releasing Mainard's arm, and then before Mainard could answer, he groaned. "Never mind, I know. All of them. I remember them myself, all hanging together and looking as if they expected to be summoned to answer for some crime. So, they heard about the tally sticks and that Gerlund was Bertrild's goldsmith, and one of them pried Gerlund's mouth open and learned about the other precious item he held, the packet."

He stood thinking, then narrowed his eyes and asked, "Who knew you were not going back to the Lime Street house after work yesterday?"

Without answering, Mainard started walking across the Chepe toward his shop. Bell strode after him. "You told FitzRevery," he said grimly. "He was at Magdalene's on Thursday, and he came to ask you to spend a few hours with him on Friday because he knew Sabina was not with you, and you told him you were going to the Old Priory Guesthouse to be with her. . . ."

There was no counter in front of Mainard's shop. There was no sense in getting saddles, saddlebags, and reins soaked, even though they were treated to resist wetting, and the finer, softer suedes would definitely not be improved by the rain. However the door was invitingly open and they could hear Henry's voice, friendly and persuasive, rehearsing the fine points of some piece of work to a hardy customer. Mainard hurried past, his face concealed by his hood, and reached for the door to the workroom.

Bell caught his arm before he opened it. "Do not forget," he said softly. "Arrange for *all* five men to meet Sir Druerie before he returns to Swythling."

"Very well," Mainard conceded unhappily. "Guild meetings are mostly on Wednesday. I will ask them to come to my house after their meetings."

"Good enough. I will be there to make sure that Saeger does not attack Sir Druerie."

Seventeen

A nd where have you been?" Master Octadenarius, already in the workroom and in a temper as foul as the weather, snapped at Mainard as soon as he walked through the door, and, turning on Bell, asked, "What brings you here? Do you scent murder and follow it as a hound does a stag?"

"I was at home," Mainard said. "At the house on Lime Street. My—"

"Your man did not know you had gone home?" the justiciar asked sardonically.

Mainard smiled slightly. "My man is loving and loyal." He shook his head at Codi, who looked harassed and had tears in his eyes. "He did not wish to tell you that I had gone to Mistress Magdalene's, to the Old Priory Guesthouse, before Vespers yesterday, and I expected—" a look of pain crossed his face "—ah . . . hoped to spend the night." He frowned at the justiciar. "But, you must have known that. I spoke to your man outside my shop yesterday, the one who asked about Borc—"

"Who is now dead!" Master Octadenarius paused, watching Mainard's face, and then said, "You are not at all surprised, I see."

"He was when I told him," Bell put in. "I am sorry, Master Octadenarius, but I do not think it worthwhile coursing this hare. Master Mainard could not have killed Borc. His uncle-by-marriage, Sir

Druerie of Swythling, was with him at the Lime Street house from—"
he turned his head toward Mainard "—from when, Master Mainard?"

"The bell for Vespers had not yet rung from St. Mary Overy
Church when I left the Old Priory Guesthouse, and it took a little less
than a half candlemark—I did not want to press poor Jean—to walk
to Lime Street. So, I guess, you could say I was with Sir Druerie from
Vespers on."

Master Octadenarius sighed. "At least your witness this time is
more reliable than a whore. Very well, I will accept that you did not
kill the man. Why should I believe that your journeyman Codi did
not?"

Codi's mouth opened, but no sound came out. He shivered, hugging himself as if he were suddenly cold.

"Codi?" Mainard echoed, and smiled again. "Codi blanches if he
has to kill a louse. Pardon me, Master Octadenarius, but that is ridiculous. Why should Codi kill Borc?"

"To protect you?" Octadenarius asked sharply.

"From such a thing as Borc was?" Mainard asked, shaking his
head. "Besides, how could he know Borc threatened me, not that he
did. I do not believe Codi ever spoke to him."

"No, Master," Codi's voice trembled, "but I did pull him away
from Henry once."

"When was this?" Mainard asked.

"Yesterday, just before he got into the workroom. I was outside,
moving the saddle Henry had sold to that yeoman to replace it with
another, when that—that *thing* slid past Henry on the other side.
Henry reached out to stop him, but he pushed past through the door
to the shop. I had to put down the saddle, but Henry followed him,
and he turned in the doorway and struck at Henry's hand with something—mayhap a broken knife. Henry cried out, and Master Fitz-
Revery stepped out of his shop. I suppose he intended to help Henry,
but I was closer, and he just gestured to me to follow Henry. I went
in and grabbed Borc, but he twisted loose and ran into the workroom."

"Why didn't you follow him there?" the justiciar asked.

"Master Mainard is more than strong enough to deal with that
creature, and the two boys were there to call me if Master Mainard
should need help, so I bound up Henry's hand, which was bleeding,

and then went back to changing the saddles. A few moments later Borc came out and went away."

"Did you ever see or meet the man before?" Octadenarius asked.

"Not that I remember," Codi said, and then frowned. "Oh. I think I once saw him go into Master FitzRevery's shop. It was late. Henry had gone home and I was taking down the counter. I remember because he was so . . . so unlike a customer or even a messenger likely to visit Master FitzRevery."

"But you never mentioned this before?"

"Why should I?" Codi cried. "Did I know the man would die in our alley? And no one ever asked me about him before."

"Please, sir," Gisel put in, taking Codi's hand. "He couldn't have done it. We were all in the shop together and the . . . the body wasn't there at dusk when I went to pull in the latchstring on the back gate for the night. I looked out, and the alley was empty. And at night, Codi can't get out. Ever since we . . . I found Mistress Bertrild, I have bad dreams, so Codi let me and Stoc put our pallets right against his. He'd have to step on us to get out. I know we sleep sound, Lord Justiciar, but not that sound."

Bell cleared his throat. Master Octadenarius gave him a sour look. "You want to stand out in the rain to look at the body? Go ahead. And how do you come to be here anyway? You never answered that."

"I had gone to the Old Priory Guesthouse this morning to. . . ." Bell's voice faltered as he remembered the miller's blood running over his hands and why he needed to be with Magdalene on the previous morning; he cleared his throat again. "To discover if her whores had learned anything more about the five men who could have taken Codi's knife. She had just told me that Bertrild herself had been in the workshop that day and could have taken the knife herself—apparently she was in the habit of picking up this and that in the hope of causing trouble—when Stoc, the younger apprentice, came to find Master Mainard to tell him about the body in the alley. The boy was soaked and overworn from running all the way, and it so happened I had my horse, so I told him I would fetch Master Mainard. Magdalene said she would keep Stoc and get him dry and warm. He was terrified. He had found the body and said something about Borc's face . . . ?"

Octadenarius sighed again. "Likely Brother Samuel at St. Catherine's will explain it. Go look if you like."

Bell promptly went out the back door, across the yard, and out the gate, which was standing open. A miserable watchman huddled against the fence, holding a worn piece of leather over his head. "I have permission to look," Bell said, and lifted the tattered, torn, and stained blanket that had been thrown over the body.

The face was indeed something that could frighten a boy unaccustomed to death. It even startled Bell because it was twisted in a terrible grimace, and the vomit that had dried around the mouth was full of dirt as was a broad bruise on the forehead. There might have been other bruising, but Borc's face had been filthy to begin with and what might be dried blood was indistinguishable from old smears of grease and gravy that had run and mingled in the rain.

The tunic had been rucked up so the braies were exposed. As with most corpses, Borc had wet and soiled himself, but Bell stood staring at the stained garments, his brows knitted in a puzzled frown. Something was wrong, different. In another moment he knew what it was. Not only the upper part of the braies were soiled, the part around the anus and penis, but the legs, the hem of the garment, and the stockings beneath it, too, were marked with filth. That meant the body had been upright when urine and feces were released.

A man does not stand upright when death relaxes the body's control. No, but for some fear can bring about the same result. Was Borc held upright as he was killed? after he was killed? Bell blinked. How was he killed? The head seemed round. There was no blood—well, maybe there was. Between the rain and old stains it was hard to tell. But the face? Was that grimace one of fear, or was it a twisting of the muscles as in a fit? Was the bruise deep enough . . . ?

Nonsense! How could a body have a bruise on its forehead and dirt around its mouth and be lying on its back?

"Watchman," Bell said, "did you turn the body over?"

"Didn' touch it a'tall. Didn' even see it, 'till you took off the blanket."

Bell guessed that Codi had put the blanket over the body and that Octadenarius had not bothered to examine it at all. It was not really an abandonment of his duty. He said he had made arrangements for the body to be carried to the brothers of St. Catherine's Hospital; Brother Samuel would examine it and tell him the cause of death. But how had it come to fall on its face hard enough to make those bruises and now be lying on its back? And when had it been turned?

It had been raining for hours. . . . Bell nudged the body with one boot; the flesh gave a little, and the body was not so rigid that it would lift in one piece like a board of wood. As it was, he could not shift it far enough to see whether the ground underneath was wet or dry. He made a horrible face as he leaned closer—Borc stank even worse in death than he had in life—to pull the blanket back over the corpse.

The change in angle of vision showed him a pile of rubbish beyond the watchman's feet and lying beside that . . . surely that was the neck of a flask. A flask and Borc connected immediately in Bell's mind. He went over to look and found a handsome leather flask, its gold-decorated stopper still tied to the neck by a finely braided gold silk cord. When he shook it, a small amount of liquid sloshed within. The watchman was looking at him in amazement.

" 'eard somethin' fall when I backed up against the wall, but I didn' see nothing," he said. "Too bad. I coulda done wit a spot t'warm me."

Bell looked from the flask to the corpse. "You do not know how lucky you are that you didn't take a 'spot' out of this flask." He twitched his head at the body and slid the flask under his cloak. "I think he did."

"Excuse me," he said to Octadenarius when he was back inside the workshop, "but I must ask Codi a question."

"By all means," the justiciar replied sourly. "The answers I am getting are doing me no good."

"Codi, did you touch the body at all after Stoc told you it was there?"

"No, Sir Bellamy." The man shuddered. "I only went as far as the gate. When I saw him . . . it . . . I told Stoc to run to the Old Priory Guesthouse to fetch back Master Mainard, and I sent Gisel for Master Octadenarius. Then I took one of the old blankets out of the shed and sort of threw it over the body. I didn't touch it. I didn't even go near it."

"And it was lying as it is now, face up?"

Codi shuddered again. "Yes."

"Do you know when it started raining?"

"I happen to know that," Octadenarius said. "I left my bed just before dawn for the usual reason and looked, as I often do, out of the window. The path was dark with wet but not under the trees where they overhang it, so it could not have been raining hard or long. Say the rain began in earnest at dawn. But why does it matter?"

"Because Borc fell forward, onto his face—there are bruises to show that—but he was lying on his back when Stoc found him. The child said something about his face, which he would not have been able to see if Borc was lying face down."

"So someone turned him over." Octadenarius shrugged. "Any passerby might have done so to see if he could help."

"I am not so sure of that," Bell said, his lips twisting with distaste. "I am not sure I would have touched anyone who smelled like that, but if the ground is dry under the body, the turning would have been done before dawn . . . when it is not very likely that a casual passerby would have been abroad."

"True enough," the justiciar said. He cast an irritated glance at Mainard, Codi, and Gisel, all standing close together in a defensive half circle, and another at Bell.

"One more question," Bell said, withdrawing the flask from under his cloak. "Does anyone know this flask?"

His glance was fixed on Gisel who examined what Bell held with innocent interest before he shook his head. Codi took a little longer, coming closer to look carefully at one of the designs.

"Mercer," he said. "That's the guild symbol. "I've seen it on some things Master FitzRevery has—a leather cup, I think. But I've never seen a flask like that." Codi glanced at his master, who had stiffened up. "It's not Master FitzRevery's own seal," he added hastily. "It's the guild seal. Any mercer could have a cup or a flask like that."

"Mainard?" Bell urged.

Mainard shook his head. "I've never seen such a flask in Perekin's shop or home."

"Where was it?" Octadenarius asked.

"Beside a heap of rubbish where the watchman was standing. Oh, don't blame him. Likely it was covered with dirt when you told him to watch the body, and the rain washed some of it away so that I noticed."

"You would notice," the justiciar said. "Bell, you think too much. You see too much."

"My chamber is very neat, too," Bell said, grinning. "I do not like anything to be out of place or unexplained. A flask like this in a rubbish heap needs explaining—and maybe the answer is within. There is still some liquid left."

"Poison?"

"That, Brother Samuel or one of his fellows will have to tell us. I am not so desperate for an explanation that I will drink any myself." Bell grinned again.

Octadenarius grimaced. "For the trouble you have given me in this matter, I should demand it of you. If Borc died of poison, he might have drunk it anytime during the day."

"That, too, Brother Samuel may be able to tell us—quick or slow acting—according to how long it takes for his animal to die."

"When did he die, do you think?"

Bell shook his head. "I would say either he died in Herlyond's shop soon after he went in or soon after he left it, or he has not been dead long. Possibly he died just before dawn. He is stiff, but not rigid. If he died yesterday afternoon, the stiffening would have had a chance to form and then start to wear away because it was warm yesterday. If he died at dawn, the stiffening would likely take longer because today it is cool and damp. Also very interesting is that he is befouled from his waist to his feet—"

"Fouling is common in sudden, violent death."

"Not fouling that runs down from hips to feet. He was standing when he was frightened enough to void or held upright after he was dead."

"Somehow," the justiciar sounded tired, "I cannot see anyone in this lot—" his glance flicked over Mainard, Codi, and Gisel "—holding a corpse upright after it was dead, or, for that matter, dropping it just outside this gate." He sighed. "It is time now to question Herlyond. Do you want to come also?"

They learned very little. Herlyond admitted freely that he had not been in the shop from early morning until past Vespers. He knew nothing of Borc and had not seen him at all the previous day. Confronted by the evidence of Octadenarius's man, the journeymen then admitted that Borc had passed through the shop. Both denied they had ever seen him before or that he had asked for money. All he had wanted was to go out through the back door because men he owed money, who wished to beat him for nonpayment, were outside. As for why they had lied about letting him pass through, that was easy. Both feared they would be punished for allowing a criminal—or a debtor—to escape.

The apprentices, who had been in the storeroom in the back, agreed that Borc had passed through the shop and out the back door. He had not stopped to eat or drink. One boy said even his swift passing through threatened to stink up the goods; they would never have permitted him even to pause to draw breath.

Bell asked about the flask, which he had carried with him, and the shock mirrored on all faces made his muscles tense and his hand drop to his sword hilt. After a moment, Herlyond said it did look like his, but his was still in his counting chamber. With Octadenarius on his heels, he went into a small room divided from the workroom and came out with an almost-identical flask.

The senior journeyman denied vociferously that he would have given a companion flask to Borc. They were expensive, he pointed out. His master had paid three shillings for his when the guild was raising funds for a charitable purpose. And when asked who else had bought similar flasks, he said most of the men in the guild had done so, or bought a cup or sometimes bought a cup and a flask. He then went into his master's office and brought out a matching cup. Bell took it in hand, but it was dry and dusty, clearly kept as an ornament as was the flask.

"Too bad there are two journeymen," Octadenarius said as they left the shop. "I cannot accuse one without having the other witness in his defense and the two apprentices, too. That is a tight-knit, happy family."

"I think we will have to wait now until we know that there *was* poison in the flask and how quickly it acted. As soon as I know, I will make a reason to visit each of the five who might be suspect and see whether any has such a flask or remembers who had one. Meanwhile, I must return to Mainard's house to retrieve my horse."

Bell smiled to himself when Octadenarius bid him farewell without the slightest sign of reluctance, plainly relieved to be rid of him. But the justiciar was an honest man, even if he was not pleased to have complicated problems added to his load of work. He took with him the carefully capped flask to be delivered with Borc's body to the monks of St. Catherine's Hospital.

The rain was no more than a drizzle by the time Bell reached the Lime Street house, which was just as well because the place was locked tight. Pounding brought Jean who called a frightened question through the door. He opened it when Bell identified himself and sent Hamo to resaddle the palfrey and bring it around. Sir Druerie, Jean told Bell when he asked, had gone up to the solar, which was now back in order, to warm his aching bones in bed. There was nothing specific Bell wanted to ask the older man, so he left him in peace, mounted, and rode toward the West Chepe where he intended to ask Master Newelyne if he remembered to whom he had spoken about Bertrild's tally sticks.

When he passed Fish Street, Bell looked over his shoulder toward the bridge, but he was not really much tempted to ride south to the Old Priory Guesthouse. Saturday was a busy day, often with extra clients to be fitted in, and he would not be welcome in the common room. Sunday was better. He knew that Magdalene and her women spent a leisurely morning over a more-than-usually hearty breakfast. If he went to early Mass, he could be with them for the meal. Magdalene would be eager to hear how Borc had died and what Sir Druerie said; the women would all pet him and praise him. . . . Bell smiled.

• • •

27 MAY
LIME STREET HOUSE

Stoc returned to Mainard's shop not long after the rain abated, calmed and well fed. Codi and Gisel seemed somewhat recovered, so Mainard decided to get over with the distasteful task Bell had demanded of him. He told Codi and the boys to get back to their work, and he went next door to tell Perekin FitzRevery about the money he had collected from Johannes Gerlund and wished to return.

"It *was* my farm," FitzRevery said, with tears in his eyes, virtually acknowledging that Genlis's notes were true. "My father did *not* swear it away to the Church. The priest—"

Mainard looked at the bitter lines around FitzRevery's mouth; those lines were new. He put a hand on his friend's arm. "Perekin, you need not explain to me. I know you. I only want to return what Bertrild wrung out of you, and I would like you to meet her uncle, Sir Druerie. He is a very good man. It is as if all the bad was concentrated in Gervase and his daughter and all the good in Sir Druerie. You will like him, and he will like you."

FitzRevery looked at the hand on his arm and licked his lips. "Wednesday, you said? After the guild dinner. Very well." He drew a deep breath and then, as if to cover over what had gone before, said briskly, "And what was going on in the alley all morning? Do not tell me your people found *another* body!"

"Yes, they did," Mainard said and was relieved at the look of horror that crossed FitzRevery's face.

He explained as much as he knew about Borc's death and left FitzRevery shaking his head. By the time he returned to his own shop, he found all the good Magdalene and her women had done Stoc was undone. He kept casting harried glances toward the back door, and Codi and Gisel were little better. Gisel hit his finger with a hammer; Stoc dropped a newly completed saddle frame; and Codi put aside the saddle seat he had planned to cut because his hands were shaking too much to produce a clean line. Mainard himself stared at the cantle he was supposed to be decorating and could not imagine how to continue the design he had started.

Thus, when Master Octadenarius returned from Herlyond's house, Mainard asked whether he could close his shop and take Codi and the boys home to Lime Street with him. Since the lay brothers arrived with their dead cart just about then and both Stoc and Gisel burst into tears, the justiciar shrugged and approved. There was no counter to take in, so Mainard sent Henry home and locked up.

At Lime Street, Mainard sent Codi and the apprentices into the kitchen to tell the cook there would be four more for dinner. He gave Codi two pence and said that if the cook did not have enough, he should buy what the boys would like from a cookshop. Seeing the relief on Codi's face, he smiled faintly, knowing Codi had expected the cook to be furious. At that moment Sir Druerie came down the stairs and the boys, seeing a guest, looked at him pleadingly. He assured them again that they could all sleep at Lime Street that night, the boys in the common room, the slaves in the kitchen, Sir Druerie in Bertrild's bed, and himself on his pallet.

Mainard had the feeling that Sir Druerie might look down on him for coddling his servants, but he would just have to ignore that. Codi and the boys were all the family he had. However, Sir Druerie paid little attention to Mainard's arrangements. He gestured Mainard into the common room and pointed toward Bertrild's chests.

"My womenfolk would be delighted to have Bertrild's clothing," he said. "They would be the envy of every other dame in our area. But these are costly garments of fine cloth and with expensive embroidery, Mainard, and you, no doubt, paid for them. Bertrild came to you with nothing but debts. I feel it unjust for me to take back her belongings."

"I do not want them," Mainard said.

Sir Druerie clicked his tongue impatiently. "Think, man, you are still young. You still need a son to inherit your business. Are you sure you do not want to keep these things, or at least some of them, for your next wife?" He laughed at Mainard's agonized expression. "Likely Bertrild soured you on womenfolk. She was, as I said, a real devil, but most women are good creatures, and you will find one, I am sure, who would make you happy."

"No. It is not that I am soured on women. The colors would not suit . . ." Mainard's voice trailed away, and the skin that could flush did so.

Sir Druerie looked at him in some astonishment. "Colors would not suit? Suit who? Have you another woman in mind already?"

Mainard took a deep breath. "I have . . . had . . . a leman . . . , a good woman. . . ."

"Have? Had? Which? Did she leave you because of Bertrild?"

"No, I sent her away—"

"To please Bertrild? That was idiotic. A wife has no business questioning what a man does so long as he provides well for her." Druerie's lips twisted. "And from the look of this house and those clothes, you certainly did that."

"No." Mainard looked down at his hands. "No, I only found Sabina after . . . after . . ." He swallowed. "Bertrild said and did things that . . . that made me incapable—"

"The evil witch! She had special torments for each person she knew."

"I did not blame her entirely. It cannot have been easy for her to lie with me. Can you imagine waking in bed and seeing my face—"

"She knew your face well before she married you. She made a bargain, and you kept your part. She should have at least given you a son or two. After that, if she did not wish to share your bed, there would be reasonably kind ways to make that clear. Do not excuse that devil to me. I suffered from her also." Then Sir Druerie smiled. "So you found a woman you like and who is satisfied to be with you. Good. But you said you sent her away?"

"When Bertrild was killed. I did not want her to be harassed."

"Hmmm. Did it never occur to you that she had a very good reason to wish to be rid of Bertrild?"

"But had less opportunity than I to do harm. I told you why I was not accused, that I was at a christening celebration. Well, Sabina was the singer there and was in plain sight of dozens of people all afternoon. Besides, she could not stab anyone."

Sir Druerie laughed aloud. "Because she is so good and sweet?"

Mainard smiled also, turning his head so the distortion of his lips and birthmarked cheek should be less obvious. "No, although sweet and good she is, but because she is blind. A knife in Sabina's hand would be useless."

"Blind! But that means she cannot cook or sew or even watch over the servants' work. Oh, well, I am sure it is very sad, but for you not all without advantage. So, how did you come to find her and make her your leman?"

"Very strangely. By my neighbor, Perekin FitzRevery, I was brought to join and become one of the principal members of a Bridge

Guild—all the Bridge Guilds are joined together for the purpose of building a new bridge across the Thames. When we have serious and private matters to discuss that the lesser members might not need to know, this guild often meets in a place called the Old Priory Guest-house, which I must tell you is a whorehouse—"

"That is a strange name for a whorehouse," Sir Druerie said, from the grin on his face vastly amused.

So Mainard told him how the Old Priory Guesthouse got its name and something about the place and the character of its whoremistress. Sir Druerie looked doubtful when Mainard spoke of what the Guest-house offered and then horrified when he named Magdalene's prices, but he did not interrupt to speak his doubts aloud.

"But one afternoon when I went there thinking to meet the others in the group," Mainard went on, "I found I had mistaken the place or time or something. In any case, Sabina came to greet me and ask what I wanted and—and I am not sure how it came about, but I found myself in her bed and . . . and fully restored to my manhood."

Sir Druerie nodded, a cynical twist to his lips. "So you bought her out of the whorehouse—"

"No, Sabina was a free woman and Magdalene . . . it is too bad you cannot meet Magdalene. She is very special."

"I have met whoremistresses," Sir Druerie said dryly.

"Not like Magdalene," Mainard retorted, raising a hand to hide his grin.

"Well, that is neither here nor there. I am glad you have a woman to tide you over, but you need a wife."

"No," Mainard said. "I will never marry again. Not unless Sabina is willing—"

"Nonsense! You cannot marry a whore. And do not begin to tell me how little she liked whoring and that she would be a good and faithful wife. Even if it were true—and that is the same tale they tell to all men, with every intention of continuing their profession as soon as their husbands are out of the house—the father of a whore's child is always in doubt. How can you leave your business to the son of a whore? How could you be sure, really sure, the child was yours?"

"I would not doubt Sabina's child." Mainard shrugged at Sir Druerie's snort. "That is not a problem for me anyway."

Sir Druerie was silent for a moment and then said, "You are fixed on this woman, are you not?"

"Yes. I will not look elsewhere if I cannot have her. I lived most of my life without a woman. My parents tried once or twice to make a match for me, but . . . I need not go into that. Anyway, I was content that way and can be again."

"Then who made the match between you and Bertrild?"

"We made it ourselves. We were old enough. I went to collect a debt that her father owed me. I had not heard he was dead, but I found Bertrild in a terrible situation. She was penniless; there was not even food in the house; and she had been threatened by other creditors. I brought in dinner from a cookshop and told her at once that I would forgive the debt—it was not large—and she was so grateful, so . . ." He shuddered. "She was so warm and gracious to me, telling me she was lonely and begging me to visit her again. Well, I knew what loneliness was, and it seemed to me that if she was so lonely that my face looked good to her, I should offer some friendship until she found more pleasing companions. Over some weeks, she seemed content with my company and finally she suggested that if I would clear her debts and support her generously, she would be glad to marry me."

Sir Druerie nodded. "She was the same when she arrived at my house, and to me, always, so smooth and pleasant. . . ." He shuddered, too, then sighed. "Mainard, I know you do not want to hear this and will not believe me, but whores are very practiced in concealing their distaste for men—and this I suspect is for all men, not you in particular. Do not offer marriage to this Sabina. As long as she knows you can cast her off if she does not please you, she *will* please you. When you are bound to her, will you, nill you, she . . ."

"She will tell me I am a monster and drive me away?" He sat quietly, his head bent in resignation, his hands lying open in his lap. "Perhaps."

Sir Druerie watched him for a moment, and tears misted his shrewd eyes. "And perhaps not," he said briskly, blinking hard. "You said the girl is blind. She cannot see you or know what you look like, so she may not know what advantage she has. She cannot have had an easy life. I tell you what. I will go tomorrow to this house and speak to her. Not being blinded by love myself, I may see more clearly than you just what kind of a woman she is. Who knows, perhaps she is worth marrying."

Mainard's head came up, but he looked doubtful. "You will not hurt or try to frighten her? Sabina is very gentle. You will not shout at her or threaten her?" And then Mainard laughed shakily. "Magdalene will kill you if you make Sabina cry. She protects her women like those Amazons of legend protected the walls of Troy."

Sir Druerie's lips twisted wryly. "Mainard, if I were to threaten someone, it would be you. The woman would immediately bow to any threat, and turn about the moment I was gone." He laughed. "You too, I fear. No, I only want to talk to her, to see what she is like. I will tell you what I learned as honestly as I know how. If you listen, you listen. If you do not, there is no more I can do for you."

"Very well. Then I will send Jean to tell Magdalene that we will come tomorrow. Magdalene does not usually take clients on Sunday, but I am sure the women may have guests if they like, so we will be welcome."

"The Old Priory Guesthouse does not entertain men on Sunday?" Sir Druerie first laughed and then pursed his lips thoughtfully. "No, do not tell the whoremistress we are coming. I would like very much to see the house and the women as they are, so to speak in a state of nature."

"We may not get in if I do not make arrangements in advance. Magdalene does not really like surprises."

"No matter. If we cannot get in and your woman cares for you, she will come out to us — unless the whoremistress keeps them prisoner?"

Mainard bit his lip. He did not really want to be refused entry to the Old Priory Guesthouse or, even if he was not refused, have Sir Druerie tell him that the beauty and goodness he saw in Sabina was false glaze like the opalescent sheen on putrid meat. He wanted to believe Sabina cared for him. Magdalene said Sabina cared only for him — but Magdalene was a whore and a sharp businesswoman. Had she told the truth? Mainard had come to respect Sir Druerie and to acknowledge that the man liked him and wished him well, but could

Sir Druerie with his prejudices judge Sabina fairly? Still, there was a chance Sir Druerie would say Sabina was fond of him. That would be a balm indeed for festering wounds.

"No, Magdalene does not confine her women at all. If for some reason Magdalene does not want us in the Old Priory Guesthouse, Sabina could come out with us. Very well, I will give the boys a free day and after dinner we will try."

Eighteen

Dulcie had hardly put the final platter on the table for the women's breakfast when the bell at the gate pealed. Magdalene said a word her women rarely heard pass her lips and rose from her place. Then she shook her head and smiled.

"It must be a message," she said. "Surely no one could want service so early in the morning."

"I don't know about that," Ella said, drawing away to the end of the bench as Diot began to cut food for her. "Often the friends who stay all night wake up with an erect standing man and want to play an early game."

Magdalene laughed, took her cloak, and pulled the hood over her head because the morning was chilly and misty. What Ella said was true enough, but by the time most men had risen and dressed and relieved their bladders, that urge would be gone. She thought it more likely that it was a response from William about the information she had sent him or, perhaps, Mainard, who could not wait any longer to see Sabina. Or Bell . . . No, it was too early for Bell.

She unlatched the gate and pulled it toward her, just as a loud crash sounded from the grocer's house across the road. The hooded head of the broad-shouldered man who had rung the bell was turned away from her, drawn to the noise. Magdalene suffered an odd dichotomy of feeling: joy for Sabina and a vague disappointment for herself.

"Mainard! You are early, but very wel—"

"Are you expecting Mainard?" Bell turned toward her, away from the loud voices coming from the grocer's shop along with the occasional tinkle of broken crocks.

"Well, I hoped. . . . I wonder why—Ah! You are both big men, and that is Mainard's cloak you are wearing, or one very like it."

"It *is* Mainard's. I was soaked through by the time I got to his house yesterday, so he lent me his clothes and his cloak. I sent the clothing back with one of the bishop's servants last night, but I forgot the cloak and also forgot to tell the servant to get mine from Mainard." He cocked his head as a crash, a woman's shriek, and a man's howl of pain drifted across the road. "Never mind that, I think we should go inside before that argument comes out and I feel obliged to prevent murder being done, although—" he winced as there was another crash and another male howl "—I am not sure who it is I would have to protect."

Magdalene stepped back, and when Bell had passed her, closed the gate behind him. She hesitated a moment, although Bell had started for the house, looking at the bell pull and wondering if she should pull it in. Then she sighed and left it where anyone could ring; there was the possibility that Mainard would come or she would hear from William.

"What news?" she asked as she took off her cloak and hung it.

"Borc was poisoned with lily of the valley. Leaves, stems, and flowers were cut small and wine poured over them in a flask. Brother Samuel says he does not think the plants were steeped more than a few hours, but that was more than long enough."

"That is unfortunate," Magdalene said, putting out her hands to take Bell's cloak.

He took it off but did not hand it to her. "Why? Borc could surely be spared more than most."

Magdalene giggled. "Do not be so silly. I didn't mean it was too bad that *Borc* was poisoned. I meant it was too bad that poison was used—from such a common plant, too. I had hoped the manner of his death would point to someone, but poison can be given and not take effect for hours—"

"Not lily of the valley. From what Brother Samuel said, it acts very fast."

"How fast? If he was outside Mainard's gate, does that mean the drink had to be given him in Mainard's house? Could he have come from, say, FitzRevery's?" She put out her hand toward the cloak again, and when he did not give it to her, asked, "Are you going to hold that all morning? I swear no one here will try to steal it. It would trail on the ground, even for me, and I am the tallest."

He laughed. "No. I wanted to leave it with Sabina to be returned to Mainard. I doubt I will need it later, and Mainard will return mine."

"Just put it beside her on the bench. Do you wish to join us to break your fast?"

"Indeed I do, thank you. I went to early Mass for the purpose of joining you."

While he spoke, he went around the table, patted Sabina on the shoulder, and laid the cloak on the bench between her and Letice. Sabina's hand went to the cloak instantly and she gathered it close, her fingers stroking it as if it were a living part of the man and could feel her caress. Then she slid down closer to Letice, leaving a space for Bell to sit.

"As to the poi—" he looked across the table at Ella and said, "—the drink given to Borc, it would have acted too fast for him to come from anywhere else, possibly even from Mainard's shop, but it was in a flask, and he could have carried that with him from any-where at all."

"So his death tells us nothing."

"Not nothing. For example, did you know that lily of the valley was poisonous?"

"Of course I did. Everyone who lived on—" she stopped, then continued, "—as I did learned what plants could not be picked for salad or for greens to be added to a pottage. But I did not know that it worked so fast."

Bell glanced up once from the slices of cold meat and wedges of cheese and pasty he had moved from central platters to his trencher, but he did not catch her up on her near slip. "Everyone who lived on a farm," she might have been about to say, or "everyone who lived on

an estate with a garden." He knew how dangerous lily of the valley
was. It was off in a fenced corner in his mother's garden with the
nightshade, foxglove, hemlock, bryony, and other dangerous plants that
could be used as medicinals in small amounts. But he was not yet
ready to confront Magdalene about her past; perhaps he would never
be ready because he did not want to know.

"You knew and I know, but I suspect that many people raised in
a city . . . Ella, love, what do you know about lily of the valley?"

"It has a sweet scent, and the little flowers are very pretty. Is there
something special I should remember about it?" Ella's lovely brow
creased with anxiety, for she often forgot things.

He looked at Magdalene, who shook her head infinitesimally and
then he smiled at Ella and said, "No, pet. I just wondered if you knew
about the plant. Magdalene does not have any in her garden, does she?
"Who else?" he asked, looking around the table.

"I know," Diot said, "but I come from a manor in the country."

Letice shook her head and then cocked it in a query, and when
Bell described the plant, she shook her head again. Sabina also shook
her head.

"But that leaves us where we were before," Magdalene said.
"FitzRevery would know as he lived at least half a year on a farm and,
of course, the invisible Saeger would know for the same reason. Josne?
Possibly. We do not know where he was from the time he left Norwich
until he reappeared in London. Herlyond? He came from a city,
Southampton, and so far as we know came directly to London, so it
is again possible but not certain. FitzIsabelle, unlikely, unless it grows
in the garden behind his house. . . . Oh!"

Bell looked up from his food. "Oh?"

"We need an excuse to look in all the gardens. I do not have lily
of the valley or any other noxious plant. If I had, we would soon be
accused of poisoning—as if a dead client was of any use to us. But
Ella is quite right. It has a very sweet scent and is pretty, too. There
are some who grow it as an ornament."

"To check the gardens is a good idea, and gives us a second string
for our bow. The bow is presently strung with Sir Druerie, who—good
Lord, I forgot to tell you that when I arrived at the Lime Street house,

it had been searched from top to bottom, every chest emptied, all the furniture upturned, pillows slit—"

"Pillows slit?" Magdalene echoed. "That does not sound like an ordinary robbery. Often after a person dies, thieves are attracted to the house in the hope that all that person's possessions will be gathered together, but an ordinary thief would steal a pillow, not slit it."

"And nothing seems to have been taken either. No, I do not think it was an ordinary thief."

"Mainard was not hurt, was he?" Sabina asked in a breathless voice.

"It would take a whole troop to damage Mainard," Bell said with a grin, "but no, he was not. He was at the shop or perhaps on his way here. Sir Druerie arrived to find the house open, the servants locked in the shed and with no idea who did it." Bell frowned. "So much has happened so fast that I did not have time to question them, but I suppose Hamo was seized and bound, the shed searched, the cook and maid drawn out by some device, possibly forced to call to Jean to come out, and then all of them thrust into the shed so the house could be searched at leisure. When I go back to watch how Sir Druerie reacts to the five Bertrild was squeezing, I will make sure the servants did not see something they do not realize is important."

"Why are you showing those five to Sir Druerie?"

"Because he is familiar with Saeger's appearance."

"Ah! And how will you get them to confront him?"

Bell looked smug. "I asked Master Mainard to invite them to his house, using the excuse that he wished to return to them what Bertrild extorted. There, he will introduce each to Sir Druerie, who will be able, I hope, to point out Saeger."

"Poor Mainard," Sabina murmured. "He will hate laying a trap that might catch a friend."

"Saeger is no friend to any man, no matter what he pretends," Bell remarked dryly. "He murdered his first wife—if she was his first—for her property, and there is some question that he killed his father-by-marriage, too."

"I know," Sabina said, "and Mainard knows also, which is why he agreed to do what you asked, but he will be very unhappy."

"I do not like to hear about robberies," Ella said. "The thieves will not come here, will they?"

"No, love, of course not," Magdalene soothed. "You know how careful we are to lock up the house. And then, there are usually some friends staying with us, and they would rush to protect you."

"No one will be here tonight," Ella said, looking from face to face for assurance.

"I will stay if I think there is any danger," Bell said, assuming that by evening Ella would have forgotten the whole discussion.

"Oh, good!" She smiled like a happy child and slid along the bench to get to her feet. "I remember you have a long, sharp sword. You will be able to keep us safe." She looked at Magdalene. "I will go clean my room now. When I am finished, can we play a game?"

"If it is quiet, love. We will see."

Letice also slid off the bench, gathering up the remains of her meal and Sabina's, which she piled at the end of the table for Dulcie to clear away. She tapped the table to draw Magdalene's attention and then signed that she was going out.

"Very well," Magdalene said, "but be careful in the street. Remember, when you were out the other morning you thought someone was following you."

Bell's head came up sharply. "Someone followed you, Letice?"

She shrugged and lifted her hands palm up to show that she was not sure, frowned, and ran off suddenly. On her slate when she returned was the word "saaf."

Bell looked at Magdalene, who said, "Safe. She means that she arrived safely."

"I don't like it," Bell said, rising from the bench. "I might have made a slip of the tongue when I was talking to the beggarmaster, who used to be whoremaster in the house where Letice worked. He may think from what I said that Letice told me for whom she changed seals and his name also. I think I will just walk along with Letice to the inn she goes to. Once she is with her friends, she will be safe enough, and I will come back. I'd like to see those documents of Genlis's again, if you don't mind, Magdalene."

"I'll get them," she said. "Will you come back here for dinner?"

He grinned broadly. "If you invite me, I will come. I am free today because the justice put off his decision on those disputed tithes. Since I do not need to stop at Swythling to look for Saeger, there is no great hurry for me to leave for Winchester. I can wait until Sir Druerie points out Saeger and perhaps have his company when I ride."

Letice came back from putting away her slate, wrapped in a cloak and veil, and Bell followed her out. Diot finished the last of her ale and said, "Do you want to put Master Mainard's cloak away in your own chamber, Sabina?"

"Oh, yes," Sabina replied and got out from behind the table, still clutching the cloak.

Diot looked at Magdalene, who shrugged, and then offered her arm to Sabina, who laid a hand lightly on it. When Diot returned to the common room, she beckoned to Magdalene who followed her into her chamber, where she shut the door. Magdalene glanced around quickly. The positions of bed and chest had been changed, and a small table with a stool had been added, but the room was in excellent order.

"I did not want to speak where Sabina could hear," Diot said. "She worries about that hulk of a man as if he were fragile as glass. However, I thought I should mention that I do not think that breaking in to Master Mainard's house was by thieves. I think it was one or more of Bertrild's victims who was looking for the documents we have. Is it safe to keep them here?"

"I thought the same myself," Magdalene agreed, "but I am not sure what to do. If I give them to Bell, he will hand them over either to the bishop or to Master Octadenarius. That might lead to a terrible death for a man like FitzRevery, which would be a great wrong if he is not guilty of killing Borc and Bertrild."

"If he carried letters to Gloucester in Normandy, that is treason."

So Diot comes from the south, Magdalene thought. Being herself from the north, an invasion from Normandy did not seem very important, but she understood Diot's reaction. It was over southern lands that battles would be fought; it was southern villages that would be raided and looted. Magdalene quickly subdued her curiousity. From where Diot came was none of her business, nor what sent her into whoredom; it could not be worse than what she herself concealed.

"I doubt it was deliberate treason," she pointed out. "Bertrild's father forced him to carry the letters. A trader in wool has no desire at all to see ships of war in the narrow sea. However, I am enough of your mind about those documents being dangerous to keep to try to get Bell to let me remove a few sentences from some of them and then give them over into his hands. I certainly do not want those men in here searching."

Diot nodded, remaining tactfully in her own room while Magdalene retrieved the documents from their hiding place. She had them all neatly separated, the bound parchments in one box and the scrolls, tied in two batches, in another. She set them beside her stool and covered them with a third box, open to show bands of ribbon and hanks of embroidery thread. Magdalene picked up her needle and began to think about what concessions she could hope to get from Bell while she waited for him to return.

<hr>

28 MAY
MAINARD'S SHOP

Mainard and Sir Druerie, having talked late into the night, overslept early Mass and barely made the later one. It took a long time to get breakfast, too, because the cook was unused to preparing for so many and, particularly, for so many young, healthy appetites. She misjudged the portions and had to make what amounted to three breakfasts before she was done.

When the boys were finally fed, Codi asked anxiously if Master Mainard would accompany them back to the shop and seemed about to burst into tears when Mainard said he had other plans for the day. Seeing his journeyman's distress, it occurred to Mainard that no work would be done even if he sent the boys back, so he told Codi to take the day off and come back to sleep at Lime Street again. They would begin anew in the new week, he promised, with everything peaceful and ordinary. Codi thanked him, said almost prayerfully that he hoped nothing exciting would *ever* happen again, and went off with the boys.

Sir Druerie went on eating without comment, although he had shaken his head when Mainard so easily yielded to his journeyman's fears. Mainard opened his mouth to point out that it was useless to try to get decent work out of skilled craftsmen when their minds were elsewhere, but instead he exclaimed wordlessly and rushed away from the table. Druerie called after him to discover what was wrong, but got no answer until Mainard returned.

"They are gone already," he said, "and I have no idea where."

"You changed your mind?" Sir Druerie asked.

Mainard, more at ease with this man than with most, wrinkled his nose. "No, only I should have told Codi to go to the shop before they set off for their holiday. The man who does the selling for me might as well not miss the Sunday trade, but he will not be able to bring out the counter or the goods. His hands are nearly useless, and he cannot carry any heavy object."

"If the shop is locked, he would not be able to get the goods anyway."

"He could get in. Master FitzRevery has a key and could let him in, but I think it an imposition to expect Perekin to carry out my counter and stock for Henry. If you will pardon me, Sir Druerie, I will walk down to the shop and open up for Henry. And since we are going to the Old Priory Guesthouse, I think I will take two or three gowns to Sabina."

"No need for pardon. I think I will accompany you. The weather is fair, and I would like to look about in the Chepe. I know I have all Bertrild's dresses and other things for my wife and daughters and daughter-by-marriage, but a new toy or two makes them so happy.... You think me too indulgent?"

Mainard laughed. "I am forever buying things for Sabina that she insists she does not need or want, so I am the last one to call you indulgent."

They finished eating in perfect amity and then strolled out. Mainard shook his head when he heard the bar being dropped in its slot behind him. It was too bad the servants should be so frightened, but he hoped the worst was over now. When they reached the corner of the Chepe, Sir Druerie looked down the street in some surprise, commenting that the market was a great deal larger than that in Winchester.

"It is only one of the markets, and actually somewhat smaller than the West Chepe. And the animal markets are not held in London.

Cattle and horses are displayed in the Smithfield twice a week. You will stay the week, at least, I hope—and of course you are welcome for as much longer as you can spare—so I can show you all the markets and more of London. My friend Master Newelyne, a cordwainer, has many connections in the West Chepe."

"Oh, yes, I will certainly stay the week. I want to lay my hands on Saeger, even if he is not the one who killed Bertrild. If he is, I will be willing enough to leave him to London justice, but if by chance a different one of those five you were describing to me murdered Bertrild, I still want Saeger for the death of his first wife. I will take him back with me and see that he hangs in Swythling."

"Bertrild was—"

"A personal devil!"

"Even so, to kill . . ." Mainard shuddered.

Sir Druerie laughed. "It is as well that you were not noble born, Mainard. It is, after all, a knight's first purpose to kill." He shook his head at Mainard's expression. "There are times when it is necessary, you know." Then he slapped Mainard on the shoulder genially. "Forget it." He gestured widely at the Chepe. "This is more interesting, but there is too much here to see just walking along. You go ahead and meet your man and help him set up for the day's work. I will look at the stalls and meet you later."

Knowing he was late already, Mainard did not argue. He bid Sir Druerie farewell, warned him that he must chaffer or he would be skinned, and urged him to come and get him if he saw something he really wanted to be sure he would get a fair price. Then he stretched his long legs and made quick work of the street between Jokel de Josne's shop, where Sir Druerie was headed, and his own. He saw Henry leaning patiently against the building.

"Sorry," he called out.

"Knew you'd be late if you let the boys sleep in Lime Street." Henry looked around. "Where are they?"

"Quaking like reeds. There was no sense sending them back here. Either they would do nothing, or they'd spoil everything they touched. I told them to go and play. I'll open and set up for you—and I'll give you a free day to make up—"

"No need," Henry said, grinning. "I like to sell. It's a real pleasure to sell your goods, Master Mainard. I never need to worry about angry customers coming back with split seams or cracked leather. If there's a fault, I know I can point it out. And my wife was glad to be rid of me today. She has some kind of women's guild coming."

While Henry spoke, Mainard removed the heavy key from his purse and pushed it into the lock. To his surprise, it would not turn. He pulled it out, put it back in, but it still would not turn. He twisted it in the other direction, thinking to free the tumblers by jostling them, but the key then turned readily. He lifted the latch and pushed, but the door was tight locked. Then he turned the key to unlock, and the tumblers moved as smoothly as they ever had. This time when he lifted the latch, the door opened.

"It was unlocked?" Henry said.

"It was unlocked," Mainard agreed, "but I could swear that I locked it when we left yesterday."

Henry stood looking at Mainard's hand on the door latch, frowning and trying to remember. Finally he shook his head. "I think you did, too, Master Mainard, but I don't know if I truly saw you lock the door yesterday, or I have seen you lock it so often that I remember all the other times."

"To tell the truth, I am no more sure than you. I have been . . . a little distracted." He shrugged. "Well, we will see if anyone has taken advantage of it."

They walked in but saw nothing much amiss. All the finished saddles ready for sale were there. One saddle was crooked on its stand and a set of reins had slipped to the floor, but the most valuable item aside from the saddles themselves, a heavily decorated, inlaid-with-ivory pair of saddlebags, lay just where Henry had left it, propped upright on a shelf behind the counter, and some silver bells and tassles for fastening to a lady's bridle were also untouched.

Henry shook his head. "You know, Master Mainard, I was upset myself yesterday, even if I tried not to show it. Two dead bodies . . . I could have knocked those reins down and brushed against the saddle and not even realized it."

"As could I," Mainard said, but he felt uneasy.

Still, he carried out the trestles and then the wide board that sat on them to make the outside counter. When the board was firmly settled, he brought out two saddles, setting one at each end of the counter, and then the odds and ends of leatherwork: the bundle of reins, several halters, several bridles, a collection of girth straps. Henry carried out his stool, which he could hook over his arms so his nearly useless hands were not necessary, and the box in which he kept farthings and a few pence to make change.

As Henry began to shift items around in what he thought was a better arrangement, Mainard went back through the shop and into the workroom. He stood in the doorway staring around, the hair prickling on the back of his neck. There was some disorder, but the boys had not cleared away as carefully as he usually demanded. Still, he *knew* someone had been in that workroom, someone had searched the shelves, gone through the piles of leather, shifted all the work on the tables, and looked through the drawers. And when he looked at his toolbox, he had proof. Someone had pried up the hasps into which the lock fitted so it could be opened.

His toolbox? That was ridiculous. If another saddlemaker wanted his tools, he would have taken the whole box. All together they were valuable; singly, they were only valuable to him. He had used them a long time, and they fitted his hands and were worn down to the angles at which he worked best—but that would be a disadvantage to another man. He did unlock the box, open it, and look in, but nothing was missing. Nothing had been missing from his house either, although that had been searched much more roughly.

Mainard closed and locked his toolbox again, looked at his worktable, and drew a sharp breath. The saddle he had been working on was ruined! He leaned closer. No, it had not been ruined, only all the stitching had been cut, the padding pulled out. . . . He stood staring at it, then turned slowly to look around the room. That was the only saddle that had been pulled apart, and it was the only saddle he had worked on since Bertrild's death. Someone who knew what was going on in his shop had opened the seams of that saddle, where he might have hidden something, opened his toolbox, searched through the shop and the workroom. He stood quietly, breathing deeply. Someone was searching for the packet he had given to Magdalene . . . someone with a key to open his shop.

He set his teeth and went into the shop and up the stair to Sabina's chambers. Here was chaos: chests emptied and furniture overturned, garments and bedding strewn everywhere. Color rose into Mainard's unblemished skin until the two sides of his face nearly matched. He stood still, fists clenched so hard the short nails bit into his callused palms, swallowing hard, fighting the impulse to rush next door and beat Perekin FitzRevery to a pulp. It was bad enough that the man had abused his trust by searching his premises and damaging his work, but to show such disdain for a woman Perekin *knew* he loved . . . cruelty, too, to disturb Sabina's furniture. It took her so long, so many bruises, to learn to move freely.

And then rage was swallowed up by alarm. What had been done in the Lime Street house was not the work of one man. To overpower the servants must have taken several working together. Five men were being bled by Bertrild. Five men had been in his shop the day that Codi's knife was stolen. What if they somehow learned that he had given that packet to Magdalene? What if they thought he had given it to Sabina to keep safe? What if they decided to wrench the secret of where the documents were from Sabina or Magdalene by force?

He left the room in chaos and hurried down the stair. He could send the servants from Lime Street to straighten it up another day, when all knew that the documents were beyond their reach. But for today, until he could arrange for the safekeeping of that packet, he had to get to the Old Priory Guesthouse to warn Magdalene. He would stay himself to protect the women there until Octadenarius or some other power had the packet.

Henry had two customers at the counter, but Mainard interrupted without a thought. Taking several farthings from his purse, he handed them to his man.

"I will not be able to come back to help you close up," he said. "I must go to the Old Priory Guesthouse. Get someone to carry the goods in and get the key from Perekin FitzRevery to lock up. Keep the key."

He had forgotten all about Sir Druerie and would have rushed to Magdalene's without even leaving a message for him, except that his guest caught at his arm as he hurried down the street and asked where he was going in such a hurry.

"The shop was searched also," he said. "They are looking for that packet I told you of. I am afraid they are growing desperate and will try to force Magdalene to give them the documents. I must go to the Guesthouse and make sure the women are safe."

Sir Druerie patted the sword at his side. "They will be safe. Lead on."

Nineteen

The gate bell pealed with such violence that Magdalene jumped to her feet, oversetting her embroidery frame, and ran out of the house to answer it. It pealed again and again, and she flung open the gate without even looking to see who was ringing. Letice must have been attacked, she thought. Perhaps Bell had been hurt defending her. They needed refuge.

She saw Mainard, his beautiful eyes wide with anxiety, his huge chest pumping, before she even realized how ridiculous her thoughts were. "Are you all right?" he gasped. "Is Sabina safe?"

"Of course we are all right," Magdalene said. "Why should we not be safe?"

"Because of what I gave you to hold," he replied, but her answer had calmed him, and he turned to look at Sir Druerie, who was leaning against the wall, still gasping for breath. "I am sorry I rushed you along so fast," he said to the older man. "Nothing like this has ever happened to me before. I was afraid my unwillingness —"

"Yes, yes," Magdalene interrupted, "but do not waste time on confessing your sins here. Bring your friend in where he can sit down and drink a glass of wine."

She held the gate wide, and tactfully stepped behind it so her presence should not embarrass the older man when Mainard almost picked him up and carried him down the path. She shut the gate and followed.

Sabina was again on the front step, calling "Mainard? Mainard? Is something wrong? Are you hurt? Did those men hurt you? Oh, who is breathing so hard?" Her hands came up, feeling for the beloved form even though she knew he was not yet close enough to touch.

"Be careful of the step!" Mainard bellowed. "I am not hurt." And then more softly. "Go in. You will be chilled."

Magdalene rolled her eyes heavenward. How those two, so devoted to each other that it made her faintly sick, could still manage not to understand they were best together, she did not know. She wished most fervently for many reasons that Bertrild's murderer would be found and that she could be rid of those accursed documents. And not least of those reasons was that there would then no longer be any excuse for Mainard not to settle matters.

She hoped Mainard would keep Sabina because the girl truly loved him, but she was no longer concerned that Sabina would be forced back into whoring. She had two or three engagements to entertain each week, and one woman had actually changed the date of a dinner she meant to give so that Sabina could sing for her guests. She would not make as much money singing as she had made whoring, but her list of clients was growing, and before the money Mainard had given her had run out, she would be able to pay for her keep and Haesel's.

By the time Magdalene entered the house and closed the door, Mainard had seated his guest at the table, and all her women had put aside their embroideries and risen to their feet. Ella cried out, "Oh, poor man," and ran to fetch a cup from the shelves against the back wall. Diot caught up a flagon of Magdalene's good wine and poured it for him, and then went to the kitchen to get a small plate of sweet cakes; experience had taught her that sugar and wine were a good restorative.

Still breathing hard, Mainard's companion only nodded his thanks, but Magdalene saw his shrewd eyes taking in everything—first Sabina and Mainard; then the women themselves in very attractive but unrevealing gowns; the stools grouped around the hearth, two with needlework set down on them; the scrubbed table; the clean floor; the neat shelves, holding only household goods, no whips, no restraints, no sexual toys.

A Personal Devil

Magdalene then also looked at Mainard and Sabina, again standing hand-in-hand, Mainard staring down into Sabina's face, which she had lifted toward him as if to facilitate his examination. Recalling his haste and anxiety and the remark he had made about "what he had given her to hold," Magdalene decided she had no more time to waste on the game of statues.

"Mainard," she said, touching his arm, "why did you run all the way here? Why were you so anxious about our safety?"

With what appeared to be a physical wrench, he pulled his gaze away from Sabina's face. "Did you hear that my house at Lime Street was searched on Friday?"

"Yes, Bell told me."

"Well, my shop was searched yesterday, searched by someone who had a key to open the door and who knew what I had been working on all last week. It certainly was not Codi or the boys. They were with me in Lime Street, and I hold the keys; Henry does not have a key—I had to go to the shop to open it for him. Nothing was taken from either place. Am I wrong in thinking those searches were for something only recently come into my possession?"

"I think not, but why should you think the Old Priory Guesthouse would be in any danger?"

"Because the searcher—no, there must have been more than one because of the way the servants were confined at Lime Street—so, searchers, could not find what they sought in my house or in my shop and might assume I had given it to my leman. I was afraid they would come here to try to force the secret out of her . . . or you."

"I thank you for your concern, but—"

"But no buts. They have all been guests here. Would you think to keep them out without a warning?"

"Ah, I see what troubled you. You feared they would come in under false pretenses and then threaten us." She smiled slightly. "I assure you they would have found nothing here and likely gone quietly away. However, I thank you again for your concern."

She twitched at his arm lightly, and tilted her head toward his companion. With her other hand she tapped Sabina's wrist. Obediently, Sabina released her grip on Mainard's hand. Although Mainard did not respond at once, first looking down at Sabina, he turned toward the table when Magdalene pulled at his sleeve a bit more insistently.

Ella was saying, "Ah, you look much better now. I hope you are restored. It was foolish for you to hurry so. We are mostly free on Sundays, so if you want—"

"Ella!" Magdalene said warningly and the girl fell silent, but no one could mistake her disappointment. "We do not solicit custom here," she said to Mainard's companion. "But Ella does love her work. No one is taking advantage of her, I assure you."

"No," Sir Druerie agreed dryly.

"Sir Druerie is not come to be a guest here, Ella," Mainard said, smiling at the girl and patting her shoulder. "He wished to meet Sabina, of whom I had spoken."

"Oh." The expression of puzzlement cleared from Ella's face. "You thought she was going to sing this afternoon and wanted to catch her before she left. That was why you hurried so fast you were all out of breath. But her engagement was yesterday. Today Sabina will be here all day." Ella smiled at Mainard and turned to Sir Druerie. "Do you wish to hear her sing, sir?"

"Later, my dear," Sir Druerie said. "Now I would like to meet your wh—Mistress Magdalene."

Magdalene stepped forward and curtsied slightly. "And you would like to be called, sir?"

"My name is Sir Druerie of Swythling—"

"I do not think you are supposed to tell us your name," Ella put in, frowning. "Not that I will remember it. I am not very good at remembering. But Magdalene always says that what you do not know cannot pop out of your mouth when you are not thinking."

"That is very true."

Sir Druerie's voice was pleasant enough, but Magdalene detected the beginning of impatience. "Ella, love," she said, "would you be good enough to go to the kitchen and try to make Dulcie understand that there will be two more for dinner—that is, two in addition to Bell, who will soon return. Altogether there will be three, beside ourselves for dinner. Can you tell Dulcie that, love?"

"Oh, yes." Ella looked toward the half-embroidered ribbon lying on her chair.

"This once, I will take care of your embroidery, and if Dulcie and Haesel are doing anything you think would amuse you, you have my permission to stay with them."

"You are very kind to that half-wit," Sir Druerie said when Ella had trotted down the corridor and disappeared into the kitchen.

"She is simple, childish, not a half-wit," Magdalene said, a slight undertone of sharpness in her voice. "Within the limits of a five-year-old, she is really quite clever. And her good humor and willingness are of considerable profit to this establishment. Now, how may I serve you?"

Sir Druerie laughed. "Mainard told me you defended your women like an Amazon. That seems to be true. Actually you cannot serve me at all, although you likely are the most beautiful woman I have ever seen. I came, as Mainard said, to meet Mistress Sabina. I wish to serve Mainard, if I can, after the damage my niece did him. Do you object?"

"Not at all," Magdalene replied without hesitation. "Sabina?"

But Sabina had already taken her staff in hand and was coming toward the table. She was pale, and Mainard stopped her, laying his hand over hers on the staff.

"You do not have to speak with him, Sabina," he said. "You do not have to do anything you do not like."

"Why should I not like to speak to your uncle-by-marriage?" she asked, smiling faintly. "If he will deign to talk to me and cares enough for you to make this effort, I can only be grateful to him." Then she turned her head toward where she knew the table was. "If you will speak, Sir Druerie, I will know where to face when I answer."

"If you do not mind, Mistress Sabina," he said, "I would like to talk to you in private. Is there such a place?"

"My own chamber is private," she said, extending the staff slowly and cautiously to be sure no person was standing in her way. "If you will come this way—"

"Sabina—" Mainard said, his voice shaking.

She turned toward him and smiled but did not speak and then went forward down the corridor toward her room with Sir Druerie trailing behind.

Magdalene drew a rather exasperated breath. When she first realized who Sir Druerie was and why he had come with Mainard, she had been furious because she thought he was Mainard's excuse for abandoning Sabina. Magdalene did not doubt that Mainard adored Sabina, but she feared that he had been hurt so deeply and so often that he simply could not bear to expose himself to hurt again. Therefore, instead of seizing the joy Sabina brought him and living in hope that she would remain his lover, he intended to run away from the relationship using as an excuse Sir Druerie's judgment that Sabina was a whore and would first betray him and then leave him.

She was less angry now. Sir Druerie had his prejudices, that was for sure, but considering them he had been remarkably patient with Ella. In addition there was genuine liking and understanding in his expression when he looked at Mainard, and he looked him straight in the face, not wincing away from its deformity. She could hope that he would perceive that Sabina truly cared for Mainard. If he did, his assurance would go a long way to giving Mainard peace.

"Would you like a cup of wine, Master Mainard?" she asked.

"No, I—I do not think I could swallow it," he said, and sat down heavily on a bench, only to spring upright again as the gate bell rang.

This was no peal, just a brief "clang-clang" to warn the house that someone was there. "That will be Bell," Magdalene said, but when she went out, Mainard was on her heels.

It was, indeed, Bell, looking very satisfied with himself as she swung the gate open. "Letice is safe with her compatriots, and they assured me—at least the most villanous looking man I've ever seen, except that Letice clearly knows him very well and trusts him—assured me that she would be accompanied home tonight."

"He is an uncle, I think, although I am by no means sure," Magdalene replied, "but I am sure that smug expression on your face has little to do with Letice's uncle."

"Oh, yes it does. He was not at all pleased when I told him who might be having Letice followed, and he said he and his friends would look into it. It may be the sheriff will—Hola, Mainard, what are you doing here?" He laughed as he said it. "Now that's a fool remark if I ever made one." Then a frown took the place of the laughter. "What I meant was why did you come to the gate with Magdalene?"

"Come inside," Magdalene said. "We do not need to tell the whole street what has been happening."

This time when she got the men seated around the table and Diot brought cups and wine, Mainard took a cup and downed it in one long swallow. Then he told Bell about the search of his shop and his conclusions. Bell listened with bright-eyed interest.

"Nothing could be better than if they do come," he said.

"Magdalene, did you bring out those documents as I asked you to do?" She nodded. "Very good. Let us spread them out on the table — enough so that anyone who suspects what they might be would recognize them."

Magdalene nodded again. "Yes, and when we see how they react, we can ask for an explanation."

"You are not going to let then in!" Mainard protested. "I will go to the gate with you and turn them away—"

"Mainard, I will *pray* that they come and welcome them gladly. Do you think I want to spend the rest of my life looking over my shoulder or guarding this house against invasion? These men must know that the proof of their misdeeds, whether desperate or mere peccadillo, is either destroyed or beyond their reach."

"Absolutely," Bell said. "When we discover which of them is Saeger, perhaps we can wring a confession out of him and be done with this matter. Once I show him the wills and the indictment and prove he will be hanged anyway for the death of his first wife, I will take everything remaining to the bishop of Winchester's house where it can be locked safely away and guarded, and we will tell the others."

"In that case, we had better look these over very, very carefully," Magdalene said as she got the two boxes holding the documents and brought them to the table. She took out the bound parchments and laid them down, flipping them over and then down again, impatiently. "I wish I knew which of these we could burn without doing harm. This business about Herlyond, for example, to expose that would be cruel and useless."

"Yet, as I told you, he acts the most guilty. And he is the likeliest to have given Borc that dose of lily of the valley. When I spoke to Brother Samuel at St. Catherine's Hospital, he could not yet tell me whether Borc died right after he visited Herlyond's shop or just before dawn on Saturday. He had to wait until the body either stiffened or softened more, and I have had no time today to learn what he discovered."

Magdalene sighed and shrugged. "I know, but does it not occur to you, Bell, that Genlis would have written these notes in the most damaging way, deliberately omitting whatever might have mitigated the offense? What if we hear good and sufficient reasons for what was done?"

"I do believe that FitzRevery's farm was not promised to the Church," Mainard said. "Or if it was, it was literally on the old man's deathbed as a result of being deliberately frightened by threats of hell. I knew old FitzRevery—not as well as I know—" he hesitated and his lips thinned "—thought I knew Perekin, but the old man was simply not the kind to give more than what was due to anyone, including God, I am very sure."

"Yet FitzRevery fits most closely into the pattern we have for the murderer, and with the threat of an accusation of treason hanging over him, he would be the most desperate to silence his accuser and destroy the evidence."

"Why do I not cut the documents apart?" Magdalene asked. "We would then have all the accusations separate, and if we felt exposure would be unjust, we could destroy just those—"

The gate bell rang.

"I will go," Magdalene said. "Diot, watch through the window. If it is anyone except the five men we hope will come, sweep all those documents back into the box and cover it in some way or carry the boxes to your chamber. If it is the five, I do not think they should see you when they first come in, Bell—"

The bell rang again, somewhat more insistently.

"You could wait in my room," Magdalene said to Bell and then turned to Mainard.

He glanced down the corridor to where Sabina had taken Sir Druerie and shook his head. "There is no sense in hiding me. They must know I am here. I told Henry, and he would tell FitzRevery if he asked. Henry never came upstairs and does not know what was done to Sabina's chamber."

The third time the ringing could be called a peal.

Diot walked with Magdalene toward the door. "If it is a client other than the five, hold them in talk a few moments so I can get to the table," she said.

As Magdalene stepped out, Diot went to the window and loosened the frame holding the sheets of oiled parchment, which let in the light but not the wind. Bell stepped into Magdalene's room, leaving the door open enough to hear and see out, not that he could see much because the walls of the corridor cut off most of his view. Mainard stood awkwardly in the middle of the room, looking alternately down the corridor and toward the door.

In a moment, Diot had pushed the frame back into place and walked to the hearth, where she picked up her embroidery and seated herself on her stool. She dropped the work to her lap and looked up as Magdalene opened the door and stepped to the side so all five men could file in. She shut the door behind them softly, and equally softly set in place the bar that locked it. Of course, the bar being inside only locked the door against those outside, but it would take a few moments to lift it from its slots and that delay might prevent the flight of a guilty man.

Ulfmaer FitzIsabelle stopped dead in his tracks when he saw Mainard. He was pushed forward by Lintun Mercer, whose eyes were turned toward the table. John Herlyond walked around them both, looking from side to side, as if he were more interested in the place than in the documents. Perekin FitzRevery saw Mainard, lifted a hand in appeal, and then dropped it without saying anything. Jokel de Josne came forward only enough to sidle toward where the door would open.

"You fool!" FitzIsabelle exclaimed, stepping toward Mainard. "What kind of an idiot gives information that might ruin a man to a bunch of whores."

"You mean I should have left it at my home or my shop so that it would be easier for you to steal it?" Mainard asked bitterly.

Lintun Mercer had walked to the table and looked at the bound sheets of parchment. Magdalene came away from the door and stood beside him. Mainard moved closer also, near enough to prevent anyone from grabbing for the documents. Mercer glanced up at Mainard, smiled, and made no attempt to touch anything. When he turned his eyes to Magdalene, however, they were narrowed.

"Why are these lying exposed for anyone to see?" he asked. "What were you intending to do with them?"

"Certainly not ask anyone to pay for keeping them secret," Magdalene said. "Master Mainard had asked, when he was told what was in the packet Johannes Gerlund was holding for his wife, if the evidence could not be destroyed. To speak the truth, I was wondering the same. Old sins, long repented and expiated, likely should be forgotten. Give me a good reason why you employed Gervase de Genlis to swear falsely, and perhaps they will be."

"That is easy enough," Jokel de Josne said immediately. "The merchants from whom I bought were gone from England, the receipts I had were in some heathen script no one could read, and two disappointed buyers were accusing me of stealing the goods. It was cheaper and easier to get Genlis to swear he was witness to the sale than to fight my accusers."

"Then why did you pay Bertrild to keep quiet?" Magdalene asked.

He shrugged. "For the same reason. It was cheaper and easier. She did not ask much the first time."

"She did not ask much?" Ulfmaer echoed. "She was bleeding me white!"

"She knew she could prove nothing against me, no matter what her father wrote," Josne said. "If you ask me, the only reason she tried to extort money from me was because I was with the rest of you when we brought Genlis here. Remember how she said we had corrupted him and caused his death?"

"There was more involved than spite," Magdalene remarked cooly. "Bertrild had collected ten pounds." She looked back at FitzIsabelle. "Perhaps more of it came from you because you robbed Gunther Granger, whose heirs would be frothing at the mouth and placing complaints with the justiciar if a hint of the loss came to them."

"There were no heirs!" Ulfmaer bellowed. "The estate would have gone to the Crown."

"Good Lord," Josne said, laughing, "then you've committed treason as well as robbing the dead."

"That for sure," Ulfmaer spat. "To which Crown should I have proffered the inheritance? To Stephen, who usurped his cousin's right? To the empress Matilda, whom we swore to uphold but who could not bestir herself to come to England? To whichever I made the payment, the other would have called that treason and support of the enemy."

He swung his head from side to side like a baited bear. Magdalene did not like Ulfmaer FitzIsabelle, but if it was true that there were no heirs, she found herself in complete sympathy with the man. She thought she would personally rather have her banker steal her money and use it to enjoy himself or support his wife and family than that it should go into the bottomless maw of the king's purse. Nonetheless, the hint of treason might have added to the impetus to permanently quiet anyone who had proof of the crime.

"Let us go, Magdalene," FitzRevery sighed. "We have been punished enough. The farm was not offered to the Church by my father, and the deed was honestly lost. If he had given it to the priest, would the priest not have brought it out and showed it when the case was argued? Because there was no deed, the judges would not give a final decision and that priest tormented me until at last I decided to find a deed. Is that so great a sin?"

"Perhaps not," Magdalene said, "but it grew, did it not? You carried letters to the rebels in Normandy."

"No!" FitzRevery shouted. "I carried a packet to a wool factor in Brugge. Yes, Genlis asked me to carry the packet, but I had no reason to suspect that there was treasonous matter in it. Genlis just asked. He did not threaten me or give me the smallest reason to suspect him of involvement with Talbot, Lovel, and FitzJohn. It was only when I came back that he came to my shop and explained what I had done."

He came forward toward the table then, but his eyes were on Mainard, not on the documents. "May God forgive me, for I know you never will, Mainard. I have violated your trust—but I was desperate. Do you know how a man convicted of treason dies? Do you know that all his possessions are confiscated? My son would have starved, my daughter been tainted." He looked down, not at the table; his eyes were empty. "It seemed such a small thing, to open the door. I did not let them damage anything except the one thing you were working on after Bertrild died. . . . Will you let us all be destroyed because we searched your house and shop?"

"This is ridiculous," Lintun Mercer said. "I was not desperate and will not be destroyed. I committed no crime. An old man was afraid to tell his daughter and son the truth about disposing of his business so he lied to them and left me with a nasty problem. Likely he did not expect to die so soon. He thought he would have time to explain to them. Why I paid? As Josne said, it was easier than adding a new doubt to the case being considered."

"But I know that seals were removed from one document and placed on another for you. You were recognized—"

"Lies," Mercer said, glaring at Magdalene. "Tell me who you have to speak against me."

"The man you paid to have the work done and the woman who did the work."

"A beggarmaster and a mute whore?" Mercer uttered a short bark of laughter without any humor in it. "As I said, I paid not out of fear but because I wanted no complications in the case to be presented to the justiciar. This is not worth discussing. If you want to bring the accusations to the justiciar, do so. I came to keep the others company."

Magdalene nodded acknowledgment and looked questioningly at John Herlyond who said, "Perhaps what I did was a crime, but I did not think so when I did it, nearly twenty years ago, and I do not think so now. I was treated unfairly by a hard, greedy master. I begged for release, but he would not free me, so I left him without permission. Because I did not wish to starve in the road, I needed a letter that would permit me to look for another master."

"How did you know that Genlis would write such a letter for you?" Magdalene asked.

Herlyond looked down, then up again, frowning. "I do not remember," he said. "Perhaps my master did business with him that I knew was not honest. Perhaps a servant of his heard me complain and hinted he would help me for a price. I had to pay him every farthing I had earned and saved over ten years. I am not sure. What can it matter twenty years later? I satisfied my second master, and I kept in mind the lessons I learned and have been, I believe, a good master to my own journeymen and apprentices."

That was certainly true. From what Bell had told her, Herlyond's journeymen and apprentices were fanatically devoted. Devoted enough to commit murder for their master? That might have been necessary if Borc was the one who had told him Genlis would write a false letter for release for him.

However, all Magdalene said was, "Yet you, too, paid Bertrild to be silent."

Herlyond sighed. "It was a mistake to do so. I see that now, but the first demand she made was small, and at the time I was busy with my sister's troubles. I did not wish to need to explain myself to my guild, and I did not want to be burdened with a fine if the court saw fit to set one. For me, too, this is no longer worth talking about."

"Except for one small matter," Bell said, as he walked into the room from the corridor. He had been quietly standing just inside the doorway of Magdalene's room while the men explained their compliance with Bertrild's extortion. His voice was dry, his tone sardonic, and he stopped at the foot of the table. "All of you say the old sins are no longer important, that there are explanations. But there are also two new murders, both connected to these documents—"

"Murders?" Jokel de Josne interrupted with a laugh. He leaned against the wall near the door, his lips twisted up on one side into a cynical leer. "Say rather an extermination of vermin. Whoever did it should be paid a fee for his trouble."

"They were human beings," Mainard said. "Not good ones, perhaps, but they deserved a chance to see the error of their ways, to confess, to repent, to be forgiven their sins."

"Bertrild? Human?" FitzRevery's voice was high and thin. "You can say that after what she did to you?"

"Yes, because unwitting and likely unwilling, she and you, not out of good will but because you wished to spite her, may have brought to me the greatest good of my entire life. God and his Merciful Mother work in Their own ways and choose what tools They will for that work."

"Pious mouthings," FitzIsabelle spat. He turned toward the table. "I want those documents destroyed. If the contents were exposed, I would be ruined. How many people will stop to think that I harmed no one, that I only wished to protect myself? They will account me greedy and untrustworthy. I did not kill the woman, I paid her."

"You may not have killed her with your own hand," Bell conceded, "but one of you five either murdered Bertrild himself or hired or forced another man to do it in order to conceal a much more serious crime than those you have explained."

"Why? Why we five?" Lintun Mercer asked. "I can see from the number of sheets and the size of the writing that many more men were accused of crimes by Genlis than us. I think what Josne said is true, that Bertrild picked us to squeeze for money not because we were most vulnerable but just out of spite."

"Why you? Because Bertrild was stabbed with two knives, and one of those knives was Codi's. Codi's knife was stolen from Mainard's shop on the nineteenth of May. The only ones who could have taken that knife were you five."

"I do not think that is true," FitzRevery said. "I know there were others in Mainard's shop both before and after we were there."

"Some were never in the workroom. Some could not have killed Bertrild for other reasons, such as not being in London at the time of her death. In any case, we know who actually killed Bertrild. It was the man who said he was Sir Druerie's messenger. The man who came muffled in a cloak. The man who Bertrild called Saeger."

"No!" Herlyond cried. "No! I did not kill her!"

Every eye in the room turned toward him.

"You mean you were the man in the cloak?" Bell asked, his hand dropping to his sword hilt.

"Yes. I was the man in the cloak, but I did not kill Mistress Bertrild, and I am not Saeger. I told you already. I had no reason to kill her."

"You hid your face. You claimed to be a messenger from her uncle. With your knife in her back, you bade her dismiss all her servants so they should see and hear nothing. And you expect us to believe that you did not kill her?"

Herlyond was breathing hard with nervousness, but he said, "I did not kill her. The rest I can explain. I was coming home from my sister's new house. There was so much dust from cleaning and scraping and painting walls that I nearly choked to death. I had intended to stay and help my sister settle into the house, but I was coughing and sneezing and she bade me go home—that was why I was muffled in the cloak. As I was riding along, I was thinking of Bertrild's second demand, and it came to me that I had rather spend the pence on my dear sister's pleasure to lift her spirits after her husband's death. Also, I thought that it was time to clear my past with my guild. I decided to go and tell Bertrild not to send Borc to my shop again."

"You could have told Borc that the next time he came."

"I did not want him in my shop again. He upset my journeymen and apprentices."

Bell's brows went up. "Enough for them to feed him lily of the valley steeped in wine?"

"No!" Herlyond exclaimed. "They would have cast him out the front door, but they had seen me give him money and were afraid for me. That was why they sent him out the back. And I do not think any of them know how dangerous lily of the valley is. They are all four from the city, and I do not have any of it in the garden. I have young children who come sometimes to the shop and play in the garden."

"Let us go back to Bertrild. Why did you say you were a messenger from her uncle?"

Herlyond shrugged. "I was exhausted from choking. I wanted a place to sit down and get a drink of water. I knew if Bertrild was there, she would likely refuse to see me, and if she were not, her servants would never let a stranger in the house, so I said I was a messenger from Sir Druerie. I knew he was Gervase de Genlis's brother. I had seen him with Sir Gervase while I waited in the stables at Moorgreen for Sir Gervase to write and sign my letter."

"But Bertrild called you Saeger."

"I had not yet put back the hood of my cloak. I suppose she mistook me for this other man. When I did lift the hood, she sort of squeaked with surprise and then said she was expecting someone else and I must leave at once. I told her I had changed my mind about paying for her silence, that I wanted my money back. She paid no attention to what I said. She did not even bother to answer me, but went to the door and shouted for her servant. Then she sent him on an errand, and told him to take someone called Hamo with him, and to send the cook and the maid to her."

"Why did she send away the servants?"

"I have no idea. I thought it was because she did not want them to hear us quarreling about the money I wanted returned."

Bell stared hard, then nodded. "But once the house was empty, you found it easy to lose your temper, draw your belt knife, and stab her in the throat."

To everyone's surprise, Herlyond laughed. "No, you are wrong. Wrong about that. Wrong about who took the knife from Mainard's shop. It was Bertrild who took Codi's knife and drew it on me! When I asked again for money, she pulled this knife from under her cloak — she had never taken it off — and said I was a cheat and a liar and what she had taken from me was rightfully hers. She looked like a madwoman and she screamed at me, I swear it was for half a candlemark, about how we had led her father into sin and we must suffer for it, and then she thrust at me with the knife."

"So then you drew your belt knife to defend yourself —"

"No. Before I thought, I thrust back at her with my whip. She was still coming for me, and the whip caught her hard on the shoulder. She fell, and I ran out. I thought she would come after me, still screaming about her father's corruption, so I pulled up my hood again, mounted, and rode away. I did not kill her! Perhaps this Saeger that she was expecting came afterward and did it."

Bell stared at Herlyond with a mixture of doubt and frustration. Little as he liked seeing his whole elaborate theory of the murder destroyed, Herlyond's story was as likely as his reconstruction of the crime, and it explained the bruise on Bertrild's shoulder, which did not fit with the knife wounds. Magdalene had told him that Stoc reported Bertrild in the shop on Friday afternoon and that both apprentices agreed she would, if she could, pick up a tool, a buckle, a pair of reins — anything that would cause trouble.

"But the stallkeepers on the alley and the grocer's wife across the street said that no one else had entered the house," Bell said.

"The alley opens onto Fenchurch as well as onto the Chepe," Mainard said. "If this Saeger came south from Fenchurch, the stallkeepers —"

"Mainard," Sir Druerie said from the corridor, "this young woman—" His voice checked as he stepped into the room and saw the unexpected crowd. His glance swept around. His eyes widened. His hand dropped to his sword hilt and he began to draw. "Saeger!" he exclaimed, moving forward.

Twenty

Every head except Lintun Mercer's swiveled right and left, looking for the person to whom the name was addressed. Mercer let out a bellow of rage so loud that everyone was frozen for one more moment. Then Bell had his knife out—a sword being utterly useless in the crowded room, which Sir Druerie was discovering—but there were too many bodies in his way. By the time he had pushed past Fitz-Isabelle, Magdalene, and Mainard, Saeger had bowled over Sir Druerie and had caught Sabina to him, pressing his knife against her neck.

Mainard howled and surged forward. The knife pressed closer, starting a tiny thread of scarlet down Sabina's long, white throat. Mainard stopped and whispered, "Don't."

"You keep them back," Saeger said to Mainard, "or I'll slit her throat. I can't die more than once, and I'm already condemned, so I've nothing to lose by killing her. But I don't want to die, so if you let me go, I'll let her go. She can't even see me to point me out."

"Don't," Mainard begged Bell, putting both his hands on Bell's shoulders and holding him still. "Don't move. He'll kill my Sabina."

"We will not interfere with you, if you do not harm her," Magdalene said, her voice soothingly soft. "You are coming near the back door. Let Sabina twist around to open the latch for you. Then, if she lies down across the corridor, you can run out the door, push it closed, and we will be delayed by Sabina blocking our path. You will have a good head start, and we will not know whether you went into the priory or out into the street."

"Damn helpful, aren't you?" he said suspiciously, but his body was already half turned, his back to the kitchen, so that Sabina could reach behind him and find the latch of the outer door.

"To speak the truth," Magdalene went on, "I don't care a pin who killed Bertrild and Borc, both of whom certainly deserved killing, and I have no particular reason to want you caught and hanged. My only interest is in the safety of my woman. I am willing to help you, if you will let her go while you are still in the house. She is dear to me—"

The words were cut off by a dull but rather loud bong, and the killer dropped like a poleaxed ox. Dulcie looked down at the man at her feet, watching suspiciously for any twitch of movement, and then turned over the long-handled skillet in her hand to examine the bottom. Behind her Haesel jumped up and down clapping her hands, and Ella cowered in a corner, whimpering about the man having a knife and hurting Sabina.

"The only doubt I ever had about working in the Old Priory Guesthouse," Diot's cool voice said, "was that I might eventually grow bored. I suppose I can lay that doubt to rest also."

Magdalene swallowed hard. "It does not happen every day, but Dulcie's pan has seen some use over the years."

Her voice was calm, although her cheeks were blanched into an unusual translucence and she clutched Genlis's documents nervously to her breast. She had caught them up right after Saeger's bellow when FitzIsabelle had reached for them. She and Diot were by now the only ones still in the common room. The front door was open, and Jokel de Josne was gone. The other men had crowded into the corridor to help? hinder? Bell, who was fastening Saeger's wrists behind his back with a cord that Dulcie had supplied.

"That pan is a lethal weapon," he said loudly to Dulcie, grinning. "I think maybe I should confiscate it."

"Nah, then. Might make a mistake wit' a new one," she said, grinning back. "Always hit 'em right with this. Not too soft—don't want 'em waken' up too soon; not too hard so they get sick. Jus' a gentle tap to make 'em behave. You leave be my pan, Sir Bell. Fries eggs good too."

He laughed and hiked Saeger to his feet. With Sir Druerie holding the man's other arm, they got him onto one of the short benches at the end of the table opposite where the documents were. Bell then tied one of his ankles to the foot of the bench, and tipped him forward over the table so he would not fall.

Mainard was holding Sabina to him, weeping, and she was patting his shoulder and assuring him she was not hurt, that it was no worse than the nicks she occasionally gave herself when cutting her food, that Magdalene would fix it right away. Magdalene, however, was busy gathering up the scrolls.

"Look at her," FitzIsabelle said, grabbing Bell by the shoulder. "Will you let a whore keep those parchments and be a threat to us for the rest of our lives?"

"No, I certainly will not let Magdalene keep Genlis's records, but not for fear any person mentioned in them would suffer from Magdalene's knowledge. I will take them with me to the bishop of Winchester's house because I do not want anyone to harass her or her women."

"I would not keep these scrolls and parchments now if I were promised a pound a day to house them," Magdalene said. "We know who killed Bertrild. . . ." Her voice faded, and she looked at Bell. "Do we know who killed Bertrild?"

"Not me," Saeger said thickly. He had lifted his head from the table and was frowning with pain, but his eyes were focused. "And I am not lying. Why should I? I cannot be hanged twice. But I do not wish to hang alone, so I will tell the truth. I went to Lime Street to kill Bertrild, I admit that. I told her to be rid of her servants, or I would not come with the money she wanted to keep silent about my true identity. But I did not kill her. She was dead when I got there."

"I didn't do it!" Herlyond exclaimed.

Lintun Mercer/Saeger shrugged. "Someone had put a knife in her throat, clean as a whistle, and she was lying on the floor covered with blood. I was so furious that I grabbed the knife that was near her hand and stuck it in her until I was tired."

Bell raised his brows. That could have been a reason for the extra knife wounds, but so could a desire to cause confusion or a vicious

spite, he thought, as Lintun Mercer/Saeger turned his head and spat
at Mainard who was cradling Sabina next to his breast.

"The crazy knife kept catching in her flesh, and I tore it out . . .
and then I saw that it was a leather-cutting knife." He laughed. "And
I remembered how that pious prig of a saddler had stood up against
me and swore that old Dockett hadn't sold me the whole business,
and I saw a way to a neat little revenge."

Bell nodded. That, at least, was true. "I suppose you didn't want
too much nosing around into Bertrild's murder either," he said. "You
say you didn't do it, but you were there and maybe someone had seen
you walk down the alley."

"Right. So I decided to drop off the body in Mainard's yard." He
laughed again. "After all, who had better reason to want Bertrild dead?"

"Where did you get the horse?" Bell asked.

"Josne has one at a stable between his place and mine. I've borrowed it before, so the hostler asked no questions. Soon as it was good
and dark, I got her out of the shed where I'd hidden her, stuck her
on the horse—wasn't easy, she was pretty stiff but at least I had her
straight—and I took her where she belonged. I moved her, but I didn't
kill her."

Bell's brows rose again in disbelief. "My, it was like a royal council.
A whole company with murder in their hearts converging on one
place. How many of you were at Bertrild's house that day?"

Saeger caught the note of doubt. "Just the one more I spoke of,"
he said, then smiled, although his brows were drawn with pain. His
gaze flicked to Perekin FitzRevery, hesitated a fraction of a moment,
and then passed to Ulfmaer FitzIsabelle. "I said I would not hang
alone. You killed her, Ulfmaer. You walked right past me in the alley."

"No!" FitzIsabelle cried. "I was never there. You are doing this to
me because I refused to write you a receipt for double the money you
paid Dockett. You wanted me to swear that he had received enough
from you to sell you his whole business. Why should I kill Bertrild? I
said that to whichever Crown I paid Gunther Granger's money, the
other would cry treason, you all know—" his eyes swept from Magdalene to Bell to Mainard "—they would never have hanged and gut-
ted me; they would only have demanded the money."

"No, that was not the reason you killed Bertrild," Saeger said. "There *was* an heir to Granger's money." He laughed. "Bertrild was the heir. Her mother, also Bertrild, was Gunther Granger's daughter." "Good God, it could be true!" Sir Druerie exclaimed. "Gervase married a girl from London with a very good dowry. Her father . . . yes, he was in the wool trade, but I don't remember his name. I do remember that Gervase was disappointed because the old man was not as generous as he hoped. Still, he made his daughter a nice present when little Bertrild was born, but she died . . . not the daughter . . . more's the pity . . . Gervase's wife. After that, the father wouldn't give Gervase another penny. Said he was the cause of his wife's death." Sir Druerie shrugged. "Could be he was."

FitzIsabelle's mouth had dropped open. When Sir Druerie stopped speaking, he closed it and swallowed. "It isn't true," he whispered, "or if it was, I didn't know. I swear I did not know. Granger never mentioned any family." Then he shook his head hard. "It doesn't matter what he says. He is a liar. I was in my shop all day on the Saturday Bertrild was killed."

"No, you were not," Saeger said with vicious satisfaction. "You went out to the cookshop to deliver your packet of money, and the cookshop is not far from Lime Street."

"Yes, I did bring the money—a whole pound!" FitzIsabelle said forcefully, a tinge of color starting to relieve the gray pallor of his face. "And if I did that, did I not expect Bertrild to be alive and well to collect it? Yes, and I remember that I walked to the cookshop with Master FitzRevery, so the only time I was alone was the little while between leaving my shop and stepping into Perekin's." He breathed a huge sigh of relief. "There! You vicious cur—no, you would give a mad dog a bad name—hang alone! I will come to watch and to laugh, I promise."

Saeger tried to rise and lunge at FitzIsabelle, his expression of rage and frustration wordlessly confirming that he had lied, but Bell cuffed him, and he fell forward onto the table, weeping and cursing. FitzIsabelle cast a single challenging glance at Bell, turned, and marched out the open door.

"You are letting him go?" Sir Druerie asked. "Do you believe him?"

"His journeyman and apprentices confirm he was in the shop," Bell replied, "and they do not love him as do Herlyond's people. They would not lie for FitzIsabelle. Besides, where can he go? He has no country estate, no friends outside the city, and he is not the type to leave everything behind when there is a good chance he can keep it all—well, all except what he stole from Granger. As to believing him . . . yes, I think I do. But it isn't important. When I deliver Mercer/Saeger to the justiciar, I am sure he will repeat his accusations, and I will report them also. Master Octadenarius will sift out the truth about Master FitzIsabelle more easily than I."

"Likely." But there was a frown on Sir Druerie's face and in a moment he went on, "Still, I think I will accompany you to this Master Octadenarius. This one—" he cast a nasty glance at Saeger "—escaped justice once, and I do not want to see him escape again. It is too bad that I do not have any of the evidence against him with me, but my word will hold him until I can obtain a copy of the indictment from home."

"No need." Bell touched his pouch. "I have that and the two wills also."

He bent and untied Saeger's leg from the bench, slapped him hard when Saeger kicked, and then yanked him upright. Sir Druerie grasped his tied wrists and pulled his arms up. Saeger howled. Sir Druerie relaxed the pressure slightly, but Saeger took the hint and stood still while Bell used the rope to make a hobble that would permit him to walk but not run.

"Hold dinner for us," Bell said to Magdalene over his shoulder as he propelled Saeger after Sir Druerie toward the door. "I am getting so hungry, I could eat you."

Mischief lightened her eyes, which had, despite her easy manner, been dark and shocked. "That is getting to be a chronic condition with you," she said.

"Well, if one of Dulcie's meals will not cure it, I will have to consider other measures."

As Bell spoke, he pushed Saeger forward on Sir Druerie's heels and pulled the door closed behind him. Magdalene stared at the door, shaking her head and muttering to herself, "Some day I will have the last word with him, I swear it."

She started to turn and saw FitzRevery rather hesitantly approaching Mainard. Magdalene stopped moving, not wanting to be noticed.

"Here is your key, Mainard," FitzRevery said.

His head still bent toward Sabina, Mainard said, "Take it back to the shop and give it to Henry. He will have to lock up if Codi and the boys do not get back before closing time."

"I am sorry," FitzRevery said very softly. "There were four against me. I am sorry. I tried to see that there was no damage done."

Mainard's head came up and his good-natured mouth was hard. "Except to Sabina's things. There you let them toss and break as if she were worthless. It will take her weeks and bruises to make her chambers her own again."

Sabina put a hand on his arm. "It does not matter, Mainard. I have Haesel now. It only means that I must carry my staff for a few days."

"I didn't know," FitzRevery said in a stricken voice. "I was so worried that Mercer—no, Saeger—and FitzIsabelle would cut up all your finished saddles and saddlebags in their search that I never went upstairs. I am sorry if my neglect will cause Sa—Mistress Sabina any distress."

If Magdalene's ears could have perked up over that "Sa—Mistress Sabina," they would have. FitzRevery had never called one of the whores "Mistress." He was kind and jolly but to his mind a whore was a whore. But clearly the form of address, to him, marked a change in Sabina's status. And if that were true, matters would soon be mended between him and Mainard, which was good. Mainard needed friends, and FitzRevery plainly valued Mainard and wished to be his friend.

"It will be easily amended," Sabina said to him politely, and then, turning her face up to Mainard, "You must be tired of holding me up, love, and my knees still feel like warm jelly. Let me sit down."

FitzRevery sighed and followed the others out.

***

Some two candlemarks later, Magdalene, Bell, Sir Druerie, Mainard, and Sabina were seated at the table finishing a very belated dinner. Diot and Ella had eaten as soon as FitzRevery left while Magdalene had been washing and bandaging Sabina's neck—more because Mainard had begun to weep each time he saw it than because the nick needed attention. She had left Sabina in her own bedchamber with its large double bed, and when she realized that Diot and Ella were gone, had sent Mainard in to her. They had not emerged from that seclusion until Magdalene had knocked on the door and told them dinner was on the table.

Magdalene was grateful for their absorption in each other so long as she did not have to watch them. She had used her privacy to deal with Genlis's documents. Perhaps Bell would be angry, but she could see no real use in inflicting more suffering that would serve no purpose. First, she cut Herlyond's name and the information about him out of Gervase's records. After some thought, she also removed the evidence against Perekin FitzRevery. She had hesitated over the material concerning Jokel de Josne, and then laughed and let it stand. Likely it could not be proven or Josne would be gone from London soon enough, and if there was more to be discovered, doubtless it should be exposed.

When she was finished, she packed everything carefully into the original covering, but without trying to reattach the seals. That would have to wait for Letice's return—if Bell would agree to that subterfuge. She rewrapped the whole in a piece of coarse cloth and sat down to wait. Fortunately it was not much longer before Bell and Sir Druerie arrived. She put off more unpleasantness, which she really felt she could not bear for the moment, by getting the meal on the table.

Everyone was so starved that conversation had been nil, except for a few comments about the murders. In exchange for somewhat better conditions in prison, Saeger had admitted to the murder of Borc. When Borc asked him for money and used his true name, Saeger had said he could do better than a few pence, that he would employ Borc, but that Borc must come back after the shop was empty. When Borc returned after dark, Saeger had spun him various tales about illegal enterprises and then suggested that he sleep in a storeroom until the journeymen and apprentices returned.

Saeger wakened Borc before dawn, and said he must finish his sleep elsewhere. When Borc protested, Saeger said he would take him to Mainard's yard, which was never locked, and give him a flask of wine to keep him warm till dawn. To that Borc agreed, and Saeger had taken along the flask of lily-of-the-valley-doctored wine and walked him to Mainard's back gate.

He told them, grinning, that he had intended Borc die in Mainard's shed with a Mercer's Guild flask clutched in his hand, but he had had to hand the flask over while he got the gate open. Then Saeger stopped laughing, Bell said, calling Borc a stupid, drunken clot who could not wait and had taken a large drink. Saeger admitted he had not known the poison would act so fast. Before he could get the latchstring of the gate out, Borc had been vomiting, voiding, and convulsing, and had cast away the flask. Saeger had turned him to his back to make sure he was dead, and having heard sounds of people stirring, decided to make himself scarce.

"He had confessed to killing Borc before, but did he ever admit killing Bertrild?" Magdalene asked.

"Not in so many words. Perhaps he still hopes to take FitzIsabelle or FitzRevery down with him, but his tongue slipped often enough for me to be sure and Octadenarius also."

Magdalene shook her head and then her whole body, as if she were shedding something unpleasant. "He just killed whoever was in his way," she said and sighed. "I am glad it is over, that Mainard is free of any suspicion. Only one loose end remains." She confessed what she had done to Bell, and waited for his reaction.

He shrugged and sighed. "I suppose I should have taken everything with me. I should have realized that you would go your own way once you had decided that enough punishment had been administered, even if it was not by the law." Then he frowned. "You did not remove the evidence of FitzIsabelle's crime, did you? After all, it is possibly Mainard's money that FitzIsabelle is holding."

"Mine?" Mainard echoed. "How can it be mine?"

"Don't be a fool, man," Sir Druerie said. "If Granger was Bertrild's grandfather, his estate rightly should have come to her in her lifetime. That would have made the estate yours. You are her heir, and it comes to you."

"How sad," Mainard said. "If he was her grandfather and she had had that money, perhaps she could have paid off the mortages on Moorgreen and had her heart's desire. But I do not want it. Let—"

"Oh, no," Magdalene said. "I am not willing for FitzIsabelle to keep his ill-gotten gains. If you do not want the money, Mainard, use it for doing good, or give it to Sabina, or—"

"Of course I will give it to Sabina. It will pay her for all the insult and pain Bertrild inflicted on her. Thank you, Magdalene, that is a wonderful idea."

"No, it is *not*," Sabina said, with more force than was normal for her. "I never heard of such an idiotic idea in my whole life. My dear Mainard, cannot you see that Magdalene is joking? You cannot give what might amount to a fortune—for I doubt FitzIsabelle would have stolen less—to a whore. Think what people would say! You would be a laughingstock."

"No, it is not so foolish," Sir Druerie said, laughing. "By all means, give it to Sabina."

His remark reduced every person at the table to silence and staring. Of them all, the last one who should have been willing to approve Magdalene's jesting suggestion was the elderly and conservative Sir Druerie. He looked around at them all in some surprise.

"If he is going to marry her," Sir Druerie continued, shrugging, "the money would come back to him anyway."

"Marry me?" Sabina said faintly. "But Mainard cannot marry me. I am a whore."

"Have you been?" Mainard asked harshly.

Sabina turned her blind face to him. "What kind of question is that? You know I was a whore before I came into your keeping—"

"I meant after?"

"No! Of course not!" Sabina drew herself up, and her voice was indignant. "You paid for my keep here and for Haesel's, and I had money from my singing. Why should I go back to work that was never to my taste?"

"To get the taste of *me* out of your mouth?"

Sabina smiled, her whole face lighting with joy. "You taste of honey and heaven to me, Mainard. You are beautiful to my hands, and I adore your funny face."

For one moment the whole table was stricken mute. Fortunately it was Mainard who found his voice first. "Then will you marry me?" he asked.

"Mainard." Her voice shook, and she paused to steady it. "You cannot mean that. I cannot bear you children. They would not only be the butt of cruel jests but, God forbid, they could be born like me, without eyes. I cannot. I cannot." And she bent her head against his breast and wept.

A long sigh whooshed out of Mainard and he clutched her closer. "Don't cry, beloved. You do not know how much you have eased my heart. That was one thing I always feared—that if we married you would want children. No more than you do I dare have a child. Not even having you for my own forever could make me willing to inflict on a child the life I have lived. You say I am beautiful to you, but the whole world is not blind."

"No heir?" Sir Druerie exclaimed. "But what will you do with your business?"

"I could leave it to my journeyman, who will be a master I hope long before I die, or if he is too well established to want another business, I could leave it to one of the apprentices. Or Sabina and I could take to ourselves one or more of the foundlings discarded by parents who cannot care for them because of death or poverty. Bertrild never understood that I did not marry her to get an heir. I wanted a woman to talk to, to laugh with, to lie with, to share my life, my worries and my pleasures."

"That I will do, Mainard," Sabina said. "Whether you marry me or keep me, I will gladly share your life in every way until I die or you drive me away."

They all lifted their wine cups to toast that statement, and Mainard softly told Sabina, who smiled and thanked them. And when the cups were emptied, Mainard said that he would like Sabina to come to Lime Street and decide whether she would like to live in that house. Sir Druerie rose to accompany them. Magdalene and Bell saw them out and then sat down at the table and stared in silence at each other.

To her amazement, Magdalene felt herself blushing. Hastily she said, "I have rewrapped Genlis's documents in their original—"

Bell reached over and put a finger over her lips. "Enough. I do not want to hear one word more about Bertrild's murder today." He looked around the room which, despite the disorder of platters and scraps not yet cleared away, of stools disarranged by the number of people who had been moving about the room, had a look of comfort and ease to it. He stared for a moment at Magdalene's embroidery frame, now carrying the start of another altar cloth or cope—some large piece of work that would take weeks or months to complete.

"You will never give up this life, will you?" he said.

She smiled. "No, never. I am me, *femme sole* in law. No one has the right to tell me what to do. I am not beholden to any man for the bread I chew, the fire in my hearth, the clothing on my body. It is said that women are weak and evil and need men to control them, but if I have sold my soul to the devil, I am going to enjoy every moment of my weakness and evilness. It will be time enough to repent when I am silver-haired and toothless." Her smile broadened into a grin. "By then I will be rich enough, I hope, that I will be able to buy absolution and a boost straight into heaven by leaving my goods and money to the Church."

He shrugged. "Evil? Perhaps it is evil for a woman to be master of herself. But weak?" He laughed softly. Then the laughter was gone and his eyes and mouth looked sad. "I love you, Magdalene, as much for your cleverness, weak and evil though it may be, as for your beauty. I can resist you no longer."

His hand had gone to his purse when he said he loved her, so Magdalene had some warning of what he would do. She knew she should refuse him. Love . . . love had been fatal to any man connected with her in the past. But Bell would be very hard to kill, she suspected, and her body was playing traitor, her nether mouth full and moist, her nipples hard and erect, and a warm softness suffusing all her muscles.

He had found five pence and held the silver coins out to her, but he would not meet her eyes, and his own showed a slight glitter along the lower lids, perhaps of tears. "Here," he said. "I wish to buy a night in your bed."

She folded his hand over the pennies and pushed it back toward his purse, smiling. "I am my own mistress, remember? I need pay share to no master, and I can take a man to my bed simply for my own pleasure. If you will come for pleasure, for laughter, knowing there may—by necessity—be others . . ." She stood up and held out her hand.

He slowly stood and stretched his own to take it, to draw her close, to kiss her. And under the rising, pulsing desire she felt for him came the little, laughing thought. "This time I had the last word."

Author's Note

I have often been asked by readers what made me choose the twelfth century as the period in which I wished to set my books. The answer is simple: The twelfth century combines the most exciting and violent political and social developments—developments not controlled by vast impersonal forces, like economics or global pressures, but directly by all-too-human people—with a beautiful simplicity of spiritual and moral values. Not that these values made people perfect. Human beings are human beings and in any period, no matter what its values, will manage to inflict upon each other every kind of misery. The reign of King Stephen of England (1135–1154) took place at just about the midpoint of this period and graphically illustrates every one of its characteristics.

Stephen's reign has been described in the *Anglo-Saxon Chronicle* (trans. by G. N Garmonsway, J. M. Dent & Sons, Ltd., London 1953) in simple words and horrible images as a period of utter disaster. "When the traitors saw that Stephen was a good-humored, kindly, and easy-going man who inflicted no punishment, then they committed all manner of horrible crimes . . . For every great man built him castles and held them against the king. . . . They burdened the unhappy people of the country with forced labor on the castles; and when the castles were built they filled them with devils and wicked men. By night and day they seized those whom they believed to have any wealth, whether they were men or women. . . . They hung them by the feet and smoked them with foul smoke. . . . They tied knotted cords around their heads and twisted it until it entered the brain. . . .

"I know not how to, nor am I able to tell of all the atrocities nor all the cruelties which they wrought upon the unhappy people. . . . Wherever the ground was tilled the earth bore no corn, for the land was ruined by such doings; and men said openly that Christ and His Saints slept."

Such a situation was the result of civil war, and while it was terrible for the poor people of England, it is a very fertile field for a novelist to plough. Civil war, however, is not only confusing to those living through it but also for those describing it and reading about it. For readers who found the glancing mention of political events in *A Personal Devil* unclear or in whom those mentions have aroused curiosity, I would like to expand, at least slightly, the historical background of the beginning of the reign of King Stephen.

In brief, William, duke of Normandy, who was called "the Bastard" in his own time and "the Conqueror" in ours, fought for and won the English throne in 1066. He ruled the country with success and surprising understanding, despite his brutality—but it was a brutal time—until his death in 1087.

William I was succeeded by his third son, also William, called "Rufus"; he only lasted for thirteen years, until he was killed (possibly murdered) by an arrow through the eye while hunting, in 1100. The priests who recorded history at that time made William II out to be a monster; more careful modern research implies he was no better nor worse than most other kings of the period, except that he insisted the Church pay the same feudal dues as any other noble and that he suffered a total lack of conviction about Christianity. The combination, plus a disinclination for female companionship, caused the bad press he received from the clergy. William II died unmarried and childless.

The heir to the throne was now William I's youngest son, Henry. A chip off the old block (he was much like his father politically, although he was called "Beauclerk" because he could read and write and seemed truly interested in learning), he ruled for thirty-five generally prosperous years. Unfortunately, his only living son was drowned in a crossing of the English Channel. For reasons too complex to go into in this very brief summary, in 1126 Henry demanded that his barons swear to accept his daughter Matilda as queen.

Women were of no importance, considered weak and evil, in medieval times. As long as Henry's powerful and ruthless hand held the scepter, the barons were quiescent, but when Henry died in 1135, they were more than willing to forget the oaths they had sworn in 1126. Both Robert of Gloucester, King Henry's bastard son, and Stephen of Blois, a nephew of King Henry's, who had spent many years in England at his uncle's court and had married the heiress of Boulogne, seemed welcome alternatives.

Stephen acted faster, however. While Robert dutifully made arrangements for his father's interment, Stephen left Boulogne as soon as he heard of Henry's death and made for London, the richest and most powerful city in the realm. What he promised the Londoners is not known, but they "elected" him king; he must have fulfilled those promises, too, because the Londoners were faithful to him until he died.

With the approval of London behind him, Stephen made a dash for Winchester, where his younger brother Henry was bishop. He was warmly welcomed, and through Henry's assistance and persuasion, Stephen was recognized as king by Robert, bishop of Salisbury, who as justiciar controlled the government of England, and by William Pont de l'Arche, who was the keeper of the royal treasury. Having in hand two vital aspects of the kingdom, Stephen appealed to the archbishop of Canterbury to anoint him king.

The archbishop demurred, citing the oath that he himself and Stephen had taken to support Matilda, but Stephen's supporters claimed that the oath had been forced upon them and was therefore null and void and moreover that King Henry had released them from that oath on his deathbed. Then Hugh Bigod, earl of Norfolk, took oath that Henry had also changed his mind about the succession on his deathbed and named Stephen his heir. (That Bigod had not been at Henry's deathbed didn't seem to trouble anyone.) Having considered these assertions and more importantly Stephen's promise to restore and maintain the freedom of the Church (and no doubt thinking of the abomination of having a woman as queen), the archbishop anointed

Stephen king of England on 22 December 1135. In medieval times this ceremony was of the utmost importance: It was believed to have *made* Stephen king.

The nobility of England was less easy to convince. Some of the barons were truly honorable men and were bound by the tenets of chivalry; they had sworn an oath to support Matilda and were resolved to hold by it. More of the barons probably hoped that rejection of Stephen would bring into power, either as king himself or as the hand and mind controlling Matilda, Robert of Gloucester, whom they knew well, admired, and trusted. Sadly, most of the nobility simply saw the period before Stephen gathered the reins of government into his hands as a time to raid freely and indiscriminately and grow rich on loot.

Help came to Stephen not from a friend or ally but from an enemy. King David of Scotland was one of those honorable men who was determined to hold by his oath to Matilda. He also saw supporting her as an opportunity to win a large chunk of English territory. David gathered an army and attacked Northumbria. Whatever doubts the nobility of England had about Stephen, they had none about their hatred of the Scots. Stephen called out the feudal army to defend the land. The barony rallied at once, and within a month Stephen was able to lead a large army north.

When David had news of the force opposed to him, he realized he could not resist. He came to meet Stephen at Durham and made submission, returning to Stephen's control the castles he had seized; however, claiming that he still held to his oath to support Matilda, he refused to swear fealty to the English king. Stephen did not force the issue, which was to breed trouble in the future.

Having taken oaths of fealty from the northern barons, Stephen traveled south with his army, accepting homage from all those who offered it and listening to complaints and pleas. He made considerable efforts to reestablish peace and stability among his subjects. And his efforts were rewarded. When Stephen held a great Court in Westminster at Easter, a contemporary chronicler (Henry of Huntington, *Historia Anglorum*, ed. Thomas Arnold; Rolls Series 74, 1879, p. 259) reports: "There had never been a more splendid [Court] held in England with regard to the multitudes who attended it, the greatness of those present, the gold, the silver, the gems, the garments, the lavishness in every respect." And at this Court, Stephen extracted oaths of fealty from all who had not previously sworn to him.

In all this time, neither Matilda nor her husband, Geoffrey of Anjou, had made any move to forward her own claim to the throne. Moreover, Pope Innocent II sent a letter recognizing Stephen as king, and shortly after the Easter Court, Robert of Gloucester came to England; he took part in high-level deliberations on the fate of Normandy and, at an equally well-attended Court in Oxford in April, Robert swore to Stephen as king. Over the summer, Stephen put down one minor and one major rebellion with seeming success, although he showed himself to be too lenient with the followers, excusing them from punishment because they claimed they had been following the orders of their overlord. Neither William I or Henry I would ever have accepted such an excuse; you obeyed your overlord *saving* your duty to the king.

However, rebellion quelled, the king's authority seemed unchallenged in England. Not so in Normandy. The council in which Robert of Gloucester had taken part about the disposition of Normandy had not borne fruit. Count Theobold of Blois (Stephen's elder brother), to whom the duchy had been offered, refused that prickly gift, and it was now Stephen's duty to go to Normandy and provide for governance of the duchy and protect it against the incursions of Matilda's husband, Geoffrey of Anjou.

At first all seemed to go well. Many of Stephen's barons accompanied him, and in May he had a conference with Louis VI of France during which he did homage for the duchy of Normandy (which meant that Louis recognized him as duke of Normandy and king of England) and made a treaty with Louis. Then disaster struck. Geoffrey of Anjou invaded Normandy and Robert of Gloucester—although he made no overt move—was suspected of favoring Geoffrey. William of Ypres, the leader of Stephen's mercenary forces, urged that Robert be ambushed.

The ambush failed, Robert having been warned, but relations between Stephen and Robert became, not surprisingly, openly strained. Worse yet, trouble broke out between the king's baronial forces and the king's Flemish mercenaries. Whether that trouble was related to the attempted ambush of Robert of Gloucester, a favorite of the barons, or not, the barons took violent offense at the favor shown the mercenaries. Recognizing the uncertain temper and loyalty of his forces, Stephen gave up any hope of attacking and subduing Geoffrey. He made a truce with him, offering two thousand marks of silver for keeping the peace.

Although Normandy was now at peace, and Stephen returned to England at the end of November 1137, the king was not completely satisfied with the accomplishment. William of Ypres was no longer in as high favor as he had been. Waleran de Meulan was now preeminent. Stephen had to drive the Scots out of Northumbria again in the spring of 1138 and then had to rush west where Geoffrey Talbot had seized Hereford Castle. Stephen drove him out, and out of his first refuge, whereupon Geoffrey ran to Bristol, the chief stronghold of Robert, earl of Gloucester. There he was safe because, soon after Pentecost, Robert had sent messengers to Stephen announcing his defiance and abandoning his oath of fealty.

In the light of this defiance and the threat that Robert of Gloucester would invade England and try to take the throne for his half-sister, Matilda, carrying letters from Geoffrey Talbot and his associates to Normandy could be considered treason. In fact, these were only the beginning of King Stephen's troubles, but the period covers that of *A Personal Devil* and an Author's Note is not the place for more history.

Finally, I wish to comment on my use of the word "English." I am well aware that in 1139 there was no "English" language and the "English" noblemen were Norman rather than native to England. For the sake of simplicity, I have used "English" to denote the native language and English baron to mean a nobleman whose chief lands were in England rather than France or Normandy.

ROBERTA GELLIS,
LAFAYETTE, INDIANA